Fateful Transitions

FATEFUL TRANSITIONS

How Democracies Manage Rising Powers,
from the Eve of World War I to China's Ascendance

Daniel M. Kliman

PENN

UNIVERSITY OF PENNSYLVANIA PRESS

PHILADELPHIA

A volume in the Haney Foundation Series, established in 1961 with the generous support of Dr. John Louis Haney

Published by
University of Pennsylvania Press
Philadelphia, Pennsylvania 19104-4112

Printed in the United States of America on acid-free paper
10 9 8 7 6 5 4 3 2 1

Library of Congress Cataloging-in-Publication Data
Kliman, Daniel M.
    Fateful transitions : how democracies manage rising powers, from the eve
of World War I to China's ascendance / Daniel M. Kliman. — 1st ed.
        p.   cm.
    Includes bibliographical references and index
    ISBN 978-0-8122-4653-7 (hardcover : alk. paper)
    1. International relations. 2. International relations—Case studies. 3. Security,
International. 4. Security, International—Case studies. 5. Great Powers. 6. Great
Powers—Case studies.
JZ1242 .K59   2014
327.09'04   2014012349

Contents

Abbreviations

ASAT   Anti-Satellite
ASEAN Association of Southeast Asian Nations
DPJ   Democratic Party of Japan
EEZ   Exclusive Economic Zone
G-20   Group of 20
GDP   Gross Domestic Product
IMF   International Monetary Fund
JMSDF Japan Maritime Self-Defense Forces
JSDF   Japan Self-Defense Forces
LDP   Liberal Democratic Party
MFA   Ministry of Foreign Affairs (China)
MMCA   Military Maritime Consultative Agreement
MTCR   Missile Technology Control Regime
NATO   North Atlantic Treaty Organization
NIC   National Intelligence Council
PLA   People's Liberation Army
QDR   Quadrennial Defense Review
R&D   Research and Development
RAF   Royal Air Force
SED   Strategic Economic Dialogue
S&ED   Strategic and Economic Dialogue
S&T   Science and Technology
UN   United Nations
USSR   Union of Soviet Socialist Republics
WTO   World Trade Organization

Chapter 1

Fateful Transitions

An age-old question—how to manage the rise of new powers—looms large for the United States, Europe, and much of Asia. Although the nature of the emerging international order remains unclear, the geopolitics of the twenty-first century has earlier parallels. Since the late 1800s, the world's major democracies have repeatedly navigated the ascendance of other nations. The choices made by democratic leaders during these fateful transitions have profoundly shaped the course of history. On the positive side, these decisions paved the way for the Anglo-American rapprochement; on the negative side, the path taken culminated in World War I, World War II, and the Cold War. This track record of limited success should give today's leaders pause as they confront a world increasingly defined by fateful transitions.

As other powers rise, democratic nations have pursued a range of strategies. Sometimes they have appeased, sometimes they have integrated the rising state into international institutions, sometimes they have built up military capabilities and alliances, and sometimes they have contained the ascendant state. On occasion, they have even switched approaches midway through a new power's emergence. This book explains the strategic choices that democratic leaders make as they navigate power shifts. It argues that an ascendant state's form of government decisively frames transitions of power: democracies can rise and reassure while autocracies cannot. As a result, the strategies adopted by democratic leaders differ depending on the regime type of the rising power.

Domestic institutions shape external perceptions of a nation's rise. On multiple levels, democratic government functions as a source of reassurance. Democracy clarifies intentions: decentralized decision-making and a free press guarantee that information about a state's ambitions cannot remain secret for long. In addition, checks and balances coupled with internal transparency create opportunities for outsiders to shape a rising power's trajectory. Other states can locate and freely engage with multiple domestic actors who all have a hand in the foreign policy of the ascendant state. Thus, democratic government mitigates the mistrust a new power's rise would otherwise generate.

Autocracy has the opposite effect. By policing the media and confining foreign policy decisions to a select few, authoritarian government creates a veil of secrecy that obscures a rising power's intentions. Moreover, in a centralized and opaque political system, opportunities to shape strategic behavior are slim. Enforced secrecy prevents external powers from identifying and subsequently exploiting rifts within the government. And outsiders have few domestic groups to engage because autocratic rule cannot tolerate independent centers of influence. Consequently, autocracy amplifies the concerns accompanying a powerful state's emergence.

Regime type sets the boundaries for how democratic leaders formulate strategy. A democracy tends to accommodate when an ascendant state upholds rule of law and provides for domestic transparency. In an environment defined by relative trust and adequate information, a democracy can safely appease the ascendant state to remove points of conflict before integrating it into international institutions. By contrast, a democracy is likely to favor a different approach at the outset of an autocracy's rise. Integration remains attractive as a tool for restraining and potentially reshaping an autocracy as it becomes more powerful. However, the existing climate of uncertainty and mistrust tends to compel a democracy to pair integration with hedging: developing military capabilities and alliances as a geopolitical insurance. This two-pronged approach is inherently fragile. If over time integration clearly fails to moderate a rising autocracy's external behavior, a democracy will shift to containment.

The argument connecting power transitions, regime type, and strategy finds affirmation in a series of historical junctures beginning with the eclipse of Pax Britannica. At the turn of the twentieth century, Great Britain entered a period of relative decline as the United States and Germany burst onto the global scene. Although both of these emerging giants challenged Great Britain on diverse fronts, its strategies toward each sharply differed. Confident in American goodwill and perceiving significant opportunities to shape the United States into a pillar of the global order it had established, London appeased Washington, systematically eliminating all sources of tension with the rising power of the Western Hemisphere. Autocratic Germany, however, elicited a different British response. Wary of Berlin's intentions and skeptical of London's capacity to influence German foreign policy through internal lobbying, British leaders initially opted for integration and hedging. But when international institutions proved unable to limit German bellicosity, they transitioned to containment.

The British approach toward Germany's resurgence under Nazi rule followed a similar course. German autocracy initially masked Adolf Hitler's true intentions. Unsure whether they were dealing with the megalomaniacal Hitler of *Mein Kampf* or a reformed and responsible statesman, British leaders attempted to integrate Germany into a new European order while simultaneously ramping up military spending as a precaution. Once the dismemberment of Czechoslovakia demonstrated that no post-Versailles Treaty settlement could moderate German behavior, London pivoted to containment, declaring war when Hitler's armies invaded Poland.

The onset of the Cold War similarly underscores how a rising nation's domestic government frames power transitions. The Second World War catapulted the Soviet Union into a dominant position on the Eurasian landmass. Uncertainty rooted in the Soviet Union's opaque political system compelled the United States to hedge against its ally while holding out hope that Moscow would join the new postwar order. However, Moscow's temporary occupation of northern Iran, bullying of Turkey, and blockading of Berlin led Washington to conclude that integration had failed to restrain the Soviet Union. Accordingly, the United States moved toward a strategy of containing its erstwhile ally.

The ascendancy of China, which started in the mid-1990s and has accelerated since 2000, demonstrates that regime type continues to shape external perceptions of a nation's rise. Censorship and state secrecy have cast a pall of uncertainty over China's long-term ambitions, ensuring that the modernization of the People's Liberation Army (PLA) and recent episodes of assertiveness in the South and East China Seas provoke growing concern in Washington and Tokyo. Concentration of power at the apex of the Communist Party and the related absence of societal checks and balances deprive the United States and Japan of opportunities to shape China's strategic behavior by engaging with a range of domestic actors. Thus, both democratic powers have moved to integrate China into the global order while simultaneously fielding new military capabilities and reinforcing strategic ties with each other and with additional countries in Asia. Despite changes of administration in both Washington and Tokyo, neither has deviated from this two-pronged approach.

Fateful transitions past and present point to multiple insights for contemporary policymakers.

First, the leadership in Beijing has wrongly bet that alleviating mistrust abroad will not require political reform at home. Integration into the global economy and rhetorical commitments to "peaceful development" and a "harmonious world" have failed to quell mounting concerns about China's future course. These concerns are inextricably linked to China's system of one-party rule, which magnifies anxieties that, in the best of circumstances, would attend the emergence of a new superpower. The absence of domestic political reform is now becoming a strategic liability as nations wary about China's ascendance take steps that amount to quasi encirclement. Moreover, widespread mistrust threatens to ultimately constrict China's ability to take a leadership role in the international community, depriving the country of the fruits of its rise.

Second, American leaders should recognize that integration, though essential, is no substitute for more actively promoting democratic reforms inside China. Encouraging gradual political liberalization is the only way to short-circuit the cycle of mistrust, reaction, and counter-reaction that increasingly defines relations between Washington and Beijing. Because China's leadership would regard a U.S. push for overnight elections as a deeply hostile act, Washington should press for political reforms that do not inherently threaten the Chinese Communist Party. It can do so by giving consistent presidential attention to human rights and specific issues of democratic governance in China, supporting efforts that help Chinese officials strengthen their own institutions, and promoting a regional agenda that advances democratic norms in Asia.

Third, India's ruling elites should recognize that influence comes not only from wealth and military power but also from the capacity to reassure. This is an advantage India enjoys thanks to its democratic institutions and one which is overlooked by many outside observers who see the parliamentary maneuvering and popular protests associated with representative government as a challenge to sustaining India's economic takeoff. No penumbra of uncertainty surrounds India's emergence on the world stage. In addition, outsiders can influence Indian foreign policy by engaging a diverse landscape of political parties, bureaucracies, business groups, media figures, and civil society actors. Consequently, despite India's testing of nuclear weapons in the late 1990s and its accelerating military buildup, mistrust of its intentions remains low. The way is clear for India to rise into a position of global leadership.

Fourth, the United States should forge closer partnerships with rising democracies to strengthen the global order. For more than six decades, the rules-based international system has advanced peace, prosperity, and freedom. However, new challenges to the order have emerged. These include a weakened global financial architecture, expansive maritime claims in East Asia and beyond, the retrenchment of democracy in some parts of the world, and fiscal constraints in the United States and Europe. To adapt and renew the current system, Washington should look to rising democracies as the most promising partners. Unlike China or Russia, these new powers possess domestic institutions that permit the United States to work with them in an environment devoid of crippling mistrust and offer American leaders entry points into their foreign policy processes. U.S. engagement with rising democracies is critical. The choices these emerging powers make—about whether to take on new global responsibilities, passively benefit from the efforts of established powers, or complicate the solving of key challenges—may, together, decisively influence the trajectory of the current international order.

The world of the twenty-first century is a world of fateful transitions. In the years ahead, how to manage rising powers will increasingly preoccupy the foreign policies of the United States, Europe, and much of Asia. The flare-up of Japan-China tensions surrounding the Senkaku/Diaoyu island group and the revelation of widespread Chinese hacking against American government agencies and corporations have put a spotlight on whether current approaches toward the growth of Chinese power are working. Meanwhile, budgetary pressures on U.S. foreign affairs and defense spending will place an even greater premium on building partnerships with rising democracies. Within Europe, the continued weakness of many Eurozone economies after the debt crisis underscores the global power shift and focuses European capitals on how to navigate the rise of other states. Leaders in the world's established powers—and their rising-state counterparts—would do well to keep in mind how regime type frames power transitions if they wish to avoid the mistakes of their predecessors.

The Book and International Relations Theory

This book speaks to multiple strands of international relations scholarship. It reinforces the extensive literature on the democratic peace and contains new insights for academic work on relations between declining and rising states.

At the same time, the book examines whether arguments about the interplay of economic interdependence and foreign policy explain the strategic choices made by democratic leaders as they navigate power transitions.

The Democratic Peace

Scholars have devoted much attention to understanding why democracies, though about as conflict prone as autocracies, have "virtually never fought one another in a full-scale international war."[1] Potential explanations generally fall into one of two categories. Normative accounts of the democratic peace argue that democratic leaders externalize rules and practices that govern the domestic political arena, for example, nonviolent conflict resolution and "live and let live" attitudes toward negotiation. At the international level, these norms translate into mutual trust and respect among democracies, which prevent conflicts from escalating into war. However, democracies do not accord autocratic regimes the same trust and respect because the latter's type of political system lacks norms that would moderate external conduct. Thus, disputes between democracies and autocracies may result in war.[2]

The other explanation for the democratic peace emphasizes the role of domestic institutions. In democracies, leaders are accountable to legislatures, major interest groups, and the general public. According to proponents of the democratic peace, this imposes a number of constraints on foreign policy. Publics will normally be averse to bearing the costs of war.[3] Democratic institutions also give a voice to interest groups who may oppose military conflict for political or moral reasons. Mobilizing for war therefore constitutes a complex, drawn-out process as leaders try to convince the public and major societal actors to support military action. Consequently, democracies mobilize slowly and in the public eye. In crises featuring two democracies, neither need fear surprise attack—each recognizes that the other operates under similar domestic constraints. This provides ample time to peacefully resolve crises through locating mutually acceptable agreements.[4]

A different institutional argument for the democratic peace draws attention to the linkage between successful prosecution of war and political survival of elected elites. Democratic leaders should be more willing than their autocratic counterparts to devote resources to war because military defeat would erode the broad political base they require to remain in office. Recognizing that elected elites in other states confront the same incentives to expend significant resources in the pursuit of victory, democratic leaders will avoid costly conflicts with each other.[5]

The democratic peace is not without critics. Using regression analysis, Joanne Gowa observes no statistical evidence of a democratic peace prior to World War I or during the interwar period. Although the democratic peace appears statistically significant throughout the Cold War, Gowa attributes this finding to shared national interests: the Soviet threat compelled democracies to settle their differences peacefully.[6] David Spiro points to the Spanish-American War and Finland's membership in the Axis during World War II as examples of military conflicts among democracies.[7] Critiquing the democratic peace from a different angle, Christopher Layne examines "near misses" where rival democratic states nearly went to war. According to Layne, in these cases factors other than externalized norms averted military conflict.[8] Sebastian Rosato, in a critique of mechanisms underlying the democratic peace, contends that nationalist publics may demand war and that leaders can manipulate public opinion when initial support is lacking.[9] Last, Edward Mansfield and Jack Snyder put forward a major qualification to the democratic peace. Using both statistical analysis and a series of case studies, they argue that well-developed political institutions and rule of law prove conducive to peace, but elected regimes at the early phase of democratic transitions are actually war prone.[10]

Proponents of the democratic peace have answered each of these critiques. Bruce Russett and John Oneal demonstrate that the democratic peace extends throughout the twentieth century. In their statistical analysis, "When the democracy score of the less democratic state in a dyad is higher by a standard deviation, the likelihood of conflict is more than one-third below the baseline rate among all dyads in the system."[11] Other scholars have replicated Russett and Oneal's findings, and the significance of the democratic peace across time has largely ceased to generate debate.

The historical anomalies that Spiro and Layne identify have led to a more precise understanding of how the democratic peace operates. John Owen incorporates perceptions of regime type into democratic peace theory. He argues that pacific relations between democracies endure only when each state perceives the other as liberal. The Spanish-American War thus upholds the democratic peace because the United States perceived its European adversary as a monarchy. Owen also evaluates "near misses" in which democracies came close to conflict and finds that normative mechanisms actually operated to forestall war.[12] Charles Lipson proposes that democracies have a special "contracting advantage." Transparency, stable leadership succession, public accountability, and constitutional checks and balances enhance outsiders' confidence that a democracy will abide by its commitments. Re-peated interaction gradually increases confidence in another democracy's reliability as a contracting partner. Lipson thereby accounts for why "near misses" may occur between democracies, particularly at the early stage of their relationship.[13]

Rosato's challenge to the democratic peace has not withstood close scru-tiny. David Kinsella notes that Rosato mischaracterizes the democratic peace. The theory extends to interactions between democratic states, yet Rosato treats it as an argument for democratic avoidance of war in all circumstances. In addition, Rosato tries to falsify the democratic peace by pointing to his-torical anomalies that existing scholarship has already addressed.[14] Branislav Slantchev, Anna Alexandrova, and Erik Gartzke call attention to methodo-logical flaws in Rosato's analysis. Rosato casts the democratic peace as an in-violable law of international relations, yet it is a theory that predicts broad tendencies, not the foreign policy choices made by any given democracy. Slan-tchev and his coauthors also uncover selection bias in Rosato's choice of evi-dence to refute the democratic peace.[15] Michael Doyle critiques Rosato from a perspective rooted in the writings of the philosopher Immanuel Kant. Doyle argues that peace among democracies reflects three interlocking factors—"Republican representation, an ideological commitment to fundamental human rights, and transnational interdependence"[16]—and that by treating each factor separately, Rosato fails to grasp the actual logic of the democratic peace.

Significant flaws have emerged in the analysis underlying Mansfield and Snyder's qualification of democratic peace theory. John Oneal, Bruce Russett, and Michael Berbaum use their own statistical model to evaluate whether democratization increases the likelihood of conflict. Their findings contradict those of Mansfield and Snyder: "democratization reduces the risk of conflict and does so quickly."[17] Vipin Narang and Rebecca Nelson show that states with fragile institutions experiencing democratic transitions have almost never initiated war. They demonstrate that the relationship between incomplete democratization and military conflict in Mansfield and Snyder's statistical model hinges entirely on a series of wars associated with the dis-memberment of the Ottoman Empire. Narang and Nelson also challenge Mansfield and Snyder's selection of case studies. Most feature countries with stable regimes or governments trending toward autocracy, not democratizing states with weak domestic institutions.[18]

This book intersects with the evolving democratic peace scholarship in several ways. It emphasizes the primacy of institutions over shared norms in promoting peace among democracies. The argument is that the byproducts of a state's regime type frame outside perceptions of its rise. Decentralized authority and transparency work together to clarify intentions and create opportunities for the shaping of strategic behavior. Domestic institutions thus enable democracies to rise and reassure. The book's focus on institutions rather than common values helps to move the democratic peace away from normative arguments grounded in Anglo-American political culture. Outside Great Britain and the United States, democratic leaders may not attribute ideological significance to the domestic arrangements of other nations. Yet the structural consequences of regime type should influence how democracies across different traditions and historical legacies relate to ascendant states.

The other contribution the book makes to the democratic peace is to extend the theory to an arena traditionally dominated by realism, an approach to international relations that downplays the impact of domestic political arrangements and prioritizes factors such as military capabilities and geography. These two factors, according to proponents of realism, should exert maximal influence over a state's foreign policy during power transitions. Thus, the book affirms the democratic peace under conditions that should be least conducive to the theory.[19]

Power Transitions

Scholarship on power transitions has its origins in Thucydides' *History of the Peloponnesian War*, a chronicle of the struggle between Sparta and an ascendant Athens. The starting premise of most work on power transitions is that the "relative strengths of the leading nations in world affairs never remain constant, principally because of the uneven rate of growth among different societies."[20] International relations theorist Robert Gilpin builds on this premise to conceive the arc of history as "successive rises of powerful states that have governed the system and have determined the patterns of international interactions and established the rules of the system."[21] In his account, war occurs when a declining but still dominant state confronts a rising power. Invariably, the rising power will seek to alter international rules, the global hierarchy of prestige, and the distribution of territory among states. The reason is that a disjuncture exists between the rising power's newfound preeminence and an international system reflecting the preferences of the now declining state. This embattled nation will attempt to right the balance of power; failure to reverse the power transition results in war. If victorious, the newly dominant power, having displaced the leading state, will set about creating a new international system more favorable to its interests.[22]

Perhaps the most developed line of argument in the scholarship on power transitions is located in the work of A. F. K. Organski. In Organski's view, differential rates of industrialization produce an international system where the distribution of benefits lags behind changes in the balance of power. The probability of war hinges on two variables: the magnitude of the gap between the dominant state and the rising power, and the rising power's degree of satisfaction with the existing international order. When the dominant state retains an unbridgeable lead, the prospects for war are negligible. No matter how revisionist, a weak nation has little recourse but to accept the current international order. However, as the dominant state declines, the likelihood of war increases with the rising power's level of dissatisfaction.[23] No longer unassailable, the flagging leader begins to question its ability to defeat the rising power in future conflicts. On the flipside, the rising power becomes ever more confident that war with the dominant state will bring about an advantageous reordering of the international system.

Organksi and scholars building on his work remain divided over the sequencing of power transitions and war. Originally, Organksi argued that rising powers initiate war before overtaking the dominant state. But in a later book, Organski and Jacek Kugler contend that wars only occur after the power transition is complete.[24] Kugler and Douglas Lemke assert that the probability of war peaks at the moment of parity between the declining and rising states, while Robert Powell finds that the likelihood of war rises throughout the course of power transitions.[25]

Disagreements over the timing of conflict point to several areas of weakness in the foundational scholarship on power transitions. The advent of nuclear weapons calls into question the merit of examining power transitions largely from the perspective of war. The costs of conflict become prohibitive when both the dominant state and the rising power possess nuclear weapons. A dissatisfied and powerful state may wish to overturn the existing international order, but in the nuclear age, radical redistribution of territory by force no longer presents a viable option.[26] Another oversight in the early scholarship on power transitions is the disproportionate attention accorded to choices made by the rising state. Woosang Kim and James Morrow acknowledge this: "We do not ask the question of why dominant states do not crush nascent challengers far in advance of their rise to power. The literature, to our knowledge, has never addressed this question, so we do not."[27]

Not all the early scholarship falls into one or both of these analytical traps. Stephen Rock examines how reconciliation occurs between major powers. Through several case studies, including the Anglo-American power transition, he finds that compatible geopolitical goals and a common culture and ideology promote reassurance.[28] Yet his approach leaves unanswered how a state might gauge a rising power's intentions. Randall Schweller focuses on why democracies experiencing relative decline refrain from preventive war. He suggests they will accommodate other democracies as they rise and form defensive alliances against ascendant autocracies. However, Schweller offers only a cursory explanation for these choices, observing that because of shared values and common external enemies, democracies inevitably regard relations with each other as positive sum.[29] In a study on the origin of great power conflict, Dale Copeland asserts that dominant states perceiving a sharp decline in their relative standing may resort to preventive war if they confront a single rising power.[30] The focus on the dominant state's strategy is useful, but the nuclear age would appear to rule out preventive war as a tool for navigating power transitions.

In recent years, a new wave of scholarship has significantly enriched the power transitions literature. Schweller in the opening chapter of an edited volume on China's ascendancy distills history and theory to describe potential responses to a new power's rise. Although some of these strategies blur together in practice, the menu of policy options he articulates represents a major step forward.[31] David Edelstein too focuses on how states navigate unfavorable power shifts. He asserts that a declining but still dominant state will pursue cooperation if the ambitions of a new power appear susceptible to external manipulation. In drawing attention to beliefs about a rising state's intentions, Edelstein makes a significant contribution.[32] Yet his perspective overlooks how such beliefs ultimately reflect a new power's regime type. Paul MacDonald and Joseph Parent examine a particular approach to relative decline: retrenchment. Surveying eighteen historical junctures, they find that a majority of great powers retract their strategic commitments when their position within the hierarchy of nations falls.[33] A question that lingers is the extent to which the authors' expansive definition of retrenchment sheds light on the concrete choices that states make during power shifts.

The new wave of scholarship also offers a more sophisticated treatment of power transitions and war. John Ikenberry points out that the probability of conflict will vary depending on the type of international order a state established before its decline. If the order subordinates other countries, a rising power will have few avenues to secure its interests other than war. But in the case of a "liberal order" that features rules-based governance and well-developed international institutions, an ascendant state will possess avenues to increase its voice and influence and consequently experience fewer pressures to pursue forcible change.[34] In a study on the origins of peace, Charles Kupchan argues that the path to reconciliation begins with a unilateral concession and that enduring friendship between nations requires "compatible social orders and cultural commonality."[35] Although his analysis extends beyond power transitions, it contains important insights for how declining and rising states might avoid conflict.

Robert Art, forecasting the future of U.S.-China relations, observes that insecurity does not invariably accompany transitions of power. He contends that war is most likely when declining and rising states present a real or perceived threat to each other, and that the insecurity of the declining state matters most.[36] Asking whether China's ascendance will result in war, Charles Glaser takes a related approach. In his perspective, the severity of the security dilemma—the cycle of action and reaction in which the pursuit of security by one state triggers a countervailing response from another—can vary during power transitions. When defense and deterrence are easy, and states perceive each other as motivated by a desire for security rather than dominance, changes in the balance of power can unfold with a reduced likelihood of conflict.[37] William Wohlforth offers a more pessimistic view of power transitions and war. He asserts that a state's status depends on its capabilities relative to others. Leveraging research in psychology and sociology, Wohlforth argues that a clear imbalance of power among states promotes acceptance of the status quo. Power transitions muddy once-clear hierarchies and create incentives for status competition, which may translate into conflict.[38]

This book builds on the considerable advancements made by the power transitions literature over the past decade. It explains strategy formulation rather than the outbreak of war, and examines the choices of the initially dominant state. The book's focus on regime type also addresses a major oversight in the current scholarship: how national leaders form beliefs about a new power's intentions and why these beliefs evolve over time.

Economic Interdependence

Statesmen and scholars have long expounded that economic interdependence causes peace. One formulation of this argument points to mutual self-interest: nations become less inclined to fight wars as the costs of disrupting trade and investment flows increase.[39] Other arguments linking commerce to peace focus on the second-order effects of economic interdependence. The exchange of goods and ideas across borders may reshape identities. As they become increasingly cosmopolitan, citizens of commercial states are less likely to view foreigners as inherently threatening.[40] Trade may also give rise to domestic groups with a vested stake in peace. These groups can leverage their new wealth to lobby for a pacific foreign policy congruent with their commercial interests.[41] Last, economic interdependence may promote peace by offering policymakers a way to credibly telegraph their intentions without resorting to force. A state's willingness to reduce lucrative trade and investment flows constitutes a powerful signal that alleviates uncertainty about resolve. This in turn diminishes the likelihood of miscalculation during disputes.[42]

Statistical research has yielded considerable support for claims about the relationship between economic interdependence and peace. Since the mid-1990s a number of studies have found a significant correlation between high levels of trade between pairs of countries and a diminished propensity for conflict. Oneal and Russett use regression analysis to demonstrate that commercial interdependence is associated with more pacific bilateral relations before World War I, during the interwar period, throughout the Cold War, and after.[43] In their book *Triangulating Peace*, Russett and Oneal again test whether the existence of important economic ties coincides with decreased conflict between states. They find that the probability of violent disputes declines by 43 percent when each country is economically dependent on the other.[44]

This "commercial peace" is not without critics. Katherine Barbieri uses regression analysis to show that higher economic interdependence enhances the risk of conflict between countries.[45] Copeland argues that expectations about future trade determine whether commercial ties foster peace or foment war. His logic is that a deep trading relationship can only underpin peace if both states foresee its continuation; if they anticipate a breakdown in future trade, highly dependent states fearing that the resulting economic loss will diminish their relative power may come to regard war as an attractive option.[46]

Proponents of the commercial peace have refuted each of these critiques. A number of scholars have suggested that Barbieri's measure of economic interdependence may account for the positive relationship between trade and conflict that she identifies. Oneal and Russett further question the scope of her regression analysis, which includes all potential pairs of countries. They demonstrate that Barbieri's main finding is a statistical mirage: trade only increases the likelihood of violence between states that lack the proximity or power to fight each other.[47] Oneal, Russett, and Berbaum test whether expectations of future commerce matter. Their analysis contradicts Copeland's argument. Historical trends in bilateral trade levels—a key point of reference for national leaders trying to forecast the future—appear to have minimal impact on the frequency of conflict between states.[48]

Another critique questions whether the line of cause and effect runs from trade to peace or peace to trade. Early arguments of this kind focus on how political relationships between states may facilitate commerce. Gowa and Mansfield contend that allied states are more likely to trade with each other because the gains in national wealth will strengthen their collective capabilities. Surveying most of the twentieth century, they conclude that alliances have a significant and positive influence on bilateral trade flows.[49] More recent arguments in this vein emphasize the simultaneous interaction between trade and conflict. In separate studies, Omar Keshk, Brian Pollins, and Rafael Reuveny, and Hyung Min Kim and David Rousseau reassess the commercial peace while accounting for reciprocal cause and effect. Both studies show that economic interdependence has no pacific benefit.[50]

This challenge to the commercial peace has not gone unanswered. In an early survey of the simultaneous interaction between trade and conflict, Soo Yeon Kim determines that the strongest line of cause and effect runs from commerce to peace.[51] Oneal, Russett, and Berbaum likewise demonstrate that while a two-way relationship characterizes trade and conflict, a dispute between states will only depress bilateral commerce for a short period. Controlling for several factors that might influence trade flows, they also find that alliances have no impact on commerce between states.[52] Last, Havard Hegre, Oneal, and Russett uncover methodological flaws in the two recent studies negating the commercial peace. They "show that the pacific benefit of interdependence is apparent when the influences of size and proximity on interstate conflict are explicitly considered."[53]

A subset of the literature on trade and peace explores how economic interdependence interfaces with domestic politics to shape a state's strategic choices. Paul Papayoanou maintains that extensive economic ties with a rival power will hinder a state's capacity to hedge or contain. Groups that directly benefit from commerce with the rival power will be reluctant to view it as hostile and oppose the adoption of confrontational policies. In addition, political leaders will fear the consequences of a more assertive strategy—that the rival power will sever commercial relations, resulting in painful economic dislocation at home. Papayoanou argues that democracies are more vulnerable to both of these dynamics because they accord all interests a voice in the making of foreign policy.[54] Kevin Narizny advances a related argument. Sectors dependent on an external power for their economic livelihood will champion a foreign policy of accommodation while sectors that compete with that power in third markets will prefer more hardline approaches. Sectors reliant on trade and investment with a multitude of foreign partners will advocate international law and institution building but stand ready to oppose aggressors that threaten regional or global stability. The balance of these sectors within a state's ruling political coalition will dictate its strategic choices.[55]

The commercial peace scholarship thus offers another vantage point for understanding how democratic leaders formulate strategy during power transitions. Trade and investment linkages may impose comparatively greater constraints on the rising state if its economy remains smaller than the democratic power's. Yet if trade with the rising state constitutes a sizeable percentage of the democratic power's national wealth, or if other types of economic entanglements exist, the potential loss of valuable commercial relations and the prospect of domestic blowback may overhang democratic leaders as they decide whether to appease, integrate, hedge, or contain. Except for the onset of the Cold War, all the case studies in this book feature nonnegligible economic ties between the democratic power and the ascendant state. Although the limited number of power transitions in the book provides an insufficient basis for broader claims about the role of economic interdependence, the analysis of multiple cases allows for a more nuanced understanding of the interplay between commercial ties and foreign policy.

Ordering of the Book

The remainder of the book offers an analytical framework and supporting historical evidence that, in turn, illuminate the geopolitics of the twenty-first century. Chapter 2 explains how regime type frames power shifts and sets the stage for how democratic states respond to the emergence of other powers. The next five chapters cover a period of time stretching from the late nineteenth century to the present. Chapter 3 explores the British responses to the simultaneous rise of the United States and Imperial Germany. Chapter

4 looks at Great Britain's approach to the resurgence of Germany during the 1930s. Chapter 5 focuses on how the United States in the 1940s managed the rise of the Soviet Union. Chapters 6 and 7 respectively examine how the United States and Japan have responded to the growth of Chinese power. Chapter 8 discusses the scholarly and policy implications of the book's main findings.

Chapter 2

Power Shifts and Strategy

This chapter connects power transitions, regime type, and the choices that democratic leaders make as they navigate the rise of other nations. The argument is that democracy in an ascendant state reassures while autocratic rule creates a climate of uncertainty and mistrust. Democracies can rise without sowing alarm because their domestic institutions clarify intentions and allow outsiders to shape their strategic behavior. Conversely, rising autocracies provoke anxiety because centralized control and pervasive secrecy obscure their ambitions and reduce opportunities to influence their trajectory. What this means is that democratic powers pursue different strategies as democracies and autocracies rise. They appease newly powerful democracies in order to remove points of conflict and pave the way for integration into international institutions. However, autocratic rule in a rising state necessitates a different approach. Democratic powers will avoid appeasement, and instead attempt to embed rising autocracies in international institutions while looking to military capabilities and alliances as a hedge. This approach amounts to a delicate balance between two disparate strategies. Containment becomes attractive if an autocracy's behavior as its rise continues unmistakably demonstrates the failure of integration to have a moderating effect.

Power and Perceptions

Changes in the balance of power and the balance of perceptions precede a fateful transition. Clever diplomacy or convincing rhetoric may, for a time, boost a nation's status in world affairs, but without an accompanying accumulation of economic and military assets, this ascendance will prove short lived. To rise, a state must bring about a shift in the prevailing balance of national capabilities. Yet that state's emergence may initially go unnoticed by outsiders. Fateful transitions unfold only when democratic leaders begin to perceive another nation's rise. This section unpacks the balance of power and the balance of perceptions because a detailed understanding of each is critical to identifying the universe of cases relevant to the book.

The Balance of Power

Although power lies at the heart of a vast body of international relations scholarship, its main components remain contested. Theorists such as Kugler and Organski put forward gross national product as a concise indicator of overall national strength.[1] To measure the balance of power, more recent academic work has used gross domestic product (GDP) and the Correlates of War, a composite index of state capabilities.[2]

It is tempting to simply define the balance of power as the balance of wealth using GDP. Yet when inflated by a large population size, GDP can provide a misleading indicator of national capabilities. As Fareed Zakaria observes, a state's power reflects the resources the national government can command.[3] If much of a state's population exists at the level of subsistence, a government can harness few resources despite the overall size of the economy.[4] History demonstrates the disjuncture between GDP and the balance of power. Well into the nineteenth century, China boasted the largest GDP of any nation. Yet the government of Great Britain—able to extract more resources from an industrializing economy—could impose its will on China.[5] GDP may overstate a nation's actual capabilities for another reason: the state refrains from translating economic prowess into military might. Blessed by a favorable geography and distrustful of standing armies, the United States long avoided maintaining a military commensurate with its economic clout. Contemporary Japan has yet to develop military forces proportionate to its status as the world's third-largest economy.[6] In short, GDP as a catchall indicator of national power is highly problematic.

Composite measurements of the balance of power can also mislead. The Correlates of War index contains six indicators of national capabilities: energy consumption, iron and steel production, military expenditures, military personnel, total population, and urban population.[7] These indicators are fixed: the index treats them as valid measures of national power from the nineteenth century to the present. In reality, what defines the balance of power has evolved over time. To give only one example, steel production once attested to a nation's overall level of economic development and war-making potential but long ago ceased to be a cutting-edge industry or a vital military input. The same applies to all indicators in the Correlates of War index except a state's military expenditures.

To accurately capture the balance of power requires historical context. From the late nineteenth century to the present, three indicators of national power have remained relevant: a nation's economic output, international trade, and military expenditures. Other indicators of national capability speak to the balance of power at specific junctures. In the pre-World War I period, observers looked to steel production and warship tonnage when evaluating the balance of power. The interwar years saw first-line aircraft join these two indicators as a period-specific measure of national capabilities. As the Cold War emerged, possession of the atomic bomb loomed large in contemporary assessments of power balances. Today, spending on research and development (R&D), along with GDP, international trade, and military expenditures remain seen as indicators of national strength. Table 1 summarizes how the defining characteristics of the balance of power have varied over time.

This century-plus span is rarely amenable to precise benchmarks that demarcate when changes in the balance of power amount to a state's rise. While a state's share of key capabilities should expand relative to the share of the democratic power, there is no clear-cut threshold marking the start of a

Table 1: Balance of Power

Period	Key indicators Type
All	GDP International trade Military expenditures
Prewar	Steel production Warship tonnage
Interwar	Steel production Warship tonnage First-line aircraft
Early Cold War	Atomic bomb
Present	R&D spending

power transition. The benchmark this book uses is a shift in the distribution of capabilities along multiple dimensions, with at least one dimension an enduring indicator of national power. The gap between the democratic power and the other state should narrow over time, though it need not close entirely.

The Balance of Perceptions

The balance of perceptions presents a different sort of measurement challenge. Perceptions of another state's rise usually take the form of a comparison, with democratic leaders expressing concern about their country's loss of preeminence going forward. To the degree that such concerns exist within a democratic elite, they are chronicled in public speeches, government documents, private correspondence, memoirs, newspapers, and magazines.

Various statements would indicate that democratic leaders worry about their country's relative decline. Most explicitly, they could project that another state will overtake their own as the leading regional or global power. They could also anticipate a loss of preeminence in a more circumscribed area. On the economic side, this could include relative size of GDP, dominance of major export markets, or technological leadership. On the military side, democratic leaders might worry about a loss of military superiority, the advent of parity in conventional or nuclear capabilities, or a changed balance of power in a specific region.

In a democracy, the balance of perceptions hinges on mainstream elite opinion. If a handful of prescient pessimists foresee relative decline but democratic leaders as a whole express confidence about their nation's prospects compared to another power, the balance of perceptions remains unmoved. For a shift to occur, democratic elites across bureaucratic and partisan lines should articulate concern about a diminishment of their state's dominant position. Together with a change in the balance of power, this transformation of perceptions marks the moment when a democratic state begins to confront a fateful transition.

Identifying Cases

Together, power and perceptions determine the universe of cases relevant to the book. This universe encompasses "hegemonic transitions" where a democratic power's global dominance comes under pressure from an ascendant state. Great Britain before World War I and the United States after 1945 have held international positions that approached hegemony. The book examines British strategy toward the emergence of the United States and Germany at the turn of the twentieth century, America's approach to the Soviet Union's postwar ascendancy, and the ongoing U.S. response to China's rise. These cases feature changes in the balance of power and the balance of perceptions.

However, the criteria that define fateful transitions point to a broader set of cases than these four. Although its commercial and maritime primacy had faded, Great Britain during the 1930s was still a pivotal democratic state. Nazi Germany's upending of a balance of power that favored Great Britain falls squarely within the universe of cases. So does China's recent eclipse of Japan, the most influential democracy in East Asia. Both of these cases feature a reversal in the bilateral distribution of capabilities, and perceptions of a sharp power inversion by democratic leaders.

Power and perceptions limit the universe of cases to these six. British strategy toward czarist Russia and Meiji Japan, U.S.-Japan and Anglo-Soviet relations during the interwar period, and U.S. policy toward Japan in the 1980s have some resemblance to fateful transitions, but ultimately each historical juncture fails to meet one or both of the criteria set out. These cases were considered but ultimately omitted.[8] The argument advanced by the book does not necessarily pertain when democratic leaders confront—or perceive—only limited fluctuations in the balance of power.

Democratic Strategies

Four strategic options—appeasement, integration, hedging, and containment—encompass the full range of policies that democracies have historically embraced as they navigate power transitions. These strategies vary widely in terms of the resources required and the actions involved. They do not capture polices that, while potentially effective, have no historical precedent, such as democratic leaders waging preventive war against a rising state or comprehensively encouraging an emerging power's political liberalization.[9]

Appeasement

A democracy can appease a rising state. The historian Paul Kennedy classifies appeasement as a strategy designed to avert armed conflict by "admitting and satisfying grievances through rational negotiation and compromise."[10] Stephen Rock in his book *Appeasement in International Politics* presents a similar definition—a "policy of reducing tensions with one's adversary by removing the causes of conflict and disagreement."[11] He adds that appeasement may include mutual accommodation, but the appeaser takes the "initiative in offering inducements and will ultimately make greater sacrifices than its opponent."

Both Kennedy and Rock provide for a relatively expansive definition of appeasement. In any instance of international negotiations, the final outcome may be uneven, with one party making more concessions than the other. If appeasement ranges from unilateral accommodation to relative reciprocity, it becomes difficult to distinguish from other strategies that a democracy might implement. A more operational definition ought to focus on resources and actions. Appeasement is a strategy that demands few national resources and entails virtually unilateral concessions by democratic leaders in negotiations with the rising state.

Integration

Democratic leaders can decide to integrate a rising power into international institutions. These institutions can differ substantially in structure and total membership, ranging from bilateral alliances with a rising power—pacts of restraint[12]—to multilateral security or economic arrangements in which many nations in addition to the rising power participate. To varying degrees, membership in institutions creates "long-term security, political, and economic commitments that are difficult to retract."[13] Integration thus holds the potential of altering the cost-benefit calculations of a rising state in a direction that renders competitive behavior less attractive. A strategy of integration also endows an ascendant state with a "place at the table" where it may voice concerns and cooperate with other nations in shaping the future global order.[14] Participation in international institutions has the potential to reshape a rising power's interests, though this outcome is far from assured.

The institutional toolkit available to democratic leaders has evolved over time. During the late nineteenth and first half of the twentieth centuries, international regimes were few and weak; for the most part, integration consisted of bilateral pacts or attempts to construct multilateral arrangements from scratch. In the post-World War II era, the establishment of a robust architecture of international governmental organizations has given democratic leaders a much larger set of institutions in which to embed rising states.[15]

Integration demands modest resources from a democratic power, namely, the time and attention government officials take to negotiate treaties, sustain consultative mechanisms, and manage multilateral regimes. Implementation of an integration strategy should feature efforts by democratic leaders to incorporate a rising state into new or preexisting international institutions.

Hedging

A democracy can hedge against another power's ascendancy. What hedging actually entails remains somewhat nebulously defined in international relations scholarship and security studies. Without explicitly using the term, Randall Schweller notes the potential for strong states to "mix concessions with credible threats, to use sticks as well as carrots" when confronting a rising power.[16] Rock similarly points to the possibility of "combining appeasement with deterrent threats in a mixed influence strategy."[17] Unsurprisingly, work on China's ascendance features the most detailed definitions of hedging. Assessing relations between Washington and Beijing, Evan Medeiros defines hedging as "policies that, on one hand, stress engagement and integration mechanisms and, on the other, emphasize realist-style balancing."[18]

Each of these scholars, though capturing aspects of hedging, falls short of an operational definition. When classified as a mixed strategy that harnesses threats and concessions, hedging blurs into coercive bargaining. The definition that Medeiros offers, on the other hand, combines two distinct approaches to a new power's rise: hedging as well as integration. Resources and actions provide a more precise framework. Hedging is a strategy that demands considerable diplomatic attention and financial investment from democratic leaders. Its execution involves policies designed to establish diplomatic or military leverage against the rising state, such as the redeployment of existing military assets, the development of new military capabilities, and the pursuit of alliances.[19]

Containment

The term "containment" originated in 1947 with George Kennan's efforts to devise a U.S. approach toward the Soviet Union.[20] It initially meant checking Soviet expansion on the Eurasian landmass, and has since become synonymous with America's strategy throughout the Cold War. Yet containment, as a strategy available to democratic leaders, existed long before the dawn of U.S.-Soviet rivalry. Its execution has always carried a steep cost, in time, in treasure, and potentially, in the lives of a nation's citizens. Containment goes well beyond hedging; it is a strategy of arresting another power's rise by imposing economic sanctions, using military capabilities and alliances to deter aggression, and if necessary, taking military action to roll back territorial conquest.

Regime Type and Power Transitions

During power transitions, democratic leaders should, in theory, always prefer integration over other approaches. Integration demands modest resources while holding out the hope of modifying behavior and reshaping interests. No other strategy for navigating a new power's rise offers such a favorable tradeoff of resources to outcomes. Although less costly, appeasement cannot create enduring incentives for responsible international conduct. Nor can appeasement promote a convergence of interests where the rising state gradually takes on the preferences of the democratic power. Hedging delivers none of the benefits associated with integration and demands substantial resources. Even if democratic leaders try to rely mostly on alliances—to hedge on the cheap—they can only attract and retain partners by fielding some military capabilities.[21] For a democracy, containment should hold negative appeal. Imposing economic sanctions against a rising state means forgoing trade and investment opportunities and terminating existing commercial ties. Additionally, deterring territorial expansion requires an expensive peacetime military, while rolling back aggression carries a steep human cost.

Yet from the late nineteenth century to the present, democratic leaders have tried every strategy in their toolkit. They have paired integration with hedging, appeased, contained, and sometimes alternated among strategies during the course of a new power's emergence. In a world of complexity, no single factor explains this variation, but one factor does stand out: the regime type of the rising power.

Democracy and Power Transitions

Democracy functions as a source of reassurance on multiple levels. In a democracy, authority is dispersed across a number of decision-makers, either through constitutionally enshrined checks and balances, or through deeply respected traditions of rule of law. Either way, a diverse array of domestic actors plays a role in foreign policymaking. At the same time, an essential element of democratic government is transparency. Transparency describes the visibility of a state's policymaking process. Under democratic rule, a government's daily proceedings largely occur in the open. Debates about policy take place in the public eye. And, because democracy places a premium on transparency, the press enjoys legal safeguards.[22]

The combination of decentralized authority and transparency prevents a democracy from concealing its true intentions. With numerous domestic actors privy to foreign policy deliberations, information inevitably leaks, making secrecy about strategic level decisions virtually impossible. Moreover, because transparency operates as a domestic norm, "any embassy can subscribe to the major newspapers that provide day-to-day investigative services on the policymaking activities" of a democratic government.[23] Outsiders may fail to predict every perturbation in a democracy's foreign policy, but they will have a clear understanding of its broader objectives.[24]

Beyond clarifying intentions, the institutions underpinning democracy also generate opportunities for access—the shaping of strategic behavior by cultivating, lobbying, and manipulating influential groups in another state.[25] By opening up the foreign policymaking process to a large number of domestic actors, decentralized authority creates conditions conducive to access. The diffusion of power under democratic rule increases the likelihood that outsiders can locate sympathetic groups who have a hand in foreign policy. In addition, enlarging the circle of decision-making virtually guarantees that internal disagreements will surface, a development that outsiders can exploit, for example, by promoting deadlock to prevent an undesired policy shift.[26]

In a democracy, transparency works in tandem with decentralized authority to create access opportunities. Publicly available information enables outsiders to locate sympathetic domestic groups to cultivate. Also, the activities of a free press lay bare foreign policy disagreements that would otherwise go unnoticed. Transparency thus allows outsiders to become intimately familiar with the contours of another country's internal debates, a prerequisite for access. Last but not least, transparency at home extends to dealings with foreigners. Because a democracy accepts considerable information flows, its citizens can more or less freely engage with the representatives of other states. This high degree of latitude is essential for outsiders to leverage points of access.

During a power transition, democratic government in the rising state reduces mistrust. Outsiders can draw upon diverse sources speaking to the emerging power's intentions. They need not conflate ambitions with military forces deployed, a formula guaranteed to generate mistrust because any ascendant state will eventually translate some of its newfound wealth into military power.[27] Information about intentions is one source of reassurance; the

Table 2: Democracy and Power Transitions

Institutions	Implications
Decentralized authority	Clear intentions
Transparency	Many access opportunities

other is the existence of access opportunities. The ability to shape strategic behavior constitutes the ultimate safeguard against the disruptions accompanying a new power's emergence. A rising democracy may harbor expansionist ambitions, but leaders in the other democratic power can partner with sympathetic domestic actors and leverage internal divisions to moderate its external objectives over time. Table 2 summarizes how democracy in an ascendant state can function as a source of reassurance.

Autocracy and Power Transitions

A state under autocratic rule lacks the reassurance mechanisms outlined above. Autocracy centralizes power, confining foreign policy decisions to an elite few, or even to a single individual. In addition, to maintain control over the population, an autocracy limits the flow of information.[28] Secrecy is pervasive. The government walls off its daily proceedings from public view: policy debates unfold behind closed doors. The need for information control renders a free press intolerable to an autocracy. Whatever media exist operate under state supervision and without meaningful legal protection.

The institutions central to authoritarian government obscure a state's intentions. With foreign policy an exclusive domain, the details of internal discussions remain closely held. Add to this sweeping state secrecy laws, and the potential for information leaks is low. Straitjacketed media have little capacity to report on policy deliberations within an autocracy, and because of state controls, outsiders largely discount whatever information the media do convey. Centralized authority and nontransparency thus generate considerable uncertainty about a state's ambitions.

The institutions associated with autocratic government also deprive outsiders of opportunities to shape strategic behavior. Centralized authority is inimical to access. Foreign policy decisions at most involve a handful of domestic actors. Business and civil society groups that might become points of access in a democracy are relegated to the sidelines. The concentration of power that underpins autocracy also decreases the probability of internal divisions that outsiders can exploit.

Nontransparency further restricts opportunities for access. Pervasive secrecy and the consequent lack of a free press prevent outsiders from understanding the landscape of power within an autocracy. It is difficult to determine who to cultivate, who to lobby, and who to manipulate. And obtaining such information would prove of little value because nontransparency applies to how citizens of an autocracy relate to foreigners. A regime that prizes secrecy will regulate interactions with outsiders, particularly on sensitive issues like foreign policy. There are inherent limits to engaging domestic actors within an authoritarian state.

Autocracy exacerbates the concerns accompanying a powerful state's emergence. The problem created by a lack of transparency is less the possibility of a surprise attack and more the uncertainty that overhangs a rising autocracy's ambitions. Outsiders confront an unanswerable question: will the ascendant state be content to peacefully accumulate influence or will it use force to rewrite international rules of the road? The new power's military capabilities will inevitably loom large as a key indicator of intentions when external observers lack alternative sources of information. Against a backdrop of uncertainty, a rising power's military buildup will trigger growing mistrust. So will the dearth of access opportunities. When outsiders lack the ability to shape strategic behavior, they become highly vulnerable to the potential downside of another power's rise. Table 3 encapsulates how authoritarian rule amplifies mistrust of an ascendant state.

Implications for Democratic Leaders

The regime type of a rising state sets the broad boundaries for democratic leaders navigating a power transition. Democracy in the ascendant nation reduces risk and bolsters trust by clarifying intentions and opening up opportunities to shape strategic behavior. This removes the need for outsiders

Table 3: Autocracy and Power Transitions

Institutions	Implications
Centralized authority	Unclear intentions
Nontransparency	Few access opportunities

to hedge: democratic leaders can forgo enhanced military capabilities and strengthened alliances and pursue a course of accommodation.

Although integration offers the most favorable tradeoff between resources and outcomes, this strategy can only succeed over a long time horizon. To the extent that international institutions can impose constraints on behavior, these constraints do not emerge overnight. Rather, they strengthen over time as a rising state becomes increasingly invested in a growing array of bilateral agreements and multilateral regimes.[29] Likewise, international institutions hold the potential to reshape a rising state's interests only after an extended period of participation.

To ensure the time needed for integration to succeed, democratic leaders will tend to favor a course of appeasement at the onset of another democracy's rise. Appeasement removes points of conflict that could become future impediments to embedding a democracy in international institutions as its rise accelerates. The stability cemented by appeasement creates conditions conducive to long-term integration. In this sense, appeasement is a bridge to the strategy democratic leaders inherently prefer when confronting a new power's rise.

By contrast, at the start of an autocracy's ascendance, a democracy will likely favor a different, less accommodating approach. A rising autocracy's opaque intentions and lack of access opportunities generate risk and foster mistrust. Democratic leaders will shy away from appeasement, which offers insufficient protection against the possibility that an autocracy will grow into a powerful adversary. Containment will, at least initially, appear to carry an excessive price tag. Democratic leaders will therefore favor a two-pronged approach. They will try to integrate the rising autocracy in the hope that international institutions will constrain its behavior and ultimately transform its interests. At the same time, they will develop military capabilities and alliances to hedge against the uncertainty accompanying the autocracy's emergence on the world stage.

This dual strategy is inherently fragile. It will endure so long as the rising autocracy's behavior demonstrates restraint—a sign to democratic leaders that the combination of integration and hedging remains sufficient. However, if over time the rising autocracy engages in diplomatic or military brinksmanship, democratic leaders will increasingly question the viability of integration. Lacking alternative sources of information that might offer a more nuanced view of the rising autocracy's behavior, they will have little recourse but to treat diplomatic and military brinksmanship as a decisive indicator of antagonism. The apparent failure of integration coupled with perceived evidence of the

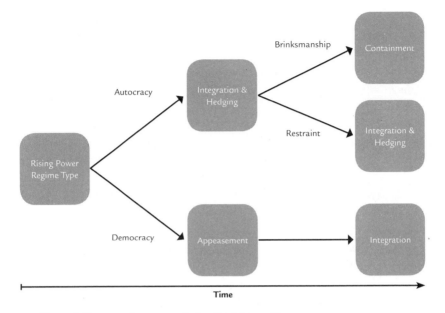

Figure 1. Democratic strategy during fateful transitions.

other state's hostility will motivate a shift to containment. Figure 1 visualizes how democratic leaders select strategies during power shifts.

The decision-making process illustrated in Figure 1 revolves around the clarity of a rising state's intentions and the availability of access opportunities. Democratic leaders make choices based on these *byproducts* of regime type, not on their perceptions of a new power's form of government.[30] As they navigate power transitions, democratic leaders may never refer to the rising state's regime type as a driver of strategy, and they may even dismiss common values as a foundation of foreign policy. Yet the rising power's domestic institutions still frame leaders' choices, because they are responding to whether they possess information about the other state's ambitions and whether they can locate opportunities to influence that state's strategic behavior from within.

Defining Regime Type

Regime type will reappear in subsequent chapters as a key factor that shapes power transitions. It is therefore important to define regime type in a way that is historically consistent and relevant to the book's main argument. One potential measure of regime type is Polity IV, a quantitative dataset commonly used in scholarship on the democratic peace. This dataset aggregates indicators of executive recruitment, executive independence, and political competition into a single numerical score. The positive end of the polity scale (+10) denotes a strongly democratic regime, while the negative end (–10) indicates a strongly autocratic regime. Although polity scores at either extreme accurately capture regime type, the middle of the scale offers a more "muddled" picture of a state's domestic institutions.[31] Polity IV data therefore serves as a first cut when assessing the regime type of an ascendant state. To ensure accuracy—and more closely link measurements of democracy and autocracy to the book's argument—the diffusion of political authority and domestic transparency provide a second set of criteria for defining the regime type of the rising power.

The World Bank Database of Political Institutions contains a robust methodology for measuring centralization of power within a regime. This database calculates the number of checks and balances by counting domestic actors legally endowed with veto authority and political parties essential to maintaining a governing coalition.[32] To qualify as decentralized, a regime must contain at least three checks and balances. This threshold is based on the fact that no country commonly regarded as a democracy has less than three checks and balances in the database.[33] A regime qualifies as centralized when only a single check and balance exists. Two checks and balances indicate a transitional domestic power structure. The World Bank database has an inherent limitation: it only starts in 1975. However, the coding procedure is easily replicable for the historical case studies contained in this book.[34]

Freedom of the press provides a valid measurement of the level of transparency in a regime. The NGO Freedom House conducts a regular worldwide survey of state interference in the media that codes countries as free, partly free, and unfree. Since its inception, the survey has evolved to include twenty-three questions across three categories—the legal, political, and economic environments in which the media operate. A subset of the twenty-three questions suffices to capture how much freedom of the press a rising state permits.[35] This abbreviated survey for evaluating state control over the media contains six questions listed in Table 4.

Conclusion

Power transitions are fraught moments in international relations, yet they differ depending on the domestic institutions of the ascendant state. Democratic

Table 4: Freedom of the Press

Legal environment

1. Does the constitution contain provisions designed to protect freedom of the press? (Y=0; N=1)
2. Do the penal code, security laws, or any other laws restrict reporting and are journalists punished under these laws? (Y=1; N=0)

Political environment

3. Are media outlets' news and information content significantly determined by the government or a particular partisan interest? (Y=1; N=0)
4. Is there official censorship? (Y=1; N=0)
5. Are journalists or media outlets subject to extralegal intimidation or physical violence by state authorities? (Y=1; N=0)

Economic environment

6. Are significant portions of the media owned or controlled by the government? (Y=1; N=0)

Score: Free=0; Partly Free=1–2; Unfree=3–6

leaders at these pivotal junctures make strategic choices that ultimately hinge on the rising state's type of regime, which determines the transparency of that state's intentions and the existence of access opportunities. This critical insight has repercussions for today's established and emerging powers. However, it is incomplete without a concrete grasp of how regime type has framed power transitions and influenced the formulation of strategy, an understanding that only history can provide. The next chapters explore six cases in which democratic states have confronted fateful transitions.

Chapter 3

Pax Britannica Eclipsed

As the United States, Europe, and much of Asia navigate the rise of new powers, the British experience at the turn of the twentieth century is instructive. Although the Pax Britannica ended on the battlefields of the First World War, the eclipse of British power occurred earlier. Between 1870 and 1914, Great Britain steadily lost ground to two emerging giants: post-Civil War America and a unified Germany. This was the product of differential economic growth rates and the military capabilities such superior economic performance afforded. Once the United States and Germany surpassed Great Britain economically, its days as the world's dominant maritime power were numbered.

The unwinding of British primacy is more than a cautionary tale; it is the only period before the current era to feature a democracy and an autocracy rising in parallel. While democratic government in the United States reassured Great Britain, allowing for appeasement, the uncertainty and mistrust generated by Germany's autocratic system compelled Great Britain to initially integrate and hedge. As growing conflict accompanied Germany's continued ascendance, the British had no recourse but to abandon this dual strategy for containment. The eclipse of Pax Britannica amply demonstrates how regime type shapes fateful transitions and sets the boundaries for how democratic leaders formulate strategy.

The Balance of Power

At its apogee in 1870, Great Britain stood head and shoulders above all rivals. The British economy was the workshop of the world while the Royal navy ruled every ocean traversed by international commerce. Yet within little more than three decades, the balance of power had radically changed. Both the United States and Germany surpassed Great Britain in economic size and steel production and substantially closed the gap on all other indicators of national power.

Gross Domestic Product

British economic predominance evaporated at the turn of the twentieth century as the United States and Germany emerged as leading powers. Great Britain in 1870 had the largest GDP of any Western nation. The United States, with a GDP more than 98 percent of Great Britain's, was close behind. Germany, a relative latecomer to the industrial revolution, had about 72 percent of Great Britain's national wealth. Although Great Britain's GDP increased from 1870 to 1913, the economies of the United States and Germany grew at a much faster pace. During this period, British economic growth averaged 1.6 percent annually, while the U.S. economy expanded at a per annum rate of 5 percent, and Germany grew at 4.7 percent.[1] Uneven growth rates brought about a marked shift in the distribution of national wealth. By the eve of World War I, Great Britain's GDP ranked behind that of the United States and Germany. Having surpassed Great Britain in 1872, the United States by 1913 had an economic output equivalent to 230 percent of British GDP. Germany, starting from a smaller base, overtook Great Britain in 1908, and by 1913, had a GDP 5 percent larger.[2]

International Trade

British commercial supremacy, once beyond challenge, became increasingly tenuous as U.S. and German involvement in international trade expanded. In 1870, the volume of British trade exceeded that of the United States and Germany combined. The trade conducted by each of these states stood at 38 percent of Great Britain's total. Between 1870 and 1913, British trade grew in absolute terms but experienced relative decline as the United States and Germany penetrated foreign markets traditionally dominated by Great Britain. U.S. exports to Europe, Japan, and China surged; German exports advanced in Europe, Latin America, and China.[3] By 1913 the value of U.S. trade had grown to 73 percent of Great Britain's, while German trade, rising even more rapidly, was 85 percent.[4]

Military Expenditures

Military expenditures (as opposed to naval expenditures) never constituted a major pillar of British primacy. Nonetheless, it is worth noting that on this dimension of national power, Germany, and subsequently the United States, closed an initial gap with Great Britain.

Unwilling to provide for a large standing army during peacetime, Great Britain in 1870 only maintained a substantial lead in military expenditures vis-à-vis a likeminded power—the United States. For a decade and a half, U.S. military expenditures actually declined as a share of Great Britain's, dropping from 65.9 percent in 1870 to 25.6 percent in 1885. This was the result of growth in British military spending coupled with U.S. demobilization following the Civil War.[5] U.S. military expenditures rebounded thereafter. In the first half of the 1890s, per annum military allocations in the United States averaged 50 percent of Great Britain's. The Spanish American War and the Boer War produced great volatility in each state's military expenditures, so the period bracketing these conflicts is atypical. In the decade before the outbreak of World War I, U.S. annual military expenditures were about 91 percent of Great Britain's.

Unsurprisingly, Great Britain was never overwhelmingly predominant in military spending relative to Germany, a nation founded on a powerful standing army. From 1872 to 1886, Great Britain retained a modest lead in military expenditures. On a per annum basis, German allocations averaged 78 percent of Great Britain's. However, from 1887 to the start of the Boer War, each state's annual military expenditures were roughly equal. Last, between 1904 and 1913, Germany held its own in an arms race with Great Britain. During this period, German military spending on average stood at 98 percent of yearly British allocations.[6]

Steel Production

Great Britain led the first industrial revolution but eventually ceded its status as the world's workshop to the United States and Germany. Nowhere was this more apparent than in steel production. Great Britain in 1870 forged more than twice as much steel as the United States and Germany combined. The steel production of these two states was respectively 28 and 21 percent of the British total. Yet four decades later Great Britain had surrendered the jewel in its industrial crown. The United States surpassed Great Britain in 1890, and by 1913 produced four times as much steel. Germany, undergoing a similar process of rapid industrialization, overtook Great Britain a decade later than the United States, and by the eve of World War I, produced 226 percent as much steel.[7]

Warship Tonnage

Great Britain's unparalleled maritime primacy waned as the United States and Germany rose. In 1880, the Royal navy was supreme in every corner of the globe and dwarfed the navies of both powers. The U.S. fleet, after becoming a formidable force during the course of the Civil War, was sold off or allowed to rot away. The remainder, an "alphabet of floating wash-tubs" in the words of one American observer, had a tonnage 26 percent that of the Royal navy. Germany, a nation forged by Prussia, a traditional land power, scarcely possessed a navy at all. German warship tonnage in 1880 was only 14 percent of Great Britain's.[8]

However, by the eve of World War I, Great Britain's reign as unchallenged ruler of the seas had ended.[9] Beginning in the late 1880s, the United States moved to reconstitute its navy. The Spanish-American war of 1898 provided a powerful impetus for additional shipbuilding, as did the later presidency of Theodore Roosevelt.[10] Consequently, the U.S. navy in 1914 reached 36 percent of the Royal navy's warship tonnage. The expansion of the German navy, beginning in 1898 with the passage of the first naval bill, ultimately posed an even greater challenge to Great Britain's control of the ocean. From 1900 to 1905, the German navy launched fourteen battleships, sparking a maritime arms race. When Great Britain escalated the arms race by introducing a revolutionary type of capital ship, Germany soon followed suit.[11] The construction of naval armaments by both sides continued at a feverish pace, and by 1914 the German navy had 48 percent of the Royal navy's tonnage. Table 5 summarizes the eclipse of Pax Britannica that occurred as the United States and Germany ascended.

The Balance of Perceptions

British fear of relative decline, though evident among a handful of farsighted intellectuals as early as 1882, only became widespread among elites during

Table 5: Anglo-U.S. and Anglo-German Balance of Power (%)

	GDP		International trade		Military expenditures*		Steel production		Warship tonnage	
	1870	1913	1870	1913	1872	1912	1870	1913	1880	1914
United States	98	230	38	73	72	87	28	408	26	36
Germany	72	105	38	85	68	94	21	226	14	48

*German military outlays remained above peacetime levels in the immediate aftermath of the Franco-Prussian War and spiked in the year before World War I. For this reason, the comparison is military expenditures from 1872 to 1912. The long-term increase in U.S. and German military expenditures relative to that of Great Britain masks substantial short-term variation.

the mid-1890s.[12] Initially, concerns about Great Britain's loss of predominance were largely economic in nature. By the century's turning, British elites also began to foresee an erosion of their country's maritime supremacy.

Premonitions of Economic Decline

Observers at the turn of the twentieth century lacked the tools to calculate gross domestic product. Elites had no means of estimating the size of the British economy or its growth rate relative to others. Indeed, the only regular statistics collected by the British government were the Customs Department's record of exports and imports.[13] The use of trade returns as a measure of relative economic performance precluded a consensus on Great Britain's declining competitiveness. Given the fluctuations of trade returns, and the malleability of the statistics collected, no unassailable conclusions could be drawn.[14]

Early warnings of economic decline thus failed to resonate among British elites. In 1886, a royal commission reported on the "Depression of Trade and Industry." The commission observed a growing challenge to British exports, and noted that the "increasing severity of this competition both in our home and in neutral markets is especially noticeable in the case of Germany." Although relatively optimistic about Great Britain's long-term economic prospects, the commission concluded: "we cannot, perhaps, hope to maintain, to the same extent as heretofore, the lead which we formerly held among the manufacturing nations of the world."[15] The anxieties voiced by the commission went largely unheeded. A report by the Board of Trade in 1888 painted a far more sanguine picture of Great Britain's economic performance. The report argued that alarmism was unwarranted, and that British commercial primacy was uncontested.[16] Likewise, the *Times* (of London), the newspaper of elites in the Victorian age, confidently asserted in 1891 that German hopes of overtaking British trade "must soon be surrendered."[17]

However, by the mid-1890s, doubts about Great Britain's economic competitiveness had become commonplace. Parliamentary debates in 1893 and subsequent years featured repeated questions about the influx of German imports into Great Britain. No longer complacent about Great Britain's long-term economic trajectory, the *Times* in 1894 and 1895 published numerous articles detailing the advance of German commerce and the intensifying competition British business faced. The "Decay of the Iron Industry," a prominently located article in the *Times*, provides a window onto British anxieties: "the iron trade of that country [Germany] has of late years greatly improved its competitive position in reference to the iron and steel industries generally, and that it now menaces the prosperity of the English iron trade to a larger extent than has ever happened in the past."[18]

The alarm sounded by the *Times* paralleled the thinking of many, though not all Conservatives, who in 1895 assumed control of government.[19] Joseph Chamberlain, the new colonial secretary, was already convinced that Great Britain would be surpassed by its commercial rivals in the absence of strenuous efforts to shore up competitiveness.[20] The president of the Board of Trade, Charles Ritchie, also harbored doubts about Great Britain's economic situation. In 1896, the Board of Trade conducted a study comparing Great Britain to France, Germany, and the United States. Summarizing the results, Ritchie, largely referring to the United States and Germany, predicted: "their competition with us in neutral markets, and even in our home markets, will probably, unless we ourselves are active, become increasingly serious." Without improving industry, Great Britain "could scarcely expect to maintain our past undoubted pre-eminence."[21]

On the economic side, the balance of perceptions decisively shifted in the mid-1890s. From then on, a critical segment of British elites projected decline relative to the United States and Germany.

Maritime Fears

Throughout much of the nineteenth century, elites in Great Britain took the Royal navy's worldwide supremacy for granted.[22] This was particularly true vis-à-vis the United States and Germany. Continuous neglect of the American navy in the decades following the Civil War led the British government to dismiss the United States as a maritime power. A paper prepared in 1882 for the Royal Commission on Imperial Defence exemplifies this perception. It described the American navy as "contemptible," and cited budgetary pressures and tensions between Congress and the executive branch as ruling out substantial increase in U.S. maritime strength.[23]

By the late 1880s, the British government had begun to reassess the future trajectory of the American navy. The War Office and the Admiralty in an 1889 joint report noted that British maritime supremacy in the Western Hemisphere was secure, but added: "the present naval policy of the United States tends in the direction of a considerable increase in strength."[24] The steady buildup of the American fleet thereafter wrought a transformation in British perceptions of the Royal navy's predominance. In a paper written for the first lord of the admiralty in 1899, the director of naval intelligence admitted that the Royal navy's squadrons in North America, the Pacific, and the Caribbean had become "completely outclassed."[25] By the early years of the twentieth century, Great Britain's loss of maritime supremacy to the United States was considered potentially global in scope. In 1901, the first lord of the admiralty observed: "if the Americans choose to pay for what they can easily afford, they can gradually build up a navy, fully as large and then larger than ours."[26] Three years later, the British naval attaché in Washington offered a similar assessment: the United States intended to become the world's second maritime power, and might ultimately displace Great Britain as the first.[27]

Fears of losing maritime supremacy to Germany emerged during roughly the same period. Before 1896, the German navy—dwarfed by its British counterpart—aroused derision rather than alarm. However, the attitude within British official circles changed when the first naval bill was introduced to the Reichstag in 1897. Elites in Great Britain worried that a stronger German navy might join with the Dual Alliance—France and Russia—to offset the Royal navy's worldwide dominance.[28]

Unease hardened into outright alarm as the German navy grew rapidly from 1900 to 1905. During this period, British elites began to perceive the Royal navy's all-important primacy in European waters as increasingly tenuous. The Admiralty identified the emerging challenge to the Royal navy's regional predominance, and recommended that the home fleet be strengthened "if it is to be on a par with the formidable German force which is being rapidly developed in the North Sea."[29] By early 1902, concerns about Germany's potential to eclipse the Royal navy in European waters permeated much of the British government. Reflecting this, the Conservative Cabinet decided to construct a naval base on the North Sea with a fleet to "be practically determined by the power of the German navy."[30]

Last, the Admiralty's readiness to alter the venerable two-power standard speaks to changing British perceptions of the maritime balance. The two-power standard had previously meant maintaining a navy equivalent to the combined fleets of the Dual Alliance. Looking forward at the end of 1904, the Admiralty anticipated that the two-power standard would have to incorporate Germany to remain a valid measure of maritime supremacy.[31]

American Democracy, German Autocracy

Although the United States and Germany emerged as rising powers at roughly the same time, they differed in one fundamental respect: regime type.

Whereas America was a democracy, Germany, despite parliamentary trappings, remained an autocracy. This disparity is not fully reflected in the Polity IV dataset. The United States during the prewar period receives a polity score of +10, denoting a strongly democratic regime. Germany receives a polity score of +1 from 1895 to 1908 and +2 from 1909 to 1914.[32] At the middle of the polity spectrum, it is difficult to draw conclusions about regime type. On the other hand, power centralization and domestic transparency—the additional set of criteria introduced in Chapter 2—clearly distinguish American democracy from German autocracy.

During the period of its ascendance, the United States had a decentralized political system. The House of Representatives was popularly elected. State legislators, who were directly accountable to the public, elected members of the Senate until 1913. Last, the popular vote determined the makeup of an electoral college, which in turn selected the president. The combination of a competitively elected executive and a bicameral legislature meant that America at the turn of the twentieth century had more than three checks and balances.

By contrast, Germany's political system concentrated authority. The German constitution placed the kaiser at the epicenter of government, particularly in the realm of foreign policy. Although the Reichstag was competitively elected, and multiple parties including those hostile to the government held large numbers of seats, the chancellor was appointed and dismissed by the kaiser alone. Rather than chosen by parties with significant representation in the Reichstag, ministers served at the kaiser's pleasure and could not even be members of parliament.[33] Germany thus featured only one check and balance.

On regime transparency, the United States and Germany also sharply differed. This becomes readily evident when assessing freedom of the press. The U.S. media enjoyed constitutional safeguards. The first amendment included in the Bill of Rights provides that "Congress shall make no law. . . . abridging the freedom of speech, or of the press."[34] By the mid-1890s, changes in the revenue structure of newspapers—the rise of commercial advertising—had also freed editors from financial dependence on political parties.[35] The German constitution failed to enshrine journalistic freedom. As a result, the government systematically wielded charges of slander, libel, and lèse-majesté against publications that it found objectionable.[36] Employing the abbreviated survey of media freedom developed in the previous chapter, the United States receives a zero—a free press—while Germany receives a four—an unfree press.

Great Britain Appeases the United States

As the United States burst onto the global scene, Great Britain opted for a strategy of appeasement. Virtually all points of tension in Anglo-American relations from 1895 on resulted in unilateral British concessions.

In July 1895, the United States intervened in the long-running boundary dispute between British Guiana and Venezuela. Unhappy with the British response, Richard Olney, the American secretary of state, issued a dispatch to the British government demanding that London agree to arbitration. Replying five months later, the Cabinet not only refused arbitration, but also denied the right of the United States to interfere in Venezuela and rejected the broader validity of the Monroe Doctrine.[37] Infuriated by the British response, President Grover Cleveland submitted a special message to Congress in December claiming that in light of British intransigence, the United States would establish a commission to determine the true boundary, and if necessary, impose the commission's findings using "every means in its power."[38]

In the wake of Cleveland's bellicose statement, the British government steadily retreated from its original position on arbitration of the Venezuelan boundary claims. Initiating informal negotiations with the United States in January 1896 implicitly conceded an American right to intervene. But Great Britain went much farther, and in February recognized the Monroe Doctrine. Arthur Balfour, at the time first lord of the treasury, declared: "there has never been, and there is not now, the slightest intention on the part of this country to violate what is the substance and essence of the Monroe Doctrine . . . a principle of policy which both they and we cherish."[39]

Moreover, serial British concessions characterized negotiations over the scope of arbitration. Privately, the British had been willing to arbitrate with Venezuela provided that all territory within a line surveyed between 1841 and 1843 by the explorer Robert Schomburgk was excluded. Yet from the outset of negotiations, the British government backpedaled from this position, and merely proposed exempting settled areas on both sides of the line. The United States refused to exclude any territory from arbitration, and Great Britain then agreed to a preliminary enquiry to determine areas of settlement. The British suggested that ten years of inhabitation define a settlement; the Americans countered with sixty years; the resulting one-sided compromise was fifty years of occupation.[40] Thus, on both the salience of the Monroe

Doctrine and the actual arbitration procedure, Great Britain entirely acceded to U.S. demands.

In the years after the Venezuela crisis, the British government faced increasing pressure to rescind the Clayton-Bulwer Treaty, which precluded the United States from singlehandedly building a canal in Central America linking the Atlantic and Pacific Oceans. President William McKinley's annual message to Congress in 1898 called for action to construct a solely American canal. In January 1899, Congress began to consider legislation authorizing a canal through Nicaragua. The British soon gave way. Negotiations between U.S. secretary of state John Hay and British ambassador Julian Pauncefote concluded with an agreement in February 1900.[41]

Although allowing the United States to unilaterally build and operate an isthmian canal, the agreement stopped short of abrogating the Clayton-Bulwer Treaty. Moreover, the new Hay-Pauncefote Treaty restricted American freedom of action by banning fortifications, neutralizing the canal during wartime, and opening the agreement to third parties. Finding these restrictions unpalatable, the Senate only ratified the Hay-Pauncefote Treaty after adding several amendments. The British government refused to approve the modified treaty, but soon welcomed a new round of negotiations. The resulting agreement—the second Hay-Pauncefote Treaty—effectively incorporated all the Senate's amendments: the Clayton-Bulwer Treaty was explicitly abrogated; neutralization of the canal during wartime was not formally guaranteed; and the internationalization clause was removed. Beyond these concessions, Great Britain also dropped the clause prohibiting fortification.[42] By the end of the isthmian canal controversy, British capitulation to U.S. demands was complete.

The last major Anglo-American dispute at the turn of the twentieth century occurred over the ill-defined border between Alaska and Canada. The Canadians largely accepted U.S. interpretation of the boundary until the Klondike gold rush of 1896. Aiming to obtain a port giving access to the gold fields, Canada demanded that the United States submit the Alaskan panhandle to arbitration involving a neutral party. From the outset, the United States rejected arbitration. Although skeptical of the Canadian claims, the British government initially sought to extract U.S. concessions by linking the Alaskan boundary dispute to negotiations over the isthmian canal. In the face of mounting U.S. frustration, Great Britain retreated and delinked the two issues.[43]

Unable to agree on arbitration, the United States and Great Britain reached a temporary arrangement in 1899.[44] Hay reopened the dispute in 1901 by proposing the creation of a binational commission to resolve the conflicting claims. By mid-1902, President Theodore Roosevelt was determined that Great Britain should acquiesce to the U.S. formula for delineating the border. As a show of resolve and also to keep order in an unruly frontier, he dispatched a company of cavalry to the Alaskan panhandle.[45]

The British government, though hoping for international arbitration, ultimately acquiesced to the U.S. formula, and in January 1903, the two sides concluded the Hay-Herbert Treaty. The agreement stipulated that each party would furnish three "impartial jurists of repute" to determine the true boundary. While Great Britain selected legal eminences to represent Canada, the United States appointed blatantly partial commissioners, including a sitting secretary of war. Nonetheless, the British government accepted the American appointments. Moreover, when the commission became deadlocked, the British representative broke with his Canadian counterparts to support the U.S. claim.[46] Like the Venezuela crisis and the isthmian canal controversy, the Alaskan boundary dispute featured unilateral British concessions.

British appeasement of the United States, though continuing for almost a decade, was always a transitional strategy. The purpose of appeasement was to stabilize Anglo-American relations to the point where long-term integration became viable. Seen from this perspective, accommodating the United States on Venezuela was a first step toward eliminating sources of conflict. The next steps were agreement on an isthmian canal and resolution of the Alaskan boundary dispute.[47] Colonial Secretary Chamberlain's assessment of Canadian claims to the Alaskan panhandle gives a tangible sense of the rationale underlying British appeasement of the United States. "I care very little for the points in dispute, but I care immensely for the consequential advantages of a thorough understanding between the two countries and the removal of these trumpery causes of irritation."[48]

America's Rise: Democracy Reassures

Great Britain favored a strategy of appeasement because democratic rule in an ascendant United States reduced risk and bolstered trust. Operating in an open society, the British could accurately survey U.S. intentions. Observing American politics in the years preceding the Venezuela crisis, the British diplomat Cecil Spring-Rice, having served a tour in Washington, could contextualize outbursts of Anglophobe sentiment as "not so much hatred as jealousy."[49] There was "no point on which the interests of the U.S. and G.B. are diametrically opposed, and neither wishes to take the other's territory."[50] In this view, a lingering sense of inferiority might impel the United States to quarrel with Great Britain, but its intentions were at heart benign.

Democratic government in the United States also generated access opportunities the British could exploit. With diverse groups influencing American foreign policy, an "English faction" existed in Washington and New York, respectively the power and money centers of the United States. This provided a basis for shaping American strategic behavior. British officials self-consciously cultivated the English faction. For example, Spring-Rice in 1887 worked to ensure a warm London reception for the daughter of the anglophile secretary of state, Thomas Bayard.[51] The open nature of the American political system also afforded diplomats like Spring-Rice a chance to develop close ties with U.S. political elites. During his first tour of Washington, Spring-Rice was hosted by senators and senior officials, and while staying with the secretary of war, attended an impromptu cabinet meeting.[52] Friendships translated into access, and "Whatever may be said of the relations, politically speaking, of England and America, one thing is absolutely certain—in no country can we Englishmen make such friendships."[53] Relationships between Anglo-American elites meant Great Britain had allies within the U.S. government sensitive to its interests.

The Venezuela Crisis

America's democratic institutions functioned as a powerful source of reassurance during the Venezuela crisis, preventing a diplomatic row from escalating into war. As the crisis unfolded, congressional actions and media uproar indicated that the United States would only pursue war as a last resort. Within a week of Cleveland's bellicose message, the Senate and the House of Representatives unanimously voted to fund a commission to determine the boundary of Venezuela. This signaled American resolve, but also that Republican and Democratic politicians were only prepared to support war *if* Great Britain ultimately rejected the commission's findings. Popular support for war, like that of Congress, was conditioned on future British intransigence. American newspapers affirmed that "Whether There Will Be War Now Rests with England," and that when the true boundary was fixed, "if England shall overstep it, it will mean war!"[54] Congress and public opinion conveyed that the United States would only undertake military action against Great Britain after the boundary commission had rendered a decision. The restraint telegraphed by Congress and the press registered in Great Britain. Prime Minister Salisbury and Ambassador Pauncefote understood that Cleveland, in committing to a U.S. commission, had postponed an Anglo-American showdown. Likewise, Colonial Secretary Chamberlain recognized that the "American affair cannot become serious for some time. . . . Altogether it must be months before there is a real crisis."[55]

As the crisis continued, America's free press made visible changes in the U.S. government's position. Newspaper reporting suggested that the commission had a less objectionable mission than unilaterally delineating the Venezuelan boundary. On December 25, the *New York World* published a story titled "Won't Dictate the Line." The story quoted Senator George Gray, a political ally of Cleveland. According to Gray, the purpose of the commission was "solely to inform the conscience of the government and the American people. . . . The United States does not assume to delimit a frontier for Great Britain."[56] Gray's remarks were subsequently noted in the British press. Because of Gray's close relationship to Cleveland, many British officials assumed that he was speaking for the president. Consequently, the British government could ascertain a softening of the U.S. position weeks before the American ambassador in London officially communicated the commission's watered-down objective—obtaining information.[57]

The U.S. media also illuminated a shift in a key shaper of foreign policy: popular opinion. Although the initial public reaction to Cleveland's message was bellicose, antiwar sentiment soon surged. By December 20, a leading financial journal, expressing the opinion of the U.S. business community, warned that a "great mistake had been made."[58] The number of newspapers critical of Cleveland's policy rapidly increased. Joseph Pulitzer, editor of the *New York World*, spearheaded a growing reconciliation movement and on the first Sunday after the crisis, churchmen across the United States pleaded for peace.[59] The transparency of the U.S. political system enabled the British government to observe this dramatic change in public opinion.[60]

Beyond helping to stabilize the immediate crisis, America's democratic institutions obviated the need for a more hard-line British approach. Against the backdrop of an open society, President Cleveland's actions were readily understood as motivated by domestic political considerations rather than a deliberate effort to undermine British interests in the Western Hemisphere. The Democratic Party faced an uphill struggle in the presidential elections of 1896. Twisting the lion's tail was one way to generate political capital, as a considerable segment of the American population was Anglophobe. To the British government, it was clear that Cleveland and the Democratic Party had manufactured a controversy to boost the electoral prospects of his successor. As Salisbury put it, the creation of a U.S. commission was "Cleveland's electioneering dodge." Although willing to entertain the possibility that Cleveland sought a pretext for invading Canada, Salisbury was "rather skeptical" that Cleveland actually desired war.[61] Knowing that Cleveland was pandering to jingo sentiment, Great Britain did not mistakenly take U.S. interference in Venezuela as a sign of real hostility.

Likewise, enduring access opportunities within the American political system limited the potential downside of accommodation during the crisis. Cleveland and Olney, though responsible for the clash with Great Britain, were seen as hostages to jingo sentiment within the United States. By this logic, if Great Britain refrained from strengthening the hand of prowar groups, peace and an amicable settlement would prevail.[62] Moreover, the British government continued to enjoy significant support among U.S. elites. Visiting Washington in September 1896, Chamberlain concluded: "although the great majority of educated Americans are friendly to Great Britain and desirous of peace, a feeling of hostility has been sedulously encouraged among the masses of the people."[63] The best option for Great Britain was to avoid provocative action and continue to rely on its friends in the United States.

The Aftermath

In the years after the Venezuela crisis, the United States became the paramount power in the Western Hemisphere. America's democratic system reassured Great Britain that its diminished position would not be exploited. Trust permeated the final phase of the Anglo-American power transition. While negotiating over the scope of Venezuelan arbitration, the British government evinced faith in U.S. willingness to abide by international law in its relations with Latin America.[64] Although Great Britain was ostensibly neutral during the Spanish-American War, in practice, British policy, by permitting U.S. access to ports and colonies, supported the American war effort. Confident that the United States would become a force for free trade in the Far East, the British government also encouraged American annexation of the Philippines.[65] By the early 1900s, Great Britain was calling for the United States to take a more active role in South America as well. Balfour, then prime minister, wrote Andrew Carnegie urging: "These South American Republics are a great trouble, and I wish the U.S.A. would take them in hand."[66]

In public, he pursued a similar line: "We welcome any increase of the influence of the United States of America upon the great Western Hemisphere."[67] The Royal navy's withdrawal from North America and the Caribbean in 1904, leaving Great Britain's substantial interests to the mercy of a rapidly growing American navy, testifies to the depth of British confidence in American goodwill.[68]

Great Britain and Germany: Integration and Hedging

As Germany emerged on the world stage, Great Britain took steps to integrate it into international institutions. But British leaders did more than this; they also hedged.

British efforts to integrate Germany occurred during an era devoid of strong international organizations; even in Europe, international institutions were few and weak. Great Britain's integration strategy therefore relied primarily on the pursuit of bilateral arrangements. The earliest of these related to the Far East. By 1898, the territorial integrity of the Chinese empire and freedom of trade within had come under pressure from all the European powers, including Germany. Largely to constrain Germany's behavior and thereby reduce the momentum behind the partition of China, Colonial Secretary Chamberlain initiated Anglo-German alliance talks in March 1898. Even skeptics of the alliance talks like Balfour still hoped to enmesh Germany in the open trading order sustained by Great Britain in the Far East.[69] Although the alliance talks failed, the British government did secure an Anglo-German agreement on China in October 1900. The treaty pledged to uphold freedom of trade in China "as far as they can exercise influence," and both parties committed to "direct their policy towards maintaining undiminished the territorial condition of the Chinese Empire."[70]

The main focus of Great Britain's integration strategy, however, was maritime. Between 1906 and 1911, the British government pursued a naval agreement with Germany. This was a self-conscious effort to create international institutions that restrained Germany from engaging in competitive behavior, namely, challenging Great Britain's naval supremacy.[71] Before and during the Second Hague Conference of 1907, the British government promoted an agreement to limit naval armaments. Although rebuffed by Germany, the Liberal Cabinet in 1908 once again pressed for a naval agreement. Foreign Secretary Grey and David Lloyd George, the chancellor of the exchequer, met with the German ambassador in July to discuss a maritime arrangement. In August, the British directly approached the kaiser, to no avail.[72] Talks resumed in 1909 when the Liberal Cabinet responded to German overtures. Two years of largely fruitless negotiations ensued. Before the second Moroccan crisis brought the talks to a close, the two sides only managed to concur on an exchange of information through naval attachés.[73]

In parallel to seeking the integration of Germany, Great Britain also implemented a hedging strategy. As German naval power began to increase, the Admiralty moved to concentrate the Royal navy in home waters. This process of redistribution accelerated under the leadership of Admiral John Fisher and took on an explicitly anti-German cast.[74] "Germany keeps her whole fleet always concentrated within a few hours of England. We must therefore keep a fleet twice as powerful as that of Germany always concentrated within a few hours of Germany."[75] An expansion of the Royal navy occurred alongside concentration. From 1901 to 1905, the Royal navy grew by nine battleships. In February 1906, Great Britain launched the HMS *Dreadnought*, a revolutionary vessel rendering the capital ships of all other navies obsolete. Thereafter, the pace of battleship construction intensified, with Great Britain laying down eight vessels in 1909 and four in each successive year through 1911.[76]

The nonmaritime element of Great Britain's hedging strategy was to forge security ties with two European land powers: France and Russia. In April 1904, the newly established Anglo-French entente was more a measure to split Paris and Moscow than a protoalliance aimed at Berlin.[77] However, after the first Moroccan crisis erupted in 1905, the Anglo-French entente came to take on an anti-German cast.[78] Great Britain concluded an entente with Russia in 1907—a radical change in British foreign policy considering that only a few years earlier the two countries had been bitter imperial rivals in Central Asia and the Far East. The Anglo-Russian entente was an additional insurance against German ambitions. As Edward Grey, the architect of foreign policy under the Liberal Cabinet, put it: "An *entente* between Russia, France, and ourselves would be absolutely secure. If it is necessary to check Germany it could be done."[79]

Autocracy Frames Germany's Rise

Great Britain had no recourse but to integrate and hedge because Germany was a rising autocracy. Opaque intentions and a lack of access opportunities created an environment in which British leaders could not rely entirely on international institutions to constrain German behavior.

Uncertainty Breeds Mistrust

With foreign policy an exclusive domain limited to the kaiser and his clique, great uncertainty surrounded an ascendant Germany's ambitions. Writing in 1904, Spring-Rice neatly summarized this conundrum: "Germany is a mystery. Does she simply want the destruction of England . . . or does she want definite things which England can help her to get?"[80] Eyre Crowe, in a 1907 memorandum that was widely circulated within the British government, also pointed to the difficulty of ascertaining German intentions:

> It would not be unjust to say that ambitious designs against one's neighbours are not as a rule openly proclaimed, and that therefore the absence of such proclamation, and even the profession of unlimited and universal political, benevolence are not in themselves conclusive evidence for or against the existence of unpublished intentions.[81]

Would German expansion be peaceful, and economic in nature, or would Germany seek hegemony over Europe? The answer was fundamentally unclear.[82]

Unsurprisingly, German intentions became the subject of much debate within the British government. Regardless whether the Conservative or Liberal Party held power, pro- and anti-German groups struggled to assert their respective views. After 1902, Chamberlain and his son, both members of the Conservative Cabinet, argued that German intentions were inimical to Great Britain. Other ministers, however, perceived German ambitions in a more benign light. Foreign Secretary Lansdowne and Balfour, then prime minister, initially remained unconvinced by either side, but Lansdowne's attempt to use reform of the colonial administration in Egypt as a "test case" for German goodwill brought disillusionment. Angered by Berlin's recalcitrance, Lansdowne and Balfour became increasingly skeptical of German motivations.[83]

Disagreement over German intentions divided the Liberal Cabinet elected in late 1905 and became increasingly sharp as the naval arms race with Germany accelerated. During the debate over British naval requirements for 1909, Cabinet members Lloyd George and Winston Churchill rallied other ministers with favorable views of Germany to press for only four new battleships. The anti-German group, which included Grey, insisted that six dreadnoughts were necessary to retain a margin of safety over the German fleet.

The debate was heated, and at one point, Grey threatened to resign. Only a compromise brokered by Prime Minister Asquith prevented conflicting assessments of German intentions from tearing the Cabinet apart.[84]

Within the British government, the balance gradually shifted toward the anti-Germans. This upwelling of mistrust was catalyzed by the autocratic nature of Germany's regime. The lack of sources illuminating German intentions led British elites to focus on what they could observe: actions abroad and changes in military capability.

Colonial quarrels sparked initial British misgivings about Germany's trajectory. The kaiser's interference in relations between the Cape Colony and the Boers, the occupation of Chinese Kiaochow by German forces in 1897, German demands on the Portuguese colonies, and the acrimonious partition of Samoa—all were interpreted by the British Foreign Office as symptomatic of a more fundamental antagonism. By the turn of the century, Great Britain's career diplomatic corps had become a bastion of anti-German sentiment.[85] German assertiveness overseas likewise provoked growing anxiety in successive Cabinets. For Lansdowne and Balfour, German resistance to the consolidation of Great Britain's position in Egypt appeared a harbinger of deeper ill will. Similarly, Grey regarded the diplomatic crisis triggered by the kaiser's landing in Tangiers as indicative of enduring German hostility.[86]

The relentless expansion of the German fleet loomed large in British threat assessments and more than any other factor strengthened the hand of anti-German groups. Based on the technical specifications of the German fleet, Selborne, first lord of the admiralty and originally an advocate of an Anglo-German alliance, concluded in 1902 that "the German navy is very carefully built up from the point of view of a new war with us."[87] Coming to power in the midst of the first Moroccan crisis, Foreign Secretary Grey perceived Germany's willingness to limit naval armaments as a touchstone of its intentions. The fruitlessness of the naval talks amplified the mistrust Grey already harbored.[88] Minus the reassurance mechanisms of a democracy, Germany's maritime buildup cast an ominous shadow over its rise.

"The Emperor Is a Very Odd Man"

An autocratic system lent additional uncertainty to Germany's ascendance by placing the kaiser at the epicenter of foreign policy. Kaiser Wilhelm of Germany was a mercurial monarch. His instability concerned Great Britain as early as 1895, the year perceptions of Germany's rise became widespread. Reporting to London, the British Embassy in Berlin warned that the kaiser's mind was "subject to hallucinations."[89] Prime Minister Salisbury, in response to the report and other information about the kaiser, noted: "The conduct of the German Emperor is very mysterious and difficult to explain. There is a danger of his going completely off his head." Moreover, Salisbury perceived the kaiser as the source of extreme German behavior. He believed that "outrageous" German demands for territory in Africa could only reflect the kaiser's decision to go against the wishes of more responsible statesmen.[90]

In January 1896, the kaiser's impulsiveness directly fueled British mistrust of Germany's rise. After the Jameson Raid—a botched attempt by British citizens from the Cape Colony to overthrow the Transvaal Republic—the kaiser, in a fit of rage, dispatched a congratulatory telegram to the Boer president. What became known as the Kruger telegram directly challenged British interests in the Transvaal by implying recognition of the Boers' independence. Through rumor, the British government discerned that Wilhelm had disregarded the advice of the chancellor and others when sending the telegram.[91] This episode demonstrated to British leaders that German intentions could rapidly change due to the kaiser's erratic nature.

The kaiser remained a key point of uncertainty as German power expanded. In the midst of the Anglo-German alliance negotiations, Balfour observed: "The Emperor is a very odd man." The first lord of the treasury worried that failure to fulfill the expectations of "so impulsive a being" might produce an abrupt turnabout in German foreign policy—the kaiser would seek an arrangement with France and Russia, then Great Britain's chief adversaries.[92] Negotiating with Germany over the fate of Samoa in 1899, Salisbury complained: "It is a great nuisance that one of the main factors in the European calculation should be so ultra-human."[93] On reading a description of the kaiser's talks with the czar in 1905, Foreign Secretary Lansdowne echoed his colleagues: "the Kaiser's language and demeanor fills me with disquiet. What may not a man in such a frame of mind do next?"[94] Lansdowne's successor, Grey, on meeting the kaiser, concluded that he was "not quite sane."[95] Centralization of authority in the hands of the kaiser rendered German intentions doubly opaque and compounded British concerns arising from Germany's colonial assertiveness and naval buildup.

Friendless in Berlin

As the power transition with Germany moved forward, British leaders had few avenues for the shaping of strategic behavior. In a political system that centralized authority, only one point of access existed: the kaiser and his closest advisers. However, this point of access was unfriendly toward Great Britain. During his posting in Berlin, Spring-Rice noted: "the Emperor and his people are actuated by feelings of hostility against England which are only limited by the German regard for law and by the practical fear of reprisals."[96] Later reports from the British Embassy in Berlin confirmed the kaiser's animosity toward Great Britain. In 1904, the British ambassador informed Lansdowne: "I hear from other sources that the Kaiser has been generally letting out against England."[97] This message, along with news that Wilhelm had become convinced that Great Britain was planning a surprise attack, led Lansdowne to wonder whether the center of political power in Germany was not actively hostile: "They cannot seriously believe that we are meditating a coup against them. Are they perchance meditating one against us?"[98]

Keenly aware of their inability to shape Germany's foreign policy from within, British elites gravitated toward a theory of "two Germanies." The kaiser and his advisers were dangerous and warlike, while the majority of the German people were peace loving.[99] This view made inroads among even some of the pro-German members of the Liberal Cabinet. Lloyd George came to espouse the "two-Germanies" theory after a visit to Berlin in 1908. The chancellor of the exchequer was "gravely disturbed by the expressions of distrust and suspicion I had encountered. . . . It seemed to me to be ominously significant of what must be the general opinion at the time in leading German circles."[100]

If democratic rule had prevailed in Germany, the kaiser's antipathy would not have deprived Great Britain of friends in Berlin. The British government could have cultivated groups empowered by democracy such as the Reichstag and thereby offset the kaiser's malign influence over German foreign policy. Countering one domestic actor with another was in fact Great Britain's approach to the United States, where according to the logic of a "two Americas" theory, elites were sympathetic but the masses Anglophobe. This approach was impossible to carry out in Germany, where the constitution stripped the Reichstag of any role in foreign affairs. With the kaiser and his advisers unfriendly, the British government had nowhere else to turn for access.

Great Britain Embraces Containment

During the first decade of the twentieth century, a rising Germany was prickly and assertive yet unwilling to press international disputes to the brink of war.

In 1905, the diplomatic crisis Germany triggered over Morocco worried British elites but did not fundamentally shake their faith in the utility of integration. After 1910, however, frequent conflict accompanied Germany's rise. The British became disillusioned with integration and increasingly convinced of Germany's unremitting antagonism, and steadily shifted to containment.

The Second Moroccan Crisis

In July 1911, Germany sparked a crisis that raised the specter of the first large-scale European war in forty years. The epicenter of the crisis was Morocco. Eager to receive compensation for what appeared to be an impending partition of Morocco, Germany dispatched the gunboat SMS *Panther* to Agadir. The *Panther*'s presence was intended to convince France and Great Britain that Germany ought to receive concessions for any changes in Morocco's status. Moreover, the German government hoped that pressing its claim to compensation might bring about tensions that would weaken or even fracture the Anglo-French entente.[101] But Great Britain and France remained united. The crisis escalated, and foreshadowing the events of August 1914, Germany deployed troops to the Belgian border. Ultimately, all parties stepped back from the precipice and reached a settlement whereby France occupied all of Morocco and Germany received territories previously part of the French Congo.

For Great Britain, the second Moroccan crisis was a watershed moment. It compelled the civilian leadership in London to become intimately involved in war planning against Germany. While still at the Home Office, Churchill pressed for information concerning the army's strength and mobilization time frame. Foreign Secretary Grey urged the Admiralty to go on heightened alert. Richard Haldane, the civilian head of the War Office, cancelled military exercises scheduled for September because British troops might soon be needed in Europe.[102] Most important, Asquith convened a meeting of the Committee on Imperial Defence to examine "actions to be taken in the event of intervention" in a Franco-German conflict. Adjudicating between plans put forward by the Admiralty and the War Office, this select group fatefully chose sending troops to France over naval attacks against the German coast. Never before had British leaders confronted the possibility of war with Germany in such a tangible way.[103] Their faith in integration as a tool for moderating German behavior was badly shaken.

Another repercussion of the second Moroccan crisis was the ascendance of the anti-Germans within the Cabinet. Because London had few sources of insight on German intentions, the crisis convinced additional ministers of Germany's unwavering hostility. In the weeks following the *Panther*'s appearance in Agadir, Lloyd George and Churchill left the orbit of the pro-German group. As the second Moroccan crisis unfolded, they became the most rabidly anti-German members of the Cabinet. Lloyd George independently decided to include a challenge to Germany in his Mansion House speech.[104] Privately, he believed that "Germany meant war; wouldn't it perhaps be better—to have it at once?"[105] Churchill, for his part, was so forceful in advocating a formal alliance with France and Russia that Grey had to restrain him.[106] The pro-Germans had previously looked to Lloyd George and Churchill for leadership, so their departure came as a crushing blow.

Great Britain did not immediately abandon integration in the wake of the second Moroccan crisis, but efforts to embed Germany within international institutions became increasingly controversial and expectations sank. When a British mission arrived in Germany in early 1912 to discuss an agreement on naval armaments, the Foreign Office lobbied against these discussions and considered them bound to fail. Grey, though supporting the mission, was also pessimistic about the likelihood of success. As before, the talks foundered. Churchill in March 1912 proposed a "naval holiday" whereby Germany would reduce its battleship construction and Great Britain would reciprocate. Reiterated in March and October 1913, Churchill's scheme was repeatedly rebuffed.[107] By 1914, Grey, like many British leaders, had become thoroughly disillusioned, and publicly noted: "It is no good making proposals (to Foreign Powers) which they will not welcome and are not prepared to receive."[108]

While British efforts to integrate Germany after July 1911 declined, hedging took on a harder cast. Alongside keeping pace with Germany in the maritime arms race, Great Britain tightened its strategic ties with France. In November 1912, the two agreed to automatic consultations if another state threatened either party. Although the Anglo-French entente was still not an alliance, the expectation was that Great Britain would come to France's aid.[109] By April 1913, naval talks resulted in plans for the defense of France's northern coast and joint operations in the Mediterranean. By summer 1914, Great Britain was effectively committed to defending France even if the Cabinet claimed to retain flexibility.[110]

The July Crisis

Great Britain's strategy toward Germany transformed into containment as the July crisis of 1914 intensified. The crisis began in Sarajevo with the assassination of Austro-Hungarian archduke Franz Ferdinand. Carried out by Serbian nationalists, the murder exacerbated the existing antagonism between Austria-Hungary and the Kingdom of Serbia. Because each state had close ties to another European power—Germany and Russia respectively—and Russia was an ally of France, tensions could not be contained within the Balkans. When Austria-Hungary declared war against Serbia, Europe experienced a concatenation of competitive military mobilizations. Rather than waiting for Russia to transport its massive army to the eastern front, Germany prepared to strike westward against France. The planned invasion corridor ran through neutral Belgium.

This was what the British feared. In late July 1914, Great Britain queried whether Germany would respect the integrity of Belgium.[111] The German reply, coming on July 31, verged on outright rejection of Belgian neutrality. On August 2, Germany demanded that Belgium grant its troops free passage, and warned that war would otherwise ensue.[112] Two days later, Foreign Secretary Grey pressed Germany to withdraw its demands, and stated that Great Britain would take "all the steps in their power necessary to uphold the neutrality of Belgium."[113] Instead, a full-scale German invasion of Belgium followed. Great Britain in turn moved to implement a new strategy for managing Germany's troubled rise: containment. The Royal navy instituted a blockade to strangle Germany's foreign commerce while the British expeditionary force deployed to the European continent to aid the beleaguered French.[114]

The final transition to containment was swift because Germany's willingness to violate the integrity of Belgium provided irrefutable evidence of integration's failure. Within the Cabinet, the anti-Germans could at last overcome all resistance to containment. Worth highlighting are the efforts of Lloyd George, who manipulated wavering members of the Cabinet into supporting intervention on the side of France. Attending meetings held by undecided ministers, Lloyd George professed similar doubts, yet simultaneously raised the territorial integrity of Belgium as a moral issue that would obligate a declaration of war. Because of Lloyd George's efforts, the German invasion of Belgium was accepted by a near totality of the Cabinet as justification for belligerency.[115]

Even if Germany had avoided invading Belgium and attacked across its frontier with France, Great Britain would still have opted for containment, though perhaps with less rapidity. Convinced by the second Moroccan crisis that German intentions were unremittingly hostile, much of the Cabinet believed a German-dominated Europe would threaten Great Britain's very survival.[116] There was no recourse other than containment in the face of German military aggression.

Other Influences on British Strategy

America's democratic system and Germany's autocratic rule clearly provided a key backdrop to the eclipse of British power at the turn of the twentieth century. Yet different strands of international relations theory point to other factors worth exploring. As discussed in Chapter 1, economic interdependence offers another vantage point for understanding how democratic states navigate fateful transitions. So do other factors—geography and shared culture—that originate from the scholarship on power shifts. All these factors are not necessarily alternative explanations; rather, they offer a more detailed picture of British strategy.

Economic Interdependence

The power transition from Great Britain to the United States and Germany was marked by considerable economic interdependence. Anglo-American trade accounted for almost 6.5 percent of British GDP in 1885 and slightly more than 5 percent of British GDP in 1913. Another significant economic linkage existed: America was the main recipient of British capital flows, which in 1900 totaled $2.5 billion. Germany never came close to rivaling the United States as a recipient of British investment, but Anglo-German trade as a share of British GDP expanded from about 2.5 percent in 1885 to about 3.4 percent in 1913.[117] Trade interdependence with the United States should have disproportionately affected Great Britain, which by the eve of World War I had a much smaller economy. With British and German GDP comparable in size, a high level of commerce should have imposed similar restraints.

Deep economic ties appear to have played at most a secondary role in British appeasement of the United States. The Venezuela crisis of 1895 is exemplary. London financiers first reacted to Cleveland's message by dumping American securities, creating a panic in the U.S. stock market. The immediate behavior of British businessmen attests to the reciprocal effects of economic interdependence and conflict: Anglo-American commercial ties began to unravel when the overall relationship sharply deteriorated. Having unloaded some of their American holdings, bankers in London subsequently pressed for arbitration.[118] There is no evidence that the British government would have behaved differently in the absence of such lobbying efforts. For different reasons, appeasement appealed to the business community and the British government.

In retrospect, economic interdependence clearly failed to prevent Great Britain from containing Germany. During the July crisis of 1914, London bankers lobbied for neutrality, as scholars such as Papayoanou and Narizny would predict. This pressure was felt by members of the Cabinet.[119] Despite opposition from business groups, the British government decided to enter the First World War on the side of France and Russia. This decision—and the larger conflagration that engulfed all of Europe—came as a devastating surprise to contemporary believers in the pacifying effects of economic integration.

Geography

Realist theories of international relations emphasize the role of geography in shaping threat perceptions. John Mearsheimer observes that "when great powers are separated by large bodies of water, they usually do not have much offensive capability against each other. . . . Therefore, great powers separated by water are likely to fear each other less than great powers that can get at each other over land."[120] In the realist perspective, because distance impedes the projection of military force, a rising power should appear more threatening to its neighbors than to countries in other regions. By this logic, democratic leaders should oppose the ascendancy of nearby states while accommodating the rise of remote powers.

It is possible to explain British strategy toward the United States and Germany as the by-product of geography. While the growth of the United States took place across the Atlantic Ocean, Germany's emergence occurred in Great Britain's backyard. The expansion of the American navy merely threatened to overturn the balance of power in North American waters. By contrast, Germany amassed a navy a few hours' steam from British shores. With British resources increasingly strained, London could not afford to confront multiple rising powers at once and had to choose between accommodating Washington and Berlin. Unsurprisingly, British leaders decided to appease the more distant power: the United States.

There is some truth to this geographic narrative. The Boer War that lasted from 1899 until 1902 imposed an immense drain on the British treasury. It would have been difficult if not impossible for Great Britain to sustain a robust hedging strategy against both the United States and Germany. Once

British leaders came to experience severe resource constraints in the aftermath of their military debacle, choosing to appease the United States and hedge against Germany had an undeniable geographic logic.

However, Great Britain did not at first have to choose between accommodating a distant power and a rising neighbor. The outlines of British strategy toward the United States were determined during the Venezuela crisis of 1895. When British leaders initially confronted the growth of American power, they did not have to consider a highly capable German navy stationed just across the North Sea. This formidable force existed largely in the kaiser's imagination; the legislative bill that heralded the start of Germany's maritime buildup was only introduced to the Reichstag in 1897. Moreover, Great Britain during the Venezuela crisis was positioned to adopt strategies other than appeasement. Its global commitments had yet to vastly outstrip available resources and the Royal navy was still dominant in North American waters.[121] In late 1895, British appeasement of the United States was a choice, not a necessity. British strategy at this stage reflected the transparency and access opportunities created by America's democratic institutions.

The degree of trust in the Anglo-American power transition further points to the incomplete explanation that geography provides. If forced by mounting resource constraints to hedge only against neighboring Germany, British leaders should at least have harbored some trepidation about how Canada and a highly profitable "informal empire" in Latin America would fare as the United States became paramount in the Western Hemisphere. Instead, British leaders believed that future vulnerability to a regionally dominant United States would not threaten their country's interests. Only the reassurance conveyed by America's democratic institutions can account for this.

On balance, geography reinforced the impact of regime type in these two power transitions. America's location in the Western Hemisphere added to the reassurance conveyed by the transparency of U.S. intentions and the permeability of the U.S. foreign policymaking process to outside influence. Conversely, Germany's proximity to Great Britain amplified the mistrust generated by its opaque ambitions and dearth of access opportunities.

Anglo-Saxon Solidarity

Some historians have argued that a sense of racial solidarity inclined Great Britain to accommodate America's rise. In this narrative, common identity— possibly as much as democratic institutions—allowed the United States to reassure Great Britain as it emerged on the world stage.

On close inspection, this Anglo-Saxon argument is also incomplete. It is true that statements referring to "our American cousins" and "the trans-Atlantic branch of our race" permeate British newspapers and speeches from the turn of the twentieth century.[122] Anglo-Saxon solidarity was undoubtedly an important influence on public opinion in Great Britain. However, it deferred to strategic calculation within the Cabinet, and not the reverse.[123] Additionally, rhetoric of racial kinship was for a time evident in Anglo-German relations, yet notions of common identity proved insufficient to reassure Great Britain about German intentions.[124]

Likewise, the access opportunities the British identified within the United States stemmed more from a democratic system than a shared language and culture. These naturally helped to facilitate friendships among Anglo-American elites. Yet in an autocracy, a common identity would have run up against barriers to interelite friendships such as pervasive state secrecy and a stigma against interacting with foreigners. Friendships with Americans also translated into access because groups ranging from legislators to newspaper editors to businessmen could all influence U.S. foreign policy. By stripping these groups of power, autocratic rule would have precluded the British from using friendships to shape America's strategic behavior.

Conclusion

The eclipse of Pax Britannica offers a number of lessons. Post-Civil War America could reassure Great Britain because its democratic institutions clarified intentions and created opportunities to engage powerful domestic actors. This gave Great Britain sufficient confidence to appease. Germany's autocratic system not only fostered uncertainty and mistrust but also limited access. The British had little recourse but to integrate and hedge and ultimately contain as Germany became increasingly assertive. Although it would be an exaggeration to draw a straight line from Germany's regime type to the battlefields of the First World War, a lack of democracy undoubtedly rendered the rise of Germany more destabilizing.

Chapter 4

Germany Resurgent

Great Britain's strategy toward the resurgence of Germany during the 1930s is traditionally synonymous with appeasement. Recklessly credulous, British leaders offered Adolf Hitler a series of unilateral concessions culminating with the Munich Agreement, which transferred Czechoslovakian territory to Germany. Only too late, when Germany violated the Munich Agreement and occupied the heartland of the Czech state, did the British government realize the folly of its course. This appeasement narrative evolved immediately after the Second World War and poses a dilemma for the book's focus on regime type.[1] Within a year of taking power, Hitler transformed the Weimar Republic into a totalitarian state. If authoritarian rule causes a power's rise to generate mistrust, why did Great Britain appease Germany for so long?

More recent scholarship on Great Britain's response to the German resurgence under Hitler resolves this dilemma. The British did not appease: they rearmed and tried to integrate Germany into new European institutions and when that failed after Munich, transitioned to containment. Nor were British leaders entirely credulous about German intentions. The Nazi regime's centralization and lack of transparency created uncertainty that steadily hardened into mistrust. Once again, regime type framed a fateful transition.

The Balance of Power

The Versailles Treaty of 1919 upended the balance of power in Great Britain's favor. Crushing economic reparations and forced disarmament temporarily reduced Germany, restoring British primacy. The depression that engulfed the global economy in the late 1920s served to prolong British predominance over Germany, which was particularly hard hit.[2] This inherently ephemeral balance of power came to an end with the demise of the Weimar Republic. Under the new Nazi regime, Germany recovered its earlier lead in GDP and steel production and leaped ahead of Great Britain in military expenditures and first-line aircraft.

Gross Domestic Product

Measured in terms of national wealth, British dominance ended within six years of the Weimar Republic's fall. Burdened by reparation payments and ravaged by the worldwide economic depression, Germany in 1932 had an economy smaller than that of Great Britain. The GDP of the dying Weimar Republic was only 92.6 percent of Great Britain's. However, the German economy boomed after Hitler became chancellor.[3] Buoyed by public works and rearmament, Germany's GDP grew at a rate of 7.6 percent per annum until 1938, the final year of peace. The British economy emerged from the global depression at a more sluggish pace, expanding at 3.8 percent annually over the same time period. As a result, Germany's GDP in 1938 was 15 percent larger than Great Britain's.[4]

International Trade

British commercial primacy remained virtually unchanged during the course of Germany's resurgence. In 1932, Great Britain remained the foremost trader in a shrunken global economy.[5] While the worldwide depression devastated British commerce, German trade suffered an equally precipitous decline. During the last year of the Weimar Republic, the volume of German trade stood at 71 percent of Great Britain's total. Under Hitler, it never exceeded this high water mark. The Nazi economy was geared toward achieving autarky rather than commercial supremacy. German exports were directed toward Southeastern Europe to promote dependency and secure vital raw materials. With commerce subordinate to strategic goals, the volume of German trade, though growing, slipped to 68 percent of Great Britain's by 1938.[6]

Military Expenditures

An artifact of the Versailles Treaty, British predominance in military outlays evaporated with the advent of Hitler's Third Reich. The Versailles Treaty limited the Weimar Republic to an army of one hundred thousand men and a tiny surface fleet. It prohibited tanks, heavy artillery, and an air force.[7] Consequently, even at a time of historically low British military outlays, the Weimar Republic in 1932 spent only 45 percent as much on armaments. Flouting the Versailles Treaty, the new Nazi regime immediately initiated a program of rearmament. Tripling in a single year, German military expenditures in 1933 were 136 percent of Great Britain's. Although British military spending rose sharply thereafter, the Nazi regime rearmed at a more rapid pace. In the final year of peace, German military spending was almost four times that of Great Britain.[8]

Steel Production

Following the Nazi takeover, parity in steel production gave way to marked British inferiority. The earlier worldwide economic slump had brought about steep declines in British and German steel production, but German industry experienced more severe dislocations. Hence, in 1932, the Weimar Republic produced roughly the same amount of steel as Great Britain. This situation of parity was short lived. Utilizing idle capacity, Hitler's rearmament program nearly tripled German steel production. By 1938, German foundries accounted for more than twice as much steel as their British counterparts.[9]

Warship Tonnage

Despite German rearmament, British maritime supremacy remained largely intact. The Washington Naval Conference capped the Royal navy at 525,000 tons in capital ships. Against this benchmark, the Weimar Republic's navy barely registered. In 1932, it consisted of five light cruisers and twelve torpedo boats. Because Hitler's rearmament program favored the army and air force, the German navy in 1938 was still a shadow of Great Britain's. Figures on warship tonnage are not available, but a survey of each state's maritime strength attests to the Royal navy's continued predominance. Germany had three battleships to Great Britain's twelve, nine cruisers to Great Britain's sixty-two, and twenty-two destroyers to Great Britain's 159. Only in submarines did Germany outclass the Royal navy.[10]

First-Line Aircraft

During the first six years of Nazi rule, Germany completely eclipsed British air power. In 1932, Great Britain enjoyed total air supremacy over Germany. Forbidden by the Treaty of Versailles, the Weimar Republic's clandestine air force existed largely on paper.[11] On ascending to the chancellorship, Hitler devoted

Table 6: Anglo-German Balance of Power (%)

	GDP		Military expenditures		International trade		Steel production		First-line aircraft	
	1932	1938	1932	1938	1932	1938	1932	1938	1932	1939
Germany	93	115	46	398	71	68	108	214	0	295

substantial resources to establishing a German air force. As early as 1935, the Luftwaffe deployed 41 percent as many first-line aircraft as the Royal air force (RAF). The British government sought to maintain parity by embarking on a program of air rearmament, but could not keep up. As a result, when Germany invaded Poland in September 1939, the first-line strength of the Luftwaffe was nearly three times that of the RAF.[12] Table 6 depicts Great Britain's loss of predominance over Germany on multiple indicators of national power.

The Balance of Perceptions

In the wake of Hitler's rise, British elites began to predict a German resurgence. They worried that German rearmament would upend the balance of power. The indicator of national capability of greatest interest to the Cabinet, the Foreign Office, and the military services was the relative strength of Germany's air force.

As early as 1933, members of the British government were convinced that under the Nazi regime, the Luftwaffe would graduate from a paper air force to one capable of striking Germany's neighbors.[13] In a document prepared for the Cabinet less than a month after Hitler's installation as chancellor, Foreign Secretary John Simon warned: "Germany will rely for her military power above all on military aircraft."[14] Serving as de facto prime minister in the Cabinet of Ramsay MacDonald, Stanley Baldwin also perceived a nascent German challenge to the RAF's superiority. At a meeting of the Cabinet Disarmament Committee in March 1933, Baldwin is recorded as stating: "There were two things that frightened him more than anything else. The first was the liability of this country to air raids and the second was the rearming of Germany. . . . The air was the first arm which the Germans will start to build up."[15]

Over the next two years, concern that the Luftwaffe would eclipse the RAF became increasingly palpable within the Cabinet. In March and November 1934, Baldwin pledged that Great Britain would not tolerate air inferiority vis-à-vis Germany. The first promise of air parity may have been largely a response to pressure emanating from Conservative members of parliament and the public. However, the second promise—coming after intelligence reports predicted a loss of RAF superiority at the end of 1936—reflected a degree of genuine alarm in addition to political calculations.[16]

Within the Cabinet, perceptions of a shift in the balance of air power became even more pronounced in 1935. Intelligence obtained by the Foreign Office gave credence to Hitler's boast in March that the Luftwaffe had attained parity with the RAF. Once again, Baldwin publicly reaffirmed the British government's commitment to match German air strength, and this time, inaugurated a special committee to ascertain what was required to ensure parity. The committee reported to the Cabinet in May that Germany had already outpaced Great Britain in terms of first-line aircraft.[17]

The Cabinet was not alone in predicting the ascendance of the Luftwaffe. However, the Service Departments and the Foreign Office clashed over the time frame of Germany's air rearmament. In 1933, the Chiefs of Staff considered any significant change in the balance of air power temporally remote. The following year, Air Marshall Edward Ellington still maintained that Germany would only achieve parity with the RAF in 1945.[18] By contrast, the Foreign Office was certain that "Germany will proceed to the building of a formidable armament on land and *especially* in the air."[19] Convinced that the erosion of British air superiority would occur in the short term, the Foreign Office was put in the ironic position of advocating a larger air force than the Air Ministry was ready to countenance. Conflicting projections of the Luftwaffe's relative strength notwithstanding, the Service Departments and the Foreign Office were united in anticipating a future loss of air predominance. Disagreements over the timing reflected different intelligence sources and the Air Ministry's initial propensity to underestimate the pace of German rearmament.[20]

1933: The Death of German Democracy

The collapse of democratic government accompanied Germany's resurgence. The Polity IV dataset clearly delineates the swift and brutal transition that followed the Nazi takeover. In 1932, the dying Weimar Republic receives a score of +6 on the polity scale. After Hitler's rise to power in 1933, the Polity IV dataset assigns Germany a score of –9.[21] A more granular focus on domestic authority structures and the transparency of governance further underscores Germany's rapid transformation into a totalitarian dictatorship.

Once appointed to the chancellorship, Hitler immediately set about concentrating political power in his own hands. To obtain a majority in the Reichstag, he called for new elections. Although marred by violent suppression of the Communists and Social Democrats, the election in March 1933 was still competitive: intimidation of the left-wing parties failed to garner the Nazis more than 50 percent of the vote. Even with the support of the National People's Party, they held less than the two-thirds majority needed to establish a dictatorship by constitutional means. This proved a minor obstacle. By excluding the Communists and wooing the Catholic-dominated Center Party, Hitler on March 23 obtained a supermajority for a law ceding the Reichstag's powers to the chancellor. In the months that followed, all political parties except the Nazis were dissolved. On July 14, Germany was officially declared a one-party state. Legislative elections ceased to be competitive, and plebiscites marked by terror and intimidation substituted for election of the executive.[22] Using the World Bank's coding criteria, Germany from July 1933 had only one check and balance.

The German media became a captive press during the first year of Hitler's Third Reich. The constitution of the Weimar Republic had guaranteed the right of self-expression. This right was taken to encompass freedom of the press.[23] However, after the Reichstag fire of February 27, 1933, Hitler secured a decree suspending seven sections of the constitution covering individual and civil liberties. Journalistic freedom in Germany was thereby deprived of constitutional safeguards. The Reich Press Law enacted in October 1933 sounded the death knell for Germany's once vibrant press. It enabled the Nazi regime to prosecute journalists for any reporting that "tends to weaken the strength of the German Reich . . . or offends the honor and dignity of Germany."[24] Not only did official censorship become widespread, but the German government incarcerated uncooperative journalists and forced the media industry to consolidate under the leadership of a Nazi party member.[25] On the scale measuring freedom of the press developed in Chapter 2, Nazi Germany scores six—its press was unfree. With the media muzzled, governance in Germany became opaque.

The Myth of British Appeasement

After the Second World War, Great Britain's strategy toward Germany between 1933 and 1938 became synonymous with appeasement. Winston Churchill and other British officials who earlier than their peers supported taking a hard line against Hitler actively promoted this narrative.[26] However, recent scholarship by historians has discredited this depiction of British strategy. As Hitler transformed Germany into an autocracy and revitalized its economy with a program of massive rearmament, Great Britain pursued an approach that differed from straightforward accommodation. It attempted to enmesh Germany in a new set of European institutions while simultaneously rearming. British strategy was to integrate and hedge, not to appease.

The Search for a European Settlement

Given the absence of strong multilateral regimes during the 1930s, British leaders attempting to integrate Germany looked to build institutions from the ground up. This took the form of an ultimately fruitless search for a post-Versailles order in Europe that would recognize yet simultaneously restrain German ambitions. One year after Hitler's rise to power, the British government presented Germany with the first outline of a new European settlement. The proposal acknowledged Germany's right to limited rearmament: Hitler could have an army of 200,000, build light tanks, and provided that no agreement on air disarmament was concluded within two years, field an air force. Additionally, the other European powers would disarm to German levels over seven years. Intended to control the pace of Hitler's rearmament program and lay the foundation for a more enduring European order, this British proposal proved acceptable neither to Germany nor to France.[27]

Great Britain again put forward a plan for a new European settlement in 1935. This time the French were brought on board before approaching Germany. The Anglo-French vision included mutual security pacts in Central and Eastern Europe, an armament agreement, and a five-power mutual assistance pact to deter unprovoked bombing. Conveyed to the German government in a memorandum, the Anglo-French proposal came to naught. However, in June 1935, Great Britain did succeed in attaining an Anglo-German Naval Agreement. Designed to avert a maritime rivalry, the accord capped the German fleet at 35 percent of the Royal navy's warship tonnage.[28]

British efforts to secure a comprehensive settlement continued despite German obduracy. In July 1936, Great Britain acting in tandem with France and Belgium proposed a five-power conference to establish a new security arrangement in Western Europe. Germany delayed the conference indefinitely. Later in the year, Hjalmar Schacht, the president of the Reichsbank, floated an arrangement whereby Germany would adopt a more cooperative posture in Europe in exchange for colonies and economic assistance. The British government used contacts with Schacht to sound out the possibility of a new regional order encompassing mutual security guarantees, arms limitation agreements, and German reentry into the League of Nations. British officials subsequently raised the question of a general settlement with Hitler in November 1937 and March 1938. They were rebuffed each time.[29]

Concessions later construed as appeasement were actually a component of Great Britain's search for a post-Versailles settlement in Europe. British elites recognized that a resurgent Germany would not enter constraining institutions without inducements. "If we wish to achieve a comprehensive settlement . . . then we must face the fact that this settlement must take the form of a bargain. A bargain can only be achieved at a price."[30] The British government thus offered concessions to Germany, but without exception, linked them to membership in institutions that would ultimately constitute a new European order.

The British proposal in 1934 pledged to ease restrictions on the German military provided that Hitler accepted a new disarmament scheme. Likewise, the 1935 Anglo-French plan promised to abrogate limitations on Germany's armed forces if Hitler reciprocated by participating in mutual security guarantees, an armaments agreement, and an air pact. The British government also attempted to trade modification of the Rhineland's status for German accession to a ceiling on first-line aircraft. However, Hitler's unilateral remilitarization of the Rhineland in March 1936 eliminated this bargaining chip.[31]

The Cabinet's response to feelers put out by Reichsbank president Schacht also featured the expectation that German quids would accompany British quos. Although willing to consider the restitution of German colonies and economic assistance, Neville Chamberlain and Anthony Eden—prime minister and foreign secretary respectively—were adamant that such concessions be part of a general settlement. When Lord Halifax, a member of the Cabinet and confidante of Chamberlain, met with Hitler in November 1937, he explicitly tied the question of German colonies to the attainment of a new regional order. Colonies "could only be broached as a part of a general settlement by means of which quiet and security might be established in Europe."[32]

In short, what Churchill and others later framed as appeasement was actually a more complicated approach of trying to integrate Germany into European institutions.

British Rearmament

The appeasement myth overlooks what was a key dimension of British strategy toward Germany: hedging through rearmament. Great Britain did not wait until the Munich crisis of September 1938 to prepare for a military clash with the Third Reich. In fact, the reconstitution of British military strength began much earlier.

Within less than a year of Hitler's appointment to the chancellorship of Germany, the British government began to consider rearmament. In November 1933, the Cabinet founded the Defence Requirements Committee to "prepare a programme for meeting our worst deficiencies."[33] Nine months later, the Cabinet approved a substantial expansion of the RAF and allocated additional resources to the other services. All told, British military expenditures in 1934 rose 62 percent above the previous year's outlays.[34]

Between 1935 and 1938, the intensity of British rearmament accelerated. The Cabinet authorized successively larger numbers of first-line aircraft. By February 1938, aircraft orders had reached the limits of British industrial capacity.[35] The army and navy also received additional funding. In early 1936, the Cabinet endorsed a five-division expeditionary force and decided to construct five new battleships. Overall, military spending soared: Great Britain's defense outlays in 1938 were 4.6 times higher than in 1933.[36] A strategy of appeasement would not have included rearmament of this scale.

Autocracy Overshadows Germany's Resurgence

British leaders had no desire to launch an ambitious military buildup. Their highest priority was economic recovery. In addition, paying for rearmament entailed unpopular measures such as higher taxation or cutting social spending. Politically, it would have been far easier for the British government to have focused solely on attaining German acceptance of a new European settlement.[37] But because the authoritarian revolution carried out by the Nazis obscured German intentions and amplified mistrust, relying entirely on international institutions to constrain behavior posed a significant risk. As

German power increased, the only responsible choice for British leaders was to pair integration with hedging.

Hitler: Nationalist or Napoleon?

When the Nazis transformed Germany into a dictatorship in 1933, Great Britain's capacity to ascertain German intentions plummeted. The shackling of the German press and the silencing of covert channels from the Weimar period cast a pall of uncertainty over the scope of German ambitions.[38] So acute was the dearth of information that the Cabinet in mid-1936 presented Hitler with a questionnaire intended to elicit a definitive statement of German aims. In retrospect, such a statement already existed in the form of *Mein Kampf*—the manifesto penned by Hitler outlining a systematic plan of European conquest and genocide. However, few in Great Britain actually read Hitler's screed, and those who did generally found it too outlandish to believe. Additionally, British leaders were uncertain whether a book written from a prison cell in 1925 reflected the outlook of Germany's new chancellor. Cabinet Secretary Maurice Hankey in October 1933 summarized this dilemma: "Are we dealing with the Hitler of *Mein Kampf*, lulling his opponents to sleep with fair words. . . . Or is it a new Hitler, who has discovered the burden of responsible office, and wants to extricate himself, like many an earlier tyrant, from the commitments of his irresponsible days?"[39]

The question posed by Cabinet Secretary Hankey was initially unanswerable. Until 1938, Germany was too weak to execute any grand expansionist visions. And the pervasive secrecy and centralization of the Nazi regime deprived Great Britain of insights on what Germany might be planning. This did not prevent British elites from evaluating the scope of German ambitions, but a consensus was impossible. Some, like Baldwin, the acting prime minister in the Cabinet of the ailing Ramsay MacDonald, recognized the ambiguity of Hitler's intentions and refrained from passing judgment. In 1934, Baldwin's assessment of Hitler was that "no one knows what the new Germany means."[40]

Winston Churchill, though often lauded for discerning Hitler's megalomaniac aims long before anyone else, was initially ambivalent. While writing *Great Contemporaries* in 1935, Churchill, then a Conservative backbencher, observed:

We cannot tell whether Hitler will be the man who will once again let loose upon the world another war in which civilization will irretrievably succumb, or whether he will go down in history as the man who restored honour and peace of mind to the great Germanic nation and brought it back serene, helpful and strong, to the forefront of the European family circle.[41]

Other British elites were less circumspect in assessing Hitler's intentions. Yet the uncertainty created by Germany's authoritarian institutions led to multiple and contending views of Hitler. Between 1933 and 1938, many within the British government were convinced that Hitler was essentially a German nationalist. Hitler sought to reclaim the honor and sovereignty of a state emasculated by the Treaty of Versailles. While harboring territorial ambitions, Hitler would only expand the borders of the Third Reich to incorporate ethnic Germans. His goals were therefore finite and legitimated by the norm of self-determination.[42] Prominent British statesmen—Neville Chamberlain, John Simon, Anthony Eden, and Lord Halifax—initially subscribed to this view of the German chancellor.[43]

Uncertainty also allowed a darker assessment of Hitler's ambitions to be formed. Rather than merely seeking to right the injustices of the Versailles Treaty and bring his ethnic kinsmen into the Third Reich, Hitler aspired to nothing short of German mastery in Europe. Robert Vansittart, permanent under secretary of the Foreign Office, championed this interpretation of German aims.[44] By May 1933, he had already concluded: "The present régime in Germany will, on past and present form, loose off another European war just as soon as it feels strong enough."[45] Vansittart went on to initiate a long-running, sometimes bitter debate over German ambitions within the British government. His relationship with Foreign Secretary Simon became badly strained. Baldwin was also at loggerheads with Vansittart, and in 1936 attempted to remove him. Chamberlain later succeeded by promoting Vansittart to a figurehead position in the Foreign Office.[46]

However, the fall of Vansittart failed to quell mounting concerns about Hitler's aims. Unable to penetrate the internal workings of the Nazi regime, much less Hitler's mind, British elites focused on observable foreign policy changes as harbingers of future intentions. Thus, after German troops entered the Rhineland, Churchill shed his earlier ambivalence about Hitler.[47] In the wake of an even more egregious violation of the Versailles Treaty—the annexation of Austria in March 1938—he began to call for a "Grand Alliance" to thwart German expansion. Churchill rapidly became the most articulate spokesman for members of parliament critical of British strategy. This disparate and loosely knit group of lawmakers had by mid-1938 come to include disillusioned Conservative Party members, the Labour Party, and some Liberal Party members.[48]

It is important to note that Hitler's initial moves were indistinguishable from those of a German nationalist with limited objectives. Seen in this light, the apparent naiveté or wishful thinking of many Cabinet members becomes understandable. Instead, the puzzle is why a growing number of British elites concluded early on that Hitler harbored far more expansive ambitions than simply uniting all ethnic Germans under the Third Reich. What explains this puzzle is the nature of Germany's political system. With the Nazi regime a black box, there was no way for Hitler to credibly demonstrate that rearmament, the reoccupation of the Rhineland, and the absorption of Austria were not the first steps in a plan of Napoleonic conquest.

"Fantastic Hooligans and Eccentrics"

The extreme concentration of power that accompanied the advent of the Nazi dictatorship further obscured the direction of Germany's resurgence. Once Hitler eliminated alternative centers of authority, the Third Reich's foreign policy was only as predictable as the Nazi leadership. This group had, to paraphrase the historian Alan Bullock, risen from the gutter to take power.[49] Its composition and outlook concerned many in the British government.

Horace Rumbold, British ambassador to Berlin until July 1933, reported in his final dispatch that Hitler and his main lieutenants, Hermann Goering and Joseph Goebbels, were "notoriously pathological cases," that "fantastic hooligans and eccentrics" dominated the upper ranks of the Nazi hierarchy, and that "the persons directing the policy of the Hitler Government are not normal."[50] As Germany rearmed and took additional steps to subvert the Treaty of Versailles, personalization of power under Nazi rule remained a key source of uncertainty. Speaking to a deputation of Conservative Party members four months after the remilitarization of the Rhineland, Baldwin observed: "The worst of it is we none of us know what goes on in that strange man's mind; I am referring to Hitler."[51] The existence of an unconstrained and mentally unbalanced Nazi leadership thus deepened British trepidation about Germany's future trajectory.

Misplaced Faith in German "Moderates"

The structure of the Nazi regime deprived London of opportunities to shape Germany's strategic behavior. Decisions lay in Hitler's hands. He was seldom if ever influenced by direct arguments from his advisers, whom British leaders could lobby.

Nonetheless, British elites identified access opportunities in the German political system. As early as 1933, some within the British government had become convinced that extremists and moderates competed for Hitler's ear. The former group was believed to include Joseph Goebbels, the minister of propaganda, Heinrich Himmler, the chief of the SS, and Joachim von Ribbentrop, the German ambassador to London. The moderate category was thought to include Reichsbank President Schacht, Foreign Minister Konstantin von Neurath, and Werner von Blomberg, the army head. Later, Hermann Goering and his followers came to be placed in this category when the original moderates were purged.[52]

In British eyes, the existence of German moderates created an opportunity to influence the Nazi regime from within. The moderates ostensibly wanted peaceful and economically beneficial relations with Great Britain. Hitler's choices could be nudged in a favorable direction if Britain could strengthen the moderates' hand. To this end, the British government worked to bolster the moderates by communicating that German acceptance of a general settlement would bring about economic rewards and a return of colonies.[53]

Ultimately, the restraining influence of the German moderates came to naught. The potential clout of the German moderates was actually an illusion facilitated by the Nazi regime's lack of transparency and perpetuated by deliberate deception. The Nazis played up the split between extremists and moderates for British consumption. To give one example, during Lord Halifax's visit to Germany in November 1937, Goering was instructed to offer peaceful reassurances as a counterpoise to Hitler's more truculent attitude.[54] Autocratic rule allowed the Nazis to create an image of access where none in fact existed. This gambit failed to successfully reassure Great Britain because Germany's overarching intentions remained opaque.

The Road to Containment

British doubts about the effectiveness of integrating Germany deepened as Hitler steadily subverted the Treaty of Versailles while rebuffing proposals for a new European settlement. Key members of the Cabinet, however, remained cautiously hopeful that Hitler might turn out to be a German nationalist rather than a new Napoleon. This changed after mid-1938 as Hitler, emboldened by

Germany's burgeoning military, initiated a series of crises that threatened to unleash a new European war. Persuaded of Hitler's megalomaniac aims and discounting the viability of integration, the British government shifted with increasing alacrity to contain Germany's resurgence.

The Sudeten Crisis

The Sudeten crisis that erupted in September 1938 constituted a turning point in British strategy toward Germany. Its cause was the disputed status of ethnic Germans living in Czechoslovakia's Sudetenland. At Hitler's bidding, the Sudeten Germans began to agitate for autonomy. Czechoslovakia, an ally of France, initially resisted German pressure, causing tensions to flare. As the crisis intensified, the Nazi regime's pervasive secrecy obscured the scope of Hitler's demands. The British government had no option other than to wait for a declaration of German objectives. Thus, in early September, Chamberlain wrote to his sister: "on Tuesday Hitler makes his set speech and by then I suppose we may get some inkling of what is in his mind."[55] However, the address at Nuremberg offered little clarity on German designs for the Sudetenland. Afterward, Great Britain's prime minister lamented: "we have no definitive knowledge of his [Hitler's] intentions."[56]

The unchecked power Hitler wielded coupled with preexisting concerns about his mental health lent additional uncertainty to the crisis. The British ambassador in Berlin began to worry that Hitler might have "crossed the border-line of insanity."[57] Likewise, Chamberlain on September 3 observed: "Is it not positively horrible to think that the fate of hundreds of millions depends on one man and he is half mad."[58] By September 11, Chamberlain had modified his diagnosis of Hitler's mental state—the German leader was now an outright "lunatic."[59] The British government considered Hitler's personality so volatile that any warning might cause him to embrace war.[60]

To defuse the crisis, Chamberlain flew to Germany on September 15. Hitler demanded the cession of the Sudetenland to Germany and threatened to trigger a new European conflagration if his demands were not met, telling Chamberlain: "the thing has got to be settled at once. I am determined to settle it. I do not care whether there is a world war or not."[61] After this first round of shuttle diplomacy failed, Chamberlain returned to Germany on September 22. He proposed a compromise plan. Much of the Sudetenland would be apportioned to Germany while areas containing a substantial proportion of Czechs would be decided by plebiscite. Hitler's response—that the Czech government must evacuate the Sudetenland by October 1 without preconditions—came as a bitter shock and demonstrated again Great Britain's inability to penetrate the authoritarian institutions the Nazis had created.[62]

On September 29, the British, French, Italian, and German heads of state came to Munich for an eleventh-hour conference to determine the fate of the Sudetenland. The agreement that averted war provided for German occupation of most of the Sudetenland and an international commission to oversee the final transfer of territory.[63] Reflecting Great Britain's enduring search for a European settlement, Chamberlain did manage to induce Hitler to sign an Anglo-German joint declaration committing Germany to resolve all future territorial disputes through peaceful consultation. This was a quid pro quo for granting Hitler territory under Czech rule, and regarded at the time as a great diplomatic victory.[64]

The Sudeten crisis called into question a key assumption underpinning British strategy toward Germany. Until September 1938, the British government had believed that German military unreadiness created a window of time for integration. The different branches of the British military had identified 1942 as the earliest date for any German challenge to Western Europe, and retained this assessment even as Hitler rearmed and occupied the Rhineland. Chamberlain too came to ascribe similar significance to 1942, and in private letters, repeatedly observed that Germany harbored no desire for war in the short term.[65]

Hitler's willingness to risk war at the height of the Sudeten crisis compelled a reassessment of this earlier timeline. As the British government deployed the Home Fleet to war stations, began to distribute gas masks, ordered trenches dug in major cities, placed antiaircraft in the center of London, and updated plans to evacuate children from large towns, it was impossible to continue believing that a window of opportunity for integration existed.[66] Although the Munich Conference brought an end to the crisis, it amounted to only a slight retreat from the precipice. Even Chamberlain evinced little optimism about the prospects for peace. In mid-October, he observed: "We have avoided the greatest catastrophe, it is true, but we are very little nearer to the time when we can put all thoughts of war out of our minds."[67] Having experienced the harrowing Sudeten crisis, British leaders saw clearly that time no longer favored efforts to embed Germany in a post-Versailles order.

The Sudeten crisis also convinced a number of Cabinet members that Hitler's aims were Napoleonic in scale. This was evident in the growing internal dissent Chamberlain confronted as he tried to justify a negotiated resolution to the crisis. When Chamberlain returned to London after his first round of shuttle diplomacy, four Cabinet members objected to what they deemed a "complete surrender." Rumblings within the Cabinet became far more serious following Chamberlain's next meeting with Hitler. In a dramatic about-face, Foreign Secretary Halifax, until then a key supporter of transferring the Sudetenland to Germany, told the Cabinet that peace would be uncertain until the Nazis were overthrown. Halifax advocated coming to the aid of the Czechs if they chose to resist Hitler's demands. When Chamberlain asked for each minister's opinion, six dissenters backed Halifax. A significant proportion of the Cabinet had begun to conclude that Germany under Nazi rule was inevitably destined to become an adversary of Great Britain.[68]

Throughout the crisis over the Sudetenland, Chamberlain remained more optimistic about German intentions than many of his colleagues in the Cabinet. Even so, the gullible "umbrella man" portrayed in the appeasement narrative is an exaggeration. During a Cabinet meeting on September 24, Chamberlain acknowledged that Hitler might be negotiating in bad faith. At Munich, the prime minister reportedly pointed to the Anglo-German joint declaration and told his private secretary: "If Hitler signed it and kept the bargain well and good . . . if he broke it, he would demonstrate to all the world that he was totally cynical and untrustworthy."[69] Yet Chamberlain also made statements evincing faith in Hitler's self-professed limited aims.[70] His view of the German dictator defies easy categorization.

In the wake of the Sudeten crisis, hedging became the dominant element in British strategy toward Germany. Rearmament gave way to an all-out military buildup. The Cabinet approved a procurement program to boost the RAF to 3,700 fighters and 85 bomber squadrons; moved to reconstitute an expeditionary force; and authorized the creation of a 32-division army during wartime. Then, in early 1939, Great Britain began to lay the groundwork for a European coalition that would deter and, if necessary, roll back German aggression. The first step was to consolidate ties with France. On February 6, the British government publicly pledged to defend France against any attack. Anglo-French staff talks were initiated shortly thereafter. British strategy was, with increasing rapidity, shifting toward containment.

The Occupation of Prague

As part of the Munich Agreement, Great Britain and France had promised to jointly uphold the sovereignty of what remained of Czechoslovakia. In a separate Anglo-German declaration signed at Munich, Hitler had pledged that "the method of consultation shall be the method adopted to deal with any other questions that may concern our two countries."[71] Yet on March

15, 1939, without any forewarning, German troops marched into Czechoslovakia and occupied Prague, while the Slovak provinces, which had declared independence the day before, became a Nazi satellite.

In British eyes, the dismemberment of Czechoslovakia underscored the failure of integration. The Anglo-German joint declaration so dearly won at Munich had proven merely a scrap of paper. The occupation of Prague also provided irrefutable evidence that Hitler sought more than a revision of the Versailles Treaty along the lines of ethnic self-determination. By annexing a non-Germanic people, Hitler unveiled the true scope of his ambitions. British ministers concluded that Hitler would follow the course of European conquest charted by Napoleon, and the Cabinet record indicates that even Chamberlain was forced to revise his beliefs about the Nazi leader.

> The Prime Minister said that up till a week ago we had proceeded on the assumption that we should be able to continue with our policy of getting onto better terms with the Dictator Powers, and that although those powers had aims, those aims were limited. We had all along had at the back of our minds the reservation that this might not prove to be the case but we had felt that it was right to try out the possibilities of this course . . . he had now come definitely to the conclusion that Herr Hitler's attitude made it impossible to continue to negotiate on the old basis with the Nazi regime.[72]

Outside the Cabinet, the dismemberment of Czechoslovakia had a similar impact. Conservative Party members as a whole came to see Hitler as a would-be Napoleon.[73] At the Foreign Office, Vansittart's replacement, Alexander Cadogan, was compelled to admit: "It is turning out—at present—as Van predicted and as I never believed it would."[74] Throughout the British government, there was a new certainty in the near inevitability of a clash with Germany.

In the weeks and months after the fall of Prague, Great Britain began to put in place the elements of a new containment strategy. The British government instituted conscription—an unprecedented step during peacetime. Military spending surged: the armaments budget for 1939 was ultimately 323 percent above the previous year's record total.[75] On the diplomatic front, Chamberlain issued a guarantee of Polish independence at the end of March. Made before the House of Commons, this commitment established a red line for German aggression. Further red lines appeared on the map of Europe when Great Britain issued guarantees to Greece, Romania, and Turkey on April 14.[76] In late May, the Cabinet agreed to set aside decades of mistrust and a deep-seated dislike of communism to pursue an alliance with the Soviet Union. The terms put forward by Great Britain obligated the Soviet Union to defend third parties threatened by German aggression. Ultimately, an alliance proved untenable because Stalin demanded a free hand in Eastern Europe—something only Hitler was prepared to concede.[77]

As Great Britain moved to contain Germany, it abandoned the search for a post-Versailles settlement. The British government concluded that future naval arrangements were not worth pursuing, and ceased efforts to build on the Anglo-German naval agreement.[78] Chamberlain and Halifax persisted in the quest for a European settlement, but their overtures to Hitler were modest in scope, kept secret from much of the British government, and when exposed by the press, widely ridiculed.[79] By the summer of 1939, most British leaders had written off the possibility of successfully integrating Germany into international institutions.

The Polish Crisis

After Czechoslovakia, Hitler's next designs focused on Poland. In reestablishing Poland, the Treaty of Versailles had stripped Germany of territory linking East Prussia to the rest of the country. Intended to give Poland access to the Baltic Sea, this territory became a flashpoint as Hitler pressed Poland to return the free city of Danzig and the rest of the corridor. By late August 1939, massed German troops stood poised on the border of Poland and a nonaggression pact with the Soviet Union had given Hitler a free hand to strike. A final flurry of diplomacy proved futile, in part because Hitler wanted war, and also because earlier crises had led the British government to reject continuing a strategy of integration. On September 1, the German army rolled into Poland. Two days later Great Britain declared war and put in place the final element of containment: a naval blockade intended to strangle the German economy.[80]

Although the carnage of the First World War had left the British with little appetite for a new military struggle, standing aside represented an even less palatable option. By the outbreak of hostilities, London had come to conclude that Germany under Nazi rule was inherently bellicose. British wartime objectives thus encompassed the overthrow of the Nazi regime and not merely Germany's withdrawal from Poland and Czechoslovakia excluding the Sudetenland.[81] As even Chamberlain was forced to admit: "the difficulty is with Hitler himself. Until he disappears and his system collapses there can be no peace."[82]

Economic Interdependence and British Strategy

Relations between Great Britain and Nazi Germany demonstrate that trade statistics sometimes provide an inadequate picture of economic interdependence. With protectionism rampant and the Nazis aspiring to economic autarky, bilateral commerce was low; from 1932 to 1938, Anglo-German trade remained less than 1 percent of British GDP.[83] However, the legacy of British investments in the Weimar Republic created a unique form of economic interdependence. Before the global economic slump and Hitler's rise to power, London financial houses had made substantial loans to Germany. Much of this debt was frozen as part of a standstill agreement concluded in 1931. Under the agreement, Germany promised to remit interest payments while British bankers committed to extending future credit.[84]

The financial linkages perpetuated by the standstill agreement meant that the City of London—Great Britain's Wall Street—had a vested interest in stable Anglo-German relations. To protect this interest, prominent financiers and leading bankers actively lobbied the British government. It is important to separate out their influence on British strategy toward Germany.

One way business groups could have exercised influence was through convincing the Treasury to oppose rearmament. Structurally, the Treasury was more attuned to the City of London than most other segments of the British government. A number of scholars have pointed to the Treasury's role as a brake on the pace of rearmament. Until 1939, the Treasury restricted the growth of military expenditures despite objections from the military service departments and the Foreign Office.[85]

On closer inspection, however, the Treasury's attempt to control ballooning military costs appears unconnected to the work of business lobbies. Like the British military chiefs of staff, the Treasury held that any war with Germany would be protracted. A lengthy conflict would entail importing raw material and food in vast quantities. Great Britain would need ample gold reserves, substantial foreign exchange, and international creditworthiness to pay for crucial wartime imports. The Treasury therefore considered national finance a "fourth arm of defence." In this view, unlimited rearmament threatened to exhaust Great Britain's financial resources before the outbreak of war.

Fear that the "fourth arm of defence" might prematurely wither impelled the Treasury to impose limits on the growth of military spending prior to 1939, not lobbying by commercial groups anxious to maintain good relations with Germany.[86]

Another way the City of London could have shaped Great Britain's approach to Germany was through preventing termination of the standstill agreement. By guaranteeing credit to Germany, the standstill agreement provided foreign exchange that was used to purchase strategic raw materials. Perpetuating the standstill agreement meant abetting the Nazi rearmament program. It is therefore striking that the British government renewed the standstill agreement every year until the invasion of Poland. A handful of officials did call for termination of the debt-servicing arrangement in the wake of the Sudeten crisis, but they received little support. The Bank of England, the Treasury, and the Foreign Office Economic Section were all worried about the impact on certain financial houses.[87] This instance provides clear-cut evidence of how business groups shaped British strategy.

That being said, the British government's decision to renew the standstill agreement reflected more than a concern for the politically influential City of London. Terminating the agreement would have amounted to imposing sanctions on Germany. Chamberlain felt that denouncing the standstill agreement would drive Hitler irreversibly into the arms of the "extremists." For its part, the Foreign Office speculated that Hitler might even respond by declaring war.[88] The British government thus faced an unappealing decision: it could continue to facilitate German rearmament or risk triggering a military conflict. This stark choice, as much as the clout of business groups, explains why Great Britain failed to terminate the standstill agreement at an earlier date.

Conclusion

During the 1930s, Germany's regime type framed the power transition with Great Britain. The dictatorship established by the Nazis obscured German intentions. While waiting to discover whether Hitler was a nationalist or a new Napoleon, the British government rearmed and attempted to constrain Germany by enmeshing it in a new European order. As the limitations of integration and Hitler's megalomaniac ambitions became increasingly apparent, Great Britain embraced containment despite the cataclysmic losses war was expected to bring.

The Anglo-German power transition of the 1930s contains several lessons. First, perceptions of access are not, alone, sufficient to shape a democratic state's choice of strategy. For a time British leaders wrongly identified "moderates" around Hitler who could be leveraged to soften the harder edges of German foreign policy. Yet their mistaken assessment was not reflected in Great Britain's initial approach to Germany, which was to integrate and hedge. This suggests that access opportunities must deliver tangible results to function as a source of reassurance, and that ultimately, reassurance is more closely linked to the clarity of a new power's ambitions. The second lesson of this chapter relates to policy. British strategy toward Nazi Germany reveals that a democracy confronting an autocracy's rise needs to carefully determine the right mix of hedging and integration in order to build up a sufficient insurance against disaster. History would have turned out better if Great Britain had hedged more aggressively in the early years of Hitler's regime.

Chapter 5

Red Star Rising

The destruction wrought by the Second World War precipitated the rise of the Soviet Union. Powerful states on the USSR periphery were either shattered by defeat or exhausted in victory. At the same time, the Red Army advanced to the heart of Europe, placing vast new territories and large foreign populations under Soviet control. Although the United States remained the world's preeminent power, its position was no longer unassailable, particularly if the USSR could gain dominance over the industrial and natural resource concentrations located just beyond its expanded frontiers. The end of the most cataclysmic war in history had ushered in a new fateful transition.

The USSR's autocratic system shaped American perceptions of its rise from the outset, creating an environment of uncertainty and mistrust that existed even as the two countries fought as allies against Germany. Thus, the initial U.S. response to the Soviet ascendance was to integrate and hedge. After the war, the USSR's pervasive secrecy ensured that its growing assertiveness would appear to American observers a harbinger of unbridled expansionism. With Soviet enmity the new consensus in Washington, containment became the only possible course.

The Balance of Power

The encirclement of German forces at Stalingrad marked the advent of a Soviet recovery that, by the outbreak of the Korean War, had reshaped the balance of power. Over the course of seven years, the USSR overtook the United States in military expenditures, narrowed the economic gap, and cracked the secret of the atomic bomb.

Gross Domestic Product

Within a short period after World War II, the enormous disparity in national wealth between the United States and the Soviet Union began to diminish. The wartime gap between the U.S. and Soviet economies was stark. While global conflict had lifted the United States from the stranglehold of the Great Depression, the USSR was devastated by a German onslaught. Accordingly, Soviet output plummeted from 45 percent of U.S. GDP in 1940 to 21 percent of U.S. GDP in 1943. However, peacetime brought about a reversal of economic fortunes. The United States initially suffered a sharp drop in domestic demand as government spending underwent a major decline. By contrast, the Soviet economy, buoyed by postwar reconstruction, expanded at a rapid pace, averaging GDP growth of 8.5 percent per annum from 1946 to 1950. Consequently, by 1950 the USSR output amounted to 35 percent that of the United States, a considerably higher percentage than in 1943.[1]

International Trade

The Soviet rise after World War II left America's commercial preeminence untouched. During the first full year of peacetime, 1946, the USSR's foreign commerce was about one tenth that of the United States. Soviet trade continued to increase thereafter, but at a declining rate. By 1950, the USSR's foreign commerce as a U.S. equivalent was only 17 percent.[2]

Military Expenditures

Between 1945 and 1950, U.S. superiority in military spending gave way to a slight inferiority favoring the USSR. Although Soviet armaments spending rose steadily throughout the Second World War, U.S. military allocations expanded at an exponential rate as the American economy converted to a wartime footing. By 1943, Soviet military expenditures were only 11 percent that of the United States. The pattern of relative military outlays abruptly shifted after the termination of hostilities in 1945. Pressured to "bring the boys home," the U.S. government quickly demobilized. Military spending fell precipitously, and in 1948, plumbed levels not seen since the Great Depression. The USSR, however, opted for a posture of military vigilance and ratcheted up spending on armaments to the point where military allocations in 1950 were almost twice as large as 1945. By 1950, the Soviet Union was spending more on armaments than the United States.[3] The change in relative expenditures actually understates the shift in the military balance of power that occurred during the second half of the 1940s. The simultaneous drawdown of American ground

Table 7: U.S.-Soviet Balance of Power (%)

	GDP		Military expenditures		International trade		Atomic bomb	
	1943	1950	1943	1950	1946	1950	1943	1950
USSR	21	35	11	107	10	17	No	Yes

forces and continued Soviet investment in the Red army positioned the USSR to militarily dominate vital areas of the Eurasian landmass.

The Atomic Bomb

By breaking America's atomic monopoly, the Soviet Union reshaped the balance of power on what was at the time regarded as a key indicator of national capability. In 1943, the Soviet atomic bomb program lagged far behind the Manhattan Project. Indeed, the USSR's pursuit of an atomic bomb consisted largely of espionage activities conducted against the United States. This changed when U.S. atomic bombs leveled Hiroshima and Nagasaki. In response, the Soviet Union embarked on a crash effort to develop a bomb of its own. What followed was a massive mobilization of scientific talent and prison labor that delivered results in August 1949, when the USSR successfully tested a plutonium weapon.[4] Table 7 summarizes the changing U.S.-Soviet distribution of capabilities.

The Balance of Perceptions

U.S. perceptions of the Soviet Union's ascendance predated the end of World War II. Well before the fall of Berlin or the Japanese surrender in Tokyo Bay, American elites realized that victory would transform the Soviet Union's international position. The United States had entered the war not only to avenge Pearl Harbor but also to prevent the Axis from dominating Eurasia, the world's strategic heartland. Yet paradoxically, the war's successful conclusion promised to upend the Eurasian balance of power in the USSR's favor.

Diverse individuals and organizations inside the U.S. government recognized the Soviet Union's impending geopolitical gains. President Franklin Roosevelt was especially prescient. Speaking in confidence to an American journalist in December 1942, Roosevelt observed that the collapse of the Axis in Europe would render the Soviet Union "the only first-rate military power on the continent."[5] The president's Chief of Staff, Admiral Leahy, likewise foresaw that the war would redound to the Soviet Union's geopolitical advantage. In a memorandum intended for the secretary of state, Leahy underscored that the "phenomenal" growth of Soviet military power coupled with the exhaustion of British strength would give the USSR unchallenged mastery in continental Europe.[6]

Similar perceptions existed outside the White House. In 1943 and 1944, the U.S. military authored multiple studies describing the Soviet Union's transformed geopolitical position. These reports pointed to eventual Soviet dominance in Eastern and Central Europe, Northeast Asia, and even the Middle East.[7] The future author of the Long Telegram, George Kennan, also highlighted the USSR's wartime gains. Serving in Moscow as deputy chief of the U.S. mission, Kennan warned his superiors that "two hundred million people, united under the strong, purposeful leadership of Moscow and inhabiting one of the major industrial countries of the world, constitute a single force greater than any other that will be left on the European continent when the war is over."[8]

Whether Kennan's warnings directly influenced Washington is uncertain, but his anxieties paralleled the thinking of civilians heading the national security bureaucracy there. In January 1945, the "State-War-Navy" committee, a semiregular conclave of the three department secretaries or their representatives, discussed how a policy of unconditional surrender toward Germany and Japan would "unbalance the international system in the face of Soviet power."[9]

American perceptions of a shifting balance of power became even more pronounced after the final defeat of the Axis. A specter began to haunt U.S. officials—communist penetration of countries lying beyond the occupation forces of the Red Army. As seen from Washington, communist parties in Western Europe and elsewhere answered to the Soviet Union. If they took power, the USSR would control new territories without firing a shot.[10] Additional Soviet gains would further unbalance the international system and undermine America's geopolitical position, perhaps irretrievably.

This perspective was explicitly articulated in a number of U.S. government documents. A September 1946 study compiled by President Harry Truman's special counsel, Clark Clifford, and a junior naval aide, George Elsey, noted: "If the Soviet Union acquires control of one or more of these areas [Western Europe, the Middle East, China, or Japan], the military forces required to hold in check those of the U.S.S.R. and prevent still further acquisitions will be substantially enlarged."[11] Subsequent government reports laid out even more dire assessments of how continued Soviet expansion would create an imbalance of power. Drafted in March 1948, National Security Council Report 7 (NSC 7) noted:

> Between the United States and the USSR there are in Europe and Asia areas of great potential power which if added to the existing strength of the Soviet world would enable the latter to become so superior in manpower, resources, and territory that the prospect for the survival of the United States as a free nation would be slight.[12]

All Power to Stalin

The Soviet Union that emerged from the cataclysm of the Second World War was an autocracy. The Polity IV dataset makes this designation, assigning the USSR a score of -9 between 1943 and 1950.[13] Detailed examination of the USSR's internal checks and balances and degree of media freedom also indicates that under Joseph Stalin the Soviet Union had evolved into a model totalitarian state.

Brutal purges of senior Communist Party members and the decimation of the Red Army's officer corps during Stalin's reign of terror in the 1930s created an extreme concentration of power in the Soviet system. Having eliminated all elements with the potential to counterbalance his authority, Stalin thereafter dominated the Politburo—the institution at the apex of the Communist Party, which in turn controlled the Soviet state. The makeup of the Politburo was determined at Stalin's discretion. So were the Politburo's agenda, its procedures, its location, and its time of meeting. Beyond exercising institutional control over the Politburo, Stalin could punish its membership with personal humiliation, demotion, and at the extreme, death.[14] Thus, the only check and balance in the USSR was Stalin himself.

The Soviet regime also lacked transparency. Rather than uncovering the inner workings of government, the media in the USSR were a mouthpiece of the state. The Soviet constitution of 1936 guaranteed freedom of the press only "in conformity with the interests of the workers and for the purposes of strengthening the socialist system."[15] Not surprisingly then, a formidable censorship apparatus called the Glavlit operated at every administrative

level of the Soviet Union.[16] Defying the state censors could result in impris-
onment or death by shooting. Not only was the Soviet press straitjacketed;
it played the propaganda role Stalin had prescribed, serving as the "prime
instrument through which the Party speaks daily, hourly, with the working
class in its own indispensable language."[17] Using the media freedom survey
employed in previous chapters, the USSR scores at the unfree end of the
spectrum.

America's Early Approach: Integrate and Hedge

Once the defeat of the Axis powers became certain, the United States began
to respond to the Soviet Union's ascendance. American policies amounted to
integration and hedging.

  During the Second World War and the immediate aftermath, the United
States sought to enmesh the Soviet Union in institutions that would under-
gird a new international order. Among these institutions was the United Nations. Washington regarded the UN not only as a tool for managing defeated
enemies but also for "domesticating" its ally, the USSR.[18] In October 1943, the
U.S. government for the first time attained a formal Soviet commitment to the
UN concept.[19] Planning for the UN moved forward in the summer of 1944,
when representatives from the main Allied powers gathered at Dumbarton
Oaks and hammered out the organization's general structure.[20] Lingering disagreements between the United States and the Soviet Union over UN voting
representation and debate procedures were tackled during the Yalta Conference of February 1945 and finally resolved by the dispatch of presidential
envoy Harry Hopkins to Moscow. The success of the Hopkins mission paved
the way for the USSR's ratification of the UN Charter in June 1945.[21]

  The American vision of a new world order featured other institutions,
most prominently, the International Monetary Fund (IMF) and the World
Bank. U.S. officials actively courted Soviet membership in these institutions
because they promised to integrate the USSR into a capitalist global economy.
Prior to the economic equivalent of Dumbarton Oaks—the Bretton Woods
Conference—President Roosevelt successfully entreated Stalin to send a Soviet delegation. At Bretton Woods, the Americans made an all-out effort to
enlist the USSR's membership in the IMF and the World Bank. Although initially reluctant, the Soviet delegation agreed in principle to join the Bretton
Woods institutions.[22]

Another element of America's integration strategy was the creation of an international atomic energy regime. Coming in the wake of Hiroshima and Nagasaki, this was a calculated effort to restrain the Soviet Union from triggering a nuclear arms race. The first stirrings of what amounted to rudimentary nuclear arms control occurred in November 1945, when President Harry Truman, Prime Minister Clement Attlee of Great Britain, and Prime Minister Mackenzie King of Canada unveiled an agreement proposing to entrust a UN commission with the control of atomic energy. The commission would in successive stages disseminate scientific knowledge, foster the peaceful use of atomic energy, eliminate nuclear weapons, and carry out international inspections. The United States approached the USSR with this three-country proposal in December 1945 and succeeded in attaining Soviet support for internationalizing atomic energy under the aegis of the UN.[23]

U.S. efforts to integrate the Soviet Union also focused on a potential flashpoint: the fate of Germany after the war's end. As Hitler's armies retreated, the United States attempted to negotiate an agreement with the USSR concerning the treatment of occupied Germany. During the Tehran Conference in December 1943, Roosevelt and Stalin discussed how to administer Germany after it surrendered. At Yalta in February 1945, the two leaders again took up the German question. They provisionally agreed to dismember Germany, with the United States, the USSR, Great Britain, and France all receiving occupation zones. Another item of contention related to Germany—reparations— was tentatively resolved.[24] However, the Yalta formula quickly unraveled, with the United States and USSR at loggerheads over the actual amount of German reparations and the procedure for extracting it. In July 1945, the Allied leaders met in Potsdam and agreed on a new formula for reparations. The Potsdam Conference also resulted in an agreement to treat Germany as a single economic unit and established a four-power control council to govern the occupation.[25]

American efforts to win World War II had the added benefit of hedging against the USSR. By the war's end, the United States had more men under arms than the Soviet Union, its navy controlled the oceans, its strategic bombing capacity was unrivaled, and it was the sole possessor of the atomic bomb.[26] Sustaining the military edifice built up over the war was impossible, and unless the United States had sought to immediately contain the Soviet Union, unnecessary. America rapidly demobilized after September 1945, but continued to hedge against the USSR by retaining a monopoly on atomic weapons.

Stalinism and the Soviet Rise

American leaders viewed the Soviet Union's early ascendance with a growing sense of unease even though the country was a wartime ally. What accounted for this mistrust was the authoritarian character of the USSR political system.

Wartime Misgivings

With the Kremlin's deliberations cloaked in secrecy, U.S. officials in 1943 possessed scant information illuminating the Soviet Union's postwar aims. They were initially unsure what course it would choose to pursue. The Office of Strategic Services issued a report laying out two possible Soviet policies. One was "military-political" aggrandizement in Eastern Europe and possibly beyond. The other was a return to the USSR 1941 borders with no further expansion.[27] The Joint Intelligence Committee of the Joint Chiefs of Staff was even more circumspect in its assessment of Soviet aims: "We do not feel that evidence concerning Soviet intentions in Europe at this time is conclusive."[28]

Only one segment of the U.S. government in 1943 had firmly held views about the USSR's intentions—the Soviet experts at the State Department. Having served in Riga and Moscow during the interwar period, they developed a mistrust of the USSR that never abated. At first, they constituted an isolated pocket of anti-Soviet sentiment within the U.S. government. But this soon changed.[29]

The opaque nature of the Soviet regime meant that its external conduct loomed large as an indicator of intentions. Lacking alternative sources of information that might have contextualized the USSR's behavior, American elites interpreted displays of Soviet intransigence, ingratitude, paranoia, and assertiveness as ominous signs. Prominent U.S. officials in Moscow and Washington thus became progressively disillusioned about the prospects for postwar cooperation with a newly ascendant USSR.

Before his posting to Moscow as U.S. ambassador, Averell Harriman was sanguine about the USSR's intentions. Soviet behavior quickly deflated his initial optimism.[30] At the Moscow Conference of late 1943, the USSR opposed a proposal for a postwar federation of Central and Eastern European states. Harriman interpreted the Soviet position as a harbinger of sinister ambitions: "I gained the impression that Stalin wanted a pulverized Europe in which there would be no strong countries except for the Soviet Union. It seemed to me that the Russians were determined to control the smaller countries."[31] Squabbles with the Soviets over the future makeup of the Polish government,

Stalin's cynical refusal to aid the Warsaw uprising, and the USSR's failure to implement provisions of the Yalta Agreement all accelerated Harriman's disillusionment. By the time of Roosevelt's death, the American ambassador to Moscow was deeply mistrustful of Soviet intentions. In a cable dated April 5, 1945, he warned Washington that the USSR's objectives included a "unilateral security ring" in Eastern Europe and communist penetration of additional countries.[32]

General John Deane, the head of the U.S. military mission to Moscow, underwent a similar conversion. By late 1944, Soviet ingratitude over lend-lease supplies and stonewalling on joint planning for Far Eastern military operations had soured his view of the USSR. Deane came to believe that the USSR would exploit American goodwill—"gratitude cannot be banked in the Soviet Union"—and that the only way to ensure cooperative postwar relations was for the United States to adopt a tougher approach.[33]

Changing attitudes toward the Soviet Union among U.S. officials based in Moscow were mirrored in Washington. Here too, the Kremlin's black-box deliberations induced American elites to take Soviet behavior as a stand-in for intentions. Secretary of State Cordell Hull, at first optimistic about the likelihood of postwar U.S.-Soviet collaboration, was shaken when the USSR demanded an extension of the UN Security Council veto to include topics of discussion. He began to wonder "whether Stalin and the Kremlin have determined to reverse their policy of cooperation with the Western Allies."[34] For Navy Secretary James Forrestal, the USSR's territorial aggrandizement in the Baltic, Poland, and Romania set off alarm bells. From the fall of 1944 onward, he became increasingly concerned about the purpose behind Soviet power.[35] What fueled Secretary of War Henry Stimson's anxiety about the USSR was a display of profound paranoia. In March 1945, the Soviet government accused the United States of negotiating with the German High Command behind its back. This was a gross distortion of what amounted to preliminary talks for the surrender of German forces in Italy. In Stimson's eyes, Moscow's "quarrelsome" behavior appeared a troubling omen. It "indicated a spirit in Russia which bodes evil in the coming difficulties of the postwar scene."[36]

President Roosevelt's optimism about Soviet intentions waned more slowly. He initially believed that the USSR's interwar hostility to the West was largely driven by external insecurity. Having realized during the course of the Second World War that the West bore them no enmity, the Soviets would, Roosevelt expected, become responsible stakeholders in the new global order.

"They are friendly people. They haven't got any crazy ideas of conquest and so forth."[37] However, the president's optimism faded in the last weeks of his life. Roosevelt was disturbed by the USSR's unwillingness to carry out its obligations under the Yalta Agreement.[38] He was also angered by Soviet accusations that the United States sought a separate peace with Germany. Unable to penetrate the Kremlin's veil of secrecy, Roosevelt could not help but take the USSR's behavior as a sign of unfriendly intentions: "Averell is right. We can't do business with Stalin. He has broken every one of the promises he made at Yalta."[39]

Approaching the Tipping Point

Roosevelt's death opened the door for officials critical of the Soviet Union to evangelize Harry Truman, the new American president. Rushing back from Moscow, Harriman briefed Truman on the USSR. He warned that the United States faced a "barbarian invasion of Europe"—the Soviets would extinguish democracy in any European country that fell under their influence. Forrestal offered a similar opinion, telling Truman that Soviet policies in Poland were part of a larger gambit to control all of Eastern Europe. Truman absorbed the concerns of his advisers, but like them, he was not yet prepared to dismiss the hope of postwar cooperation with the USSR.[40]

Such hope ebbed during the remainder of 1945. With the USSR's authoritarian system obscuring its intentions, U.S. officials interpreted Soviet behavior in the worst light possible. At the Potsdam Conference, the American delegation perceived Soviet demands for joint control over the Dardanelles and trusteeship over Libya as part of a vast expansionist design.[41] For his part, Truman attributed dark motives to Stalin's refusal to accept internationalization of several vital waterways: "What Stalin wanted was control of the Black Sea Straits and the Danube. The Russians were planning world conquest."[42] In fall 1945, the communist insurgency in Greece and the deployment of additional Soviet troops to Iran further exacerbated Truman's fears about Soviet intentions. To him, these "began to look like a giant pincers movement against the oil-rich areas of the Near East and the warm-water ports of the Mediterranean."[43] Reality differed from Truman's assessment. The pincer had only one leg: Stalin actually refrained from aiding the Greek communists.[44] Given the opaque nature of the Soviet Union's political system, there was no way for Truman to discern this.

American mistrust of the USSR approached a tipping point in the first months of 1946. The transformation of Romania and Bulgaria into Soviet-backed police states became evident to Washington in early January. Truman, perceiving this as yet another indicator of Soviet expansionism, exploded: "Unless Russia is faced with an iron fist and strong language another war is in the making. Only one language do they understand—'how many divisions have you?'"[45] Stalin's February 9 speech proclaiming the incompatibility of communism and capitalism provided another data point for U.S. officials already dubious of Soviet intentions. Harriman concluded that the USSR's new objective was to propagate communism around the world. Forrestal appears to have decided that peaceful coexistence with the Soviet Union was impossible.[46]

The Limits of Kremlinology

The opacity of the Soviet Union's political system precluded access opportunities. The USSR's all-pervading secrecy deprived the United States of the ability to influence the only Soviet official who really mattered—Stalin. In a report dated September 1944, Kennan explained:

> They [the West] will never be able to be sure when, unbeknownst to them, people of whom they have no knowledge, acting on motives utterly obscure, will go to Stalin with misleading information and with arguments to be used to their disadvantage—information which they cannot correct and arguments which they have no opportunity to rebut.[47]

Kennan, however, was isolated in his thinking. American officials at the time believed they could shape the USSR's strategic behavior by leveraging moderates within the Kremlin. Harriman in 1944 observed: "I have been conscious since early in the year of a division among Stalin's advisers on the question of cooperation with us." The U.S. ambassador to Moscow was confident that bolstering the moderate advisers presented an opportunity to nudge Soviet foreign policy in a desirable direction. "It is our problem to strengthen the hand of those around Stalin who want to play the game along our lines."[48]

American perceptions of access changed form in the wake of the Yalta Conference. Rather than recognizing two cliques surrounding Stalin, U.S. officials came to believe that Stalin himself was an embattled moderate. Secretary of State Edward Stettinius attributed intensifying frictions with the Soviet Union to "political leaders whom Stalin had to advise on his return to Moscow. These leaders may well have told Stalin that he had 'sold out' at Yalta. They are the equivalent of our isolationists."[49] During summer and fall 1945,

Truman similarly identified Stalin as a beleaguered force for moderation. At the Potsdam Conference, the president suspected that Foreign Minister Molotov, whom he regarded as a hardliner, was withholding information from Stalin.[50] Truman accordingly feared that the death of Stalin—"a moderating influence in the present Russian government"—would be catastrophic for U.S.-Soviet relations.[51]

The access opportunities U.S. officials identified were in fact a carefully crafted illusion facilitated by the Soviet Union's authoritarian system. Unable to penetrate the Kremlin's internal deliberations, they fell for a classic good cop, bad cop routine. During negotiations, Stalin was compromising and genial while Molotov was unyielding and adversarial. The Americans imputed an independent authority to Molotov and other Soviet officials where none existed. Stalin did not have to placate his subordinates. His authority was absolute and his inclinations were less than moderate.[52]

Toward Containment

Growing American mistrust accompanied the Soviet Union's ascendance, but in early 1946, many U.S. officials had yet to discount the potential for postwar collaboration. They were confused as to the nature of Soviet intentions. It was this confusion—a byproduct of the USSR's authoritarian character—that motivated the State Department to query Kennan on the sources of Soviet conduct.[53] Kennan dispatched to Washington what became known as the Long Telegram, an eight-thousand-word cable analyzing the forces animating Soviet foreign policy. The primary takeaway from Kennan's analysis was that the USSR was implacably hostile.

> In summary, we have here a political force committed fanatically to the belief that with the US there can be no permanent *modus vivendi*, that it is desirable and necessary that the internal harmony of our society be disrupted, our traditional way of life destroyed, the international authority of our state be broken if Soviet power is to be secure.[54]

What propelled Kennan's treatise to become the consensus view in the U.S. government was Soviet behavior. As its rise continued, the USSR triggered a series of crises of escalating severity culminating in a standoff over Berlin. U.S. confidence in integration declined, steps to hedge against

Soviet ambitions increased, and inexorably, American strategy shifted to containment.

The Iran Crisis

The Iran crisis of March 1946 represented an inflection point in how the United States responded to the Soviet Union's rise. The origins of the crisis lay in the Second World War, when the Allies had stationed troops in Iran to protect its oil reserves and maintain a route for lend-lease supplies going to the USSR. The deadline for removing all troops from Iran was March 2, 1946. The British left as scheduled; the Soviets remained. On March 5, Secretary of State James Byrnes transmitted a note to Moscow requesting the withdrawal of the Red Army from Iranian soil. The reply came in the form of "exceptionally heavy Soviet troop movements" in the direction of Turkey, Iraq, and Iran's capital, Tehran. On March 6 and again on March 9, the U.S. government queried Moscow on the purpose behind the Red Army's maneuvers. It met with a wall of silence. When the UN Security Council reconvened on March 25, the United States insisted on putting the Soviet military presence in Iran at the forefront of the agenda. The Americans continued to apply diplomatic pressure until April 4, when the Soviet Union and Iran announced an agreement stipulating the withdrawal of all Red Army units by early May.[55]

Although peacefully resolved, the crisis in Iran cast doubt on the viability of integration. News of the "full-scale combat deployment" of Soviet forces in Iran sparked a war scare in Washington.[56] At the height of the crisis, an alarmed Truman told Harriman: "There is a very dangerous situation developing in Iran. The Russians are refusing to take their troops out—as they agreed to do in their treaty with the British—and this may lead to war."[57] A similar mentality prevailed across the top level of the U.S. government.[58] After confronting the prospect of war with the USSR, American officials could no longer regard integration in the same light. The window of time for enmeshing the Soviet Union in international institutions appeared to be closing.

Within the American government, the Iran crisis also cemented acceptance of the Long Telegram's core insight—the Soviet Union's innate hostility toward the United States. For Truman, the crisis was a crucial litmus test of Soviet intentions. He came away believing that the USSR would inevitably expand its sphere of domination unless it met vigorous resistance. With the Long Telegram still fresh in memory, many other American officials found the Iran crisis a decisive indicator of Soviet ambitions. Those who had previously harbored substantial misgivings were confirmed in their belief. Those who had once explained away troubling Soviet behavior as the result of external insecurity were compelled to reevaluate their views.[59]

The Iran crisis triggered a gradual transformation of American strategy. In some areas, efforts to integrate the USSR endured after March 1946. The United States continued to press the Soviet Union to formally join the IMF and the World Bank.[60] At the same time, the Americans remained committed to the creation of a de facto nuclear arms control regime and Soviet participation therein. In June, Bernard Baruch, U.S. representative to the UN Atomic Energy Commission, outlined a proposal for the establishment of an International Atomic Energy Authority that would conduct a survey of nuclear-related materials and facilities throughout the world, obtain full control over them, and punish any state that violated its mandate.[61]

However, Washington moved away from integration in one crucial area—the governance of occupied Germany. Rather than utilizing established institutional mechanisms to manage disagreements with the Soviet Union, the United States opted for unilateral action. When the USSR refused to accept a single economic administration over all of Germany, the senior U.S. commander there cut off reparations deliveries from the American zone.[62]

As the United States began to place less reliance on integration, efforts to hedge against Soviet expansionism gathered steam. In May 1946, the United States offered France a $650 million credit to buttress its struggling economy. It was hoped this would reduce support for the local communist party—a tool of Soviet influence as seen from Washington.[63] Countercurrents to postwar demobilization were also emerging as U.S. officials became increasingly dubious that integration could restrain Soviet behavior and fearful of Soviet intentions. At Truman's behest, Congress in June passed a one-year extension of the draft, though the reduction in the number of U.S. military personnel continued.[64] More significantly, starting in mid-1946, the United States stepped up its production of atomic bombs, a military capability the Soviet Union at the time had no way of matching.

The Turkish Crisis

Within six months of the Red Army's maneuvers in Iran another crisis punctuated U.S.-Soviet relations. On August 7, 1946, the USSR presented the United States with a copy of a note delivered to Turkey. The note proposed the abolition of the Montreux Convention, a multilateral treaty governing access to the Dardanelles, the strait linking the Mediterranean and the Black Seas. The USSR wanted a new regime that would include only the Black Sea

powers, thereby excluding Great Britain and France—both signatories to the
Montreux Convention. Moscow also proposed the establishment of a joint
Turko-Soviet defense system in the Dardanelles. In response to the Soviet
note the United States issued a toughly worded note of its own and encouraged Turkey to resist making concessions to the USSR. Outside diplomatic
channels, Washington dispatched warships to the Eastern Mediterranean as a
show of force. By the end of October, Soviet calls for replacing the Montreux
Convention had subsided.[65]

The onset of the Turkish crisis further reinforced American belief in
the USSR's unremitting antagonism. Without information illuminating the
Kremlin's deliberations, it was easy to interpret the Soviet Union's diplomatic
stratagem as substantiating the perspective outlined in the Long Telegram.
Thus, Truman and members of his cabinet immediately perceived the Soviet proposal to replace the Montreux Convention as evidence of a desire
to dominate Turkey, and subsequently Greece, Iran, and the entire Middle
East.[66] Conceivably, the Soviets might have harbored less ambitious designs,
but with the Kremlin a black box to outsiders, there was no way to find out.

The confrontation over Turkey also dealt a deathblow to American faith
in integration. Efforts to moderate the Soviet Union through inclusion in
international institutions had failed to prevent a second crisis that brought
the two sides close to armed conflict. As the U.S. government conducted a
review of what military forces could be brought to bear to "meet any sudden
emergency in Europe" and Acting Secretary of State Dean Acheson warned
Truman that American pushback could trigger a bellicose Soviet reaction, the
inadequacy of integration and hedging became ever more apparent.[67]

Implementing Containment

The cumulative impact of the Iran and Turkish crises was the emergence of
a new American consensus regarding the Soviet Union. Giving voice to this
consensus was the Clifford-Elsey Report, an assessment of the USSR representing the collective opinion of top-level U.S. officials. Presented to Truman
in late September 1946, the Clifford-Elsey Report discounted alternatives to
containment. "Compromise and concessions are considered, by the Soviets,
to be evidence of weakness and they are encouraged by our 'retreats' to make
new and greater demands."[68] It went on to cast the USSR as an implacable
adversary: "Soviet leaders appear to be conducting their nation on a course

of aggrandizement designed to lead to eventual world domination by the U.S.S.R."[69] Last, laid to rest was the notion that Stalin constituted a moderating force on Soviet policy. "The general pattern of the Soviet system is too firmly established to be altered suddenly by any individual—even Stalin."[70]

With this hard-line view a new consensus inside the U.S. government, the transition to a containment strategy accelerated. Starting in December 1946, the United States steadily abandoned integration. When the deadline for the Soviet Union to join the Bretton Woods institutions elapsed, the Americans ceased trying to embed the USSR into a capitalist economic order, and instead, accepted an emerging reality—two world economies, one capitalist and one communist.[71] U.S. efforts to engage the Soviet Union in nuclear arms control went into deep hibernation. The Baruch Plan was quietly shelved when it became apparent that the USSR would never allow the UN Security Council to establish a highly intrusive International Atomic Energy Authority.[72] Also in December 1946, the United States unilaterally merged its German zone with the British zone. This amounted to a further departure from the institutional mechanisms designed to coordinate the occupation of Germany with the USSR.

The end of integration coincided with America's embrace of containment. From early 1947 onward, the United States took steps to arrest the growth of Soviet power. The most important of these steps was to prevent the industrial and natural resource concentrations of the Eurasian rimland from falling under Soviet control.

In the Eastern Mediterranean, Washington strengthened Greece and Turkey against Soviet influence. By early 1947, Greece, riven by civil war and economic chaos, appeared ripe for a communist takeover. Turkey, though in better shape, faced mounting economic difficulties due to the cost of mobilizing its armed forces to keep the Soviets in check. The British, who had previously supported Greece and Turkey, were financially exhausted. Under Truman's leadership, the United States filled the void left by Great Britain and announced a program of foreign aid totaling hundreds of millions of dollars.[73]

To thwart Soviet encroachment into Western Europe, the United States initially focused on economic rehabilitation. During winter 1947 hunger stalked Western Europe. Continued economic deterioration promised to boost the fortunes of communist parties aligned with Moscow. The Americans responded with the European Recovery Program, better known as the Marshall Plan after its most prominent champion, Secretary of State George Marshall. Publicly articulated in mid-1947 and enacted by Congress in April 1948, the Marshall Plan disbursed billions in economic assistance, and proved a resounding success, both in terms of reviving the economic life of Western Europe, and in terms of dampening support for local communists.[74]

Alongside fortifying Western Europe against Soviet subversion, the United States moved to strengthen the region's capacity to resist military intimidation by the USSR. Although the British and French governments initially pressed American leaders to support a Western European pact to provide a defense against the possibility of Germany's future resurgence, senior U.S. officials perceived what would become the North Atlantic Treaty Organization (NATO) as a "security system that would co-opt German power against the Soviet Union."[75] Between July and September 1948, the United States hosted representatives from Belgium, Luxembourg, France, the Netherlands, Great Britain, and Canada for a series of discussions that culminated in a memorandum sketching out the structure of a North Atlantic alliance. The details were subsequently hammered out, and on April 4, 1949, NATO was inaugurated at a signing ceremony in Washington. For the first time in its history, the United States committed itself to go to war in defense of foreign allies. These allies initially brought few military capabilities to the table. Hence, in October 1949, the United States moved to give its allies teeth: it established a Mutual Defense Assistance Program allocating one billion dollars of military aid to its NATO partners.[76]

Occupied Germany was a microcosm of U.S. efforts to stave off Soviet inroads into Western Europe. Recognizing that German unification would only occur under terms favorable to the USSR, the United States inched toward formal partition. A new currency for the western zones was introduced in June 1948; the French zone was attached to the merged Anglo-American zones in late 1948; and finally, in May 1949, the Federal Republic was established in West Germany.[77] Beyond walling off the majority of Germany from Soviet penetration, the United States refused to budge from West Berlin, located deep in the Soviet zone. On June 24, 1948, in what became the first crisis of the new Cold War, the USSR instituted a blockade aimed at ejecting the Western powers from Berlin. The American response was a massive airlift lasting more than one year.[78] The success of the airlift and the goodwill garnered by the United States eventually led Moscow to lift the blockade.

At the opposite end of the Eurasian rimland the United States secured Japan from falling into the USSR's orbit. By early 1948, Japan was entering an economic tailspin; opportunities for Soviet subversion multiplied. To reduce popular support for leftwing groups, U.S. occupation authorities, who had previously focused on democratization and crushing the power of Japanese business conglomerates, engaged in a "reverse course." Their focus shifted to the economic resuscitation of Japan, and restrictions on big business were relaxed.[79] Once ascendant, leftwing groups in Japan went into political eclipse.

Beyond checking the USSR's external expansion, America's containment strategy also undermined the Soviet economy, the ultimate determinant of whether the Soviet Union's rise would be sustainable. At Truman's request, Congress in June 1947 gave the executive branch the authority to limit exports to the Soviet Union. By the end of 1947, oil, steel, locomotives, freight cars, and synthetic rubber—all products that would contribute to the USSR's postwar reconstruction—were subject to export controls.[80] The U.S. government further tightened restrictions on trade with the Soviet Union in January 1948 by introducing a new licensing policy that covered all American goods destined for Europe. Within three years, this policy virtually eliminated U.S. exports to the USSR. The annual value of American goods shipped to the Soviet Union plummeted from $28 million in 1948 to $700,000 by the end of 1950.[81] U.S. efforts in the international sphere paralleled the imposition of export controls at home. In late 1949, the United States, in conjunction with its new Western European allies, founded the Coordinating Committee for Multilateral Export Controls, an international organization designed to rein in exports to the Soviet Union.[82]

The containment strategy that America adopted had a domestic military component as well. In 1948, Congress passed a multibillion-dollar defense supplemental, breaking the trend of annual declines in U.S. military expenditures.[83] However, the military dimension of containment initially focused less on reconstituting American conventional forces and more on building up a deployable nuclear capability. The U.S. atomic stockpile grew manyfold, reaching 235 bombs in 1949. Concomitant with this expansion, the U.S. air force capacity to deliver bombs against Soviet targets was upgraded.[84]

By the outbreak of the Korean War in 1950, the transition to containment was complete. Unable to penetrate the secrecy of the Kremlin, U.S. officials had, quite reasonably, taken the crises of the previous years as an incontrovertible sign of the Soviet Union's unbridled ambitions. Thus, the only recourse was to limit the growth of Soviet power.

Sustaining Primacy and American Strategy

One line of argument in the power transitions literature suggests another source of U.S. strategy toward the Soviet Union: the desire to maintain dominance.[85] The Second World War transformed the international system into a bipolar order, with Germany and Japan vanquished, Great Britain financially exhausted, and the United States and the USSR the only great powers standing. But what existed was a lopsided bipolarity: the Soviet Union was far weaker than the United States, particularly in the economic sphere. Scholars like Copeland would argue that Washington had every incentive to prevent its only peer competitor from acquiring control over new territories and rebuilding its economy. Containment was a foregone conclusion.

This narrative, however, finds little corroboration in the historical record. American officials recognized the dawn of bipolarity well before they moved to contain the Soviet Union. Even as the scope of the USSR's wartime geopolitical gains became clear, the United States sought to avoid a future of confrontation. Moreover, American elites came to embrace containment only as a last resort for managing the USSR's rise. The domestic politics of containment were unfavorable. Having recently experienced conscription and economic austerity during World War II, the American public had little appetite for costly foreign policies.[86] Given the state of popular opinion, U.S. leaders would have preferred to simply integrate and hedge indefinitely. They opted for containment only when convinced that a less costly and more accommodative approach toward the USSR had failed.

Conclusion

America's response to the Soviet ascendance unfolded in a unique historical moment—a world devastated by war, escalating ideological competition, and low economic interdependence between the democratic power and the rising state. Notably, the U.S.-Soviet power transition followed the pattern set by earlier eras, with autocratic rule in the rising state amplifying mistrust. Although history contains no foregone conclusions, Soviet autocracy clearly made the advent of the Cold War more likely.

Chapter 6

Emerging Superpower

Napoleon Bonaparte reputedly warned: "Let China sleep, for when she wakes, she will shake the world."[1] Two centuries later, China's long slumber has ended. Roused by capitalist reforms enacted under Communist Party rule, China is emerging as a superpower second only to the United States. China's rise and the American response will to a significant extent define the international landscape of the twenty-first century. Before looking forward and considering how this fateful transition may evolve, it is important to understand the contours of the present and recent past. Uncertainty and mistrust have accompanied China's ascendance because one-party rule endures in Beijing. Wary of Chinese intentions and unable to locate access opportunities, successive U.S. administrations have consistently embraced integration and hedging as the optimal mix of strategies for managing the growth of Chinese power.

The Balance of Power

The unipolar moment that America enjoyed following the collapse of the Soviet Union has ended with the rise of China. The ongoing power transition between Washington and Beijing has both global and regional aspects. On the economic side, the shift is worldwide in scope: China's trade with Africa and Latin America has surged, and China's GDP, now the world's second largest, has given Beijing increased leverage within international organizations such as the IMF and the World Bank. On the military side, however, the power transition is still regional. While the United States remains the only country with the capacity to project force globally, China has come to increasingly contest American dominance in East Asia. Overall, the United

States remains the world's foremost power, but China has substantially closed the gap on a number of indicators of national capability. Unless domestic instability derails its ascent, China may equal or even surpass the United States on multiple dimensions of power.[2]

Gross Domestic Product

The changing balance between the United States and China is particularly evident in the economic sphere. In 1980, a backward China had a GDP only 9 percent of America's. Thereafter, Deng Xiaoping's far-reaching reforms unleashed an economic takeoff: China's annual growth rates averaged 10 percent annually over the next thirty years.[3] Even during the information technology boom of the late 1990s, America's GDP increased by at most 4.8 percent per annum. More recently, the U.S. economy has experienced a slow recovery from the global financial crisis while China has managed to sustain high growth. This superior economic performance has, over multiple decades, brought about a profound change in the relative distribution of national wealth. By the close of 2012, China's GDP was 75 percent that of the United States.[4] Recent projections suggest that China's economy measured in purchasing power parity terms will overtake America's in size by 2020.[5]

International Trade

America's position as the world's leading commercial power has given way to an approaching parity with China. This signifies a major shift from 1980, when China was isolated from the global economy and barely registered as a trading nation. Still adhering to the autarkic course charted by Mao Zedong, China at the time had foreign commerce equivalent to about 7 percent of what America traded. The economic reforms enacted by Deng and his successors opened the Chinese economy to foreign investment, transforming the country into a hub of global production networks. Exports soared; imports also surged as foreign-owned factories brought in subcomponents manufactured elsewhere and China's burgeoning economy suctioned up ever-larger quantities of raw materials from abroad. U.S. international trade expanded after 1980, but at a slower rate. By the start of 2013, China's presence in global commerce equaled 86 percent that of the United States.[6]

Military Expenditures

American military predominance has begun to fade as China has channeled some of its newfound wealth into building up the People's Liberation Army

(PLA). In 1990, the PLA's budget was equivalent to a mere 3 percent of U.S. military outlays.[7] Accounting for this was the decline of the Soviet threat to Chinese territory and the determination of the leadership in Beijing to prioritize economic development over military strength. Since 1990, however, China's declared military expenditures have soared, growing at double-digit rates, sometimes by as much as 18 percent per annum. Rapidly expanding military outlays have enabled China to begin projecting power in the form of a blue-water navy, accurate medium-range ballistic missiles, new stealth aircraft, drones, antisatellite weapons, and a cyber warfare capability. Official PLA budget figures lack credibility, but estimates by the Stockholm International Peace Research Institute put Chinese military spending in 2012 at approximately $157 billion. At this midrange estimate, the PLA's budget amounts to about 24 percent of what America devotes to its armed forces.[8] The gap in military expenditures, though still significant, has narrowed. With America entering a period of fiscal austerity and pressure to cut military budgets mounting, the shift in the U.S.-China military balance will likely accelerate in the years ahead.

R&D Spending

China's push to develop an innovation-based economy has diminished America's lead in research and development (R&D) spending. When first recorded in 1991, R&D expenditures in China totaled 4.5 percent of that in the United States. Thereafter, the Chinese government began to implement a national strategy intended to transform China into an innovation powerhouse. Government spending on R&D increased, while at the same time, foreign corporations were encouraged to open up R&D centers in China. As a result, between 1991 and 2006, total R&D expenditures inside China jumped 15.1 percent annually. Over the same period, R&D spending in the United States expanded at 3 percent per year.[9] Since then, China's bid to become an innovation leader has become even more pronounced, with the government aiming to dominate new, high-growth sectors such as green technology. Whether China can successfully use top-down methods to promote innovation remains an open question, but at least in terms of relative R&D spending, it has continued to advance. At the end of 2013, R&D conducted within China reached about 57 percent of that in the United States.[10] Although still short of overtaking American R&D expenditures, China has started to close what once appeared an unbridgeable gap. Table 8 depicts the changing distribution of power between the United States and China.

Table 8: U.S.-China Balance of Power (%)

	GDP		International trade		Military expenditures		R&D spending*	
	1980	*2012*	*1980*	*2012*	*1990*	*2012*	*1991*	*2013*
China	9	75	7	86	3	24	4.5	57

* This comparison uses two different datasets measuring R&D spending in purchasing power parity terms.

The Balance of Perceptions

China's rise began to register among American elites as the twentieth century drew to a close. U.S. concerns about waning predominance first emerged in the military sphere. Starting in the mid-2000s, and particularly after the onset of the global financial crisis, American fears of relative decline have also taken on an economic cast. Since mid-2011, a Chinese challenge to U.S. primacy has become a near article of faith among American elites.

Military Mastery Challenged

Until the late 1990s, U.S. military superiority over China appeared beyond challenge. For much of the decade, the PLA was a museum of aging Soviet arms—a junkyard army in the words of some American observers.[11] The Taiwan Straits crisis that spanned 1995 and 1996 only underscored Chinese military weakness. When the United States deployed two aircraft carriers to signal its displeasure over PLA missile exercises near Taiwan, China was powerless to halt the intervention.

Yet around this time, U.S. estimates of China's future military potential were beginning to change.[12] Joseph Nye, in mid-1995 an assistant secretary of defense, wrote in *Foreign Affairs*, a journal representing elite American opinion, that China's rapid economic growth would ultimately transmute into "impressive military capabilities."[13] His views were echoed within the Pentagon's Office of Net Assessment.[14] By 1997, China's latent military power had started to garner wider attention within the U.S. government. The National Intelligence Council's (NIC) forward-looking "Global Trends 2010" study noted: "China has the potential to become the region's dominant military power."[15] The 1997 *Quadrennial Defense Review* (QDR)—the Pentagon's premier defense-planning document—contained a similar assessment of China's military trajectory.[16]

Perceptions of a Chinese challenge to American military primacy intensified thereafter. Looking to the future, U.S. elites started to frame China as a possible "peer competitor"—a country that one day could field military capabilities rivaling those of the United States. In a 2000 *Foreign Affairs* piece, future national security adviser Condoleezza Rice observed that China's "military power is currently no match for that of the United States. But that condition is not necessarily permanent."[17] The 2001 QDR obliquely raised China's potential to contest American military dominance. "The possibility exists that a military competitor with a formidable resource base will emerge in the region [East Asia]."[18] By contrast, the 2006 QDR openly classified China as a possible "peer competitor": "Of the major and emerging powers, China has the greatest potential to compete militarily with the United States and field disruptive military technologies that could over time offset traditional U.S. military advantages absent U.S. counter strategies."[19]

As the PLA's modernization has continued, American perceptions of a shifting military balance have changed from expectations of the future to assessments of the present. Pointing to new Chinese capabilities such as anti-satellite weapons and accurate medium-range ballistic missiles, U.S. officials and strategists have warned of a looming challenge to American power projection in the Western Pacific.[20] Given that power projection constitutes a core mission of the U.S. navy and air force, such warnings underscore the depth of American concern about relative decline on the military side.

Eroding Economic Competitiveness

Perceptions of a Chinese challenge to American primacy emerged later on the economic side. Throughout the 1990s, China failed to rouse fears of relative economic decline. The Clinton administration initially gave little heed to China's economic ascendance. Charlene Barshefsky, then deputy U.S. trade representative, recalls: "In the early years, the Clinton administration had no genuine appreciation of China's economic potential. I don't think the Clinton administration had any expectation that China could become a power to rival the United States."[21] Reports of China's near double-digit GDP growth also met with skepticism. Believing that China cooked its statistics, the Clinton administration routinely discounted Chinese growth rates by one-third to one-half.[22]

During President Clinton's second term, the scope of China's economic expansion was recognized, but whether China could sustain breakneck GDP

growth and move beyond serving as a manufacturing base for foreign corporations remained in question. Many within the Clinton administration considered China's lack of arable land, limited water resources, energy shortages,
and rampant corruption as potential impediments to its future economic
prosperity. Likewise, an outmoded, Leninist political system appeared possibly inimical to China's long-term growth prospects.[23]

After George W. Bush entered the White House, the terrorist attacks of
September 11, 2001, wars in Afghanistan and Iraq, and the U.S. housing bubble temporarily obscured the changing positions of the American and Chinese
economies. The first segment of the U.S. government to recognize the economic challenge China posed was focused on a leading indicator of economic
power: science and technology (S&T) competitiveness. In 2007, the U.S. National Science Foundation observed: "the rapidity of China's emergence as a
major S&T player is unprecedented in recent memory."[24] The same year, the
U.S. National Academies released a report entitled "Rising Above the Gathering Storm." The report argued that America's technological leadership was
threatened by a confluence of domestic trends and overseas developments.
Among the latter was China, which according to the report, was emulating
the U.S. system of national innovation, ratcheting up R&D spending, running
a $30 billion bilateral trade surplus in advanced-technology goods, and set to
produce more scientific and engineering doctorates than the United States.[25]

The advent of the global financial crisis compelled U.S. elites to focus on
China's superior economic performance, producing a consensus on America's
diminished economic standing. *Foreign Affairs* gave voice to the new sense
of declinism: "The U.S. share of world GDP had been declining for seven
years before the financial crisis hit. And it looks increasingly likely that China's GDP will surpass the United States' at some point during the next 25–30
years."[26] The tone of the National Intelligence Council's "Global Trends 2025"
study, which was released in late 2008, was also gloomy, projecting a relative
decline in all elements of American strength, including economic power, as
China continued to advance in the global hierarchy.[27]

China's ability to weather the global financial crisis coupled with the sput-
tering recovery of the American economy reinforced perceptions of a Chinese
economic challenge. In his 2011 State of the Union address, President Barack
Obama explicitly recognized this challenge, noting: "Just recently, China became
the home to the world's largest private solar research facility, and the world's
fastest computer."[28] During the 2012 presidential election cycle, China's rise became a symbol of relative economic decline that transcended party lines. Like

the incumbent they hoped to unseat, presidential aspirants from the Republican Party spoke of a Chinese challenge to America's economic competitiveness.[29]

China: Economic Reform and Political Continuity

Although China has come a long way from the dark days of the Mao era when the state intruded into every aspect of citizen life, economic reforms have not coincided with significant political liberalization. Between the mid-1990s and 2012, the Polity IV dataset assigns China a score of –7, indicating that its political system has remained autocratic.[30] A fine-grained analysis of power centralization and domestic transparency lends additional support to this categorization of China's regime type.

Sweeping economic reforms have left the political dominance of the Chinese Communist Party (CCP) untouched. The CCP retains control over the national government through a system of interlocking personnel. The general secretary of the party serves as president, a member of the Politburo Standing Committee serves as premier, and so on.[31] The selection of China's leadership therefore occurs within the apex of the Communist Party in a process far removed from competitive elections. The National People's Congress, a deliberative body with lawmaking authority, has become more active over the past decades, but it has yet to become an independent legislature. China does not conduct popular elections for delegates to the National People's Congress. Instead, legislators are chosen via a process that weeds out candidates who lack official backing.[32] Thus, no checks and balances exist outside the CCP.

The Chinese media, though booming online and off, remain subject to a high degree of state influence. Provisions of China's constitution relating to the protection of state secrets and the "honour and interests of the motherland" establish a basis for governmental censorship.[33] All Chinese media outlets are subject to regulations delineating inappropriate types of content. In practice, this means topics like the PLA, the Communist Party's internal dynamics, ethnic unrest in Tibet and Xinjiang, Taiwanese independence, and the Falun Gong. Journalists who violate these regulations can be charged with "revealing state secrets" or "inciting subversion" and imprisoned. Online, the Chinese government requires Internet service providers to block websites featuring content deemed politically subversive. A number of major media outlets remain wholly state managed. They are run by high-ranking Communist Party cadres and tasked with conveying the official line to the public.[34] All this places China's media squarely in the unfree category of the survey developed in Chapter 2. With the press constrained, China lacks transparency.

America's Enduring China Strategies

Since China emerged as a rising power in the late 1990s, the United States has opted for a two-pronged approach: integration and hedging. Despite distinct and in some cases conflicting worldviews, the Clinton, Bush, and Obama administrations have shown remarkable consistency in their choice of China strategies.

The Clinton Administration

President Clinton's second term set the enduring outlines for America's response to the rise of China. The United States ramped up efforts to embed China in an array of international institutions with the hope of constraining behavior and ultimately transforming how the country engaged the world. But under Clinton's watch, the United States also began to hedge against the growth of Chinese power.

During the late 1990s, America's integration strategy centered on China's accession to the World Trade Organization (WTO). In Washington, the WTO was seen as a mechanism for moving China toward greater compliance with Western commercial norms.[35] For this reason, the Clinton administration sought to impose particularly stringent conditions when negotiating a bilateral market access agreement with China—a prerequisite for eventual WTO membership. After a rocky series of negotiations in which Chinese recalcitrance and U.S. domestic political considerations torpedoed a final agreement, the United States clinched a bilateral accord in November 1999.[36] China's WTO accession, however, would await the next U.S. president.

American attempts to integrate China also encompassed arms control and nonproliferation. In 1997, the Clinton administration obtained a Chinese written pledge to abstain from nuclear assistance to Iran.[37] The same year, after talks with the United States on the significance of participating in export control regimes, China joined the Zangger Committee, and thereby committed to refrain from selling a set list of nuclear items.[38] Washington tried and failed in 1998 to entice Beijing into the Missile Technology Control Regime (MTCR). A later attempt to bring China into the MTCR, occurring in the final months of President Clinton's tenure, also failed.[39]

Early American efforts to integrate China had a maritime component as well. The combination of growing PLA power projection capabilities and regular U.S. air and naval patrols along China's periphery virtually guaranteed that military encounters would occur. Recognizing this, the United States in 1998 negotiated a Military Maritime Consultative Agreement (MMCA) with China. The main purpose of the MMCA was to develop a set of rules governing interactions between each country's military units. Working groups convened under the umbrella of the MMCA initially took up the issue of maritime communications. However, China's insistence that U.S. surveillance operations in its exclusive economic zone (EEZ) contravened international law frustrated efforts to craft a formal code of conduct.[40]

While embracing international institutions as a mechanism for managing the growth of Chinese power, the United States simultaneously hedged. During the late 1990s, the Clinton administration bolstered Taiwan's capacity to resist military pressure from the mainland. In 1998, the United States announced the sale of antiship and antiaircraft missiles to the island. Further arms sales, consisting of early-warning aircraft, spare parts, antiaircraft missiles, and improved surveillance radars followed in 1999 and 2000.[41] Beyond equipping Taiwan with military hardware, the United States also worked to improve the island's military "software." Starting in 1997, Taiwanese F-16 pilots began to train at a U.S. Air Force facility in Arizona. The same year, the United States initiated an annual defense-planning meeting with Taiwanese officials.[42]

Under President Clinton, America's hedging strategy also included forging closer relationships with two key Asian powers—Japan and India. Building on earlier efforts to revitalize the U.S.-Japan alliance, Washington and Tokyo inked new guidelines for defense cooperation in 1997 and in 1999 agreed to jointly research a next-generation missile interceptor.[43] Although American relations with India hit a nadir in 1998 when New Delhi tested nuclear weapons, the Clinton administration soon backed away from punitive efforts, and instead, sought to improve ties with the world's largest democracy. Clinton's visit to India in March 2000 marked the success of this course correction and laid the groundwork for a future strategic partnership.

The Bush Administration

Although castigating the Clinton administration during the 2000 presidential campaign, George W. Bush retained the China strategies pioneered by his predecessor. As Chinese power increased between 2001 and 2009, the United States continued to integrate and hedge.

The Bush administration inherited a number of mechanisms for integrating China. First and foremost, there was the WTO. Until China joined the WTO in December 2001, the United States continued to tighten the terms of its accession and successfully pressed for a reduction of agricultural subsidies.[44] The MMCA provided a platform for regulating Chinese behavior in the military sphere. But as before, maritime rules of the road remained elusive because the Chinese side was adamant in its interpretation of international law governing access to EEZs.[45]

The nonproliferation component of integration underwent a qualitative shift during President Bush's eight years in office. No longer was Washington primarily focused on constraining Beijing's behavior. Instead, it was determined to grant Beijing a leading place at the table in a new nonproliferation regime: the Six-Party Talks. At America's urging, China in early 2003 agreed to sponsor the three-party precursor to these nuclear disarmament negotiations with North Korea.[46] By late August, the talks had come to encompass not only the United States, China, and North Korea, but also Japan, Russia, and South Korea. Throughout the years of negotiation that followed, Beijing served as the host and mediator of the Six-Party Talks.

The Bush administration's most innovative contribution to America's integration strategy was the creation of the Strategic Economic Dialogue (SED). First inaugurated in 2006 and bringing together top-ranking officials from Washington and Beijing, the SED served as a superstructure for a plethora of bilateral accords. At the May 2007 meeting, the United States concluded an agreement with China to boost the enforcement of intellectual property rights. The December 2007 meeting generated multiple accords on measures to improve product safety in China, while the June 2008 meeting launched negotiations on a bilateral investment treaty.[47] These and many other agreements that came out of the SED sought to constrain China's economic behavior in areas where it had yet to conform to global standards.

Throughout the Bush administration, the United States continued to pair integration with hedging. During his first year in office, President Bush approved a landmark arms package for Taiwan that included diesel-powered submarines, four retrofitted destroyers, antisubmarine aircraft, and mine-sweeping helicopters. However, Taiwan's inability to come up with funding for the arms package and political tensions between Taipei and Washington delayed the formal sale of most items until the end of Bush's presidency.[48]

Between 2001 and 2009, American hedging also took the form of building closer ties with a growing array of Asian powers. The United States upgraded its alliance with Japan through measures such as improving military interoperability and unveiling a new set of common strategic objectives.[49] In Southeast Asia, the United States signed a new Strategic Framework Agreement with Singapore and reset relations with Jakarta by restoring military ties suspended in response to human rights abuses committed by Indonesian troops during the 1990s.[50] Looking to transform U.S. relations with India, President Bush brokered a civil nuclear agreement in 2006. This breakthrough accord enabled the two countries to strengthen military ties, enlarge defense trade, enhance bilateral commerce and investment, and expand cooperation on global issues.[51]

In a break with his predecessor, President Bush incorporated new military elements into America's hedging strategy. One of these elements was the development and deployment of sea-based missile defense. Between 2002 and 2009, the U.S. Navy conducted a series of missile defense tests and equipped a growing number of destroyers with missile interceptors.[52] This new capability had multiple applications, not least, protecting American bases in Asia from China's expanding arsenal of ballistic missiles. Under Bush, the United States also began to concentrate its air and naval forces in the Western Pacific. The U.S. navy shifted three nuclear attack submarines to Guam and positioned missile defense capable destroyers in Hawaii and Japan. In a parallel geographic reorientation, the U.S. air force stockpiled fuel and munitions in Guam and made the stationing of combat aircraft to the island routine.[53] This enhanced military presence in the Western Pacific reinforced America's capacity to intervene in potential contingencies involving China.

The Obama Administration

When Barack Obama entered the White House in January 2009, some of his advisers were inclined to take an approach toward China that publicly emphasized integration and rhetorically downplayed hedging.[54] Beijing was initially framed as a key partner in the solving of global challenges, but over time, the Obama administration began to publicly highlight competitive aspects of the U.S.-China relationship, such as unfair trading practices and cyber espionage. Behind this rhetorical shift was a consistent approach to China: throughout the Obama presidency, Washington has pursued integration and hedging strategies.

To integrate China, the Obama administration has relied on diverse international institutions. Determined to further enmesh China in the IMF and the World Bank, it has supported the reallocation of voting rights to better reflect China's growing economic stature.[55] The Obama administration has also embraced the Group of 20 (G-20) major advanced and emerging economies as a vehicle for curbing some of China's more troubling commercial practices. President Obama has tried to use the G-20 to force China to revaluate its artificially depressed currency. Although the G-20 has stopped short of setting specific targets for exchange rates, the Chinese renminbi in recent years has appreciated significantly against the U.S. dollar.[56]

Since the advent of the Obama administration, America's integration strategy has taken on an environmental dimension. The United States has pursued a global climate accord that would regulate carbon emissions and encompass not only developed countries but also emerging economies, including China, which in 2006 became the world's largest producer of greenhouse gases.[57] During the Copenhagen Conference of December 2009, the Obama administration pressed China to accept international monitoring of its emission levels as part of a larger global accord. Although the climate pact eventually reached at Copenhagen included verification language, it only called for voluntary commitments. At subsequent meetings, such as the Warsaw Conference of November 2013, a legally binding climate accord obligating China to meet specific emissions targets has remained an unfulfilled U.S. aspiration.[58]

The Strategic Economic Dialogue—now the Strategic and Economic Dialogue (S&ED)—has become a fixture of U.S. efforts to integrate China. Like the Bush administration, Obama's has used this high-level gathering as a catalyst for bilateral accords targeting Chinese economic practices that diverge from global commercial norms. The S&ED has yielded agreements on the protection of intellectual property rights and government procurement standards, though whether Beijing can or will enforce these agreements remains an open question.[59]

The Obama administration's push to enmesh China in a web of international institutions has moved forward in synch with a robust hedging strategy. While less inclined to sell weaponry to Taiwan, the Obama administration has hedged in other ways.[60] By standing with Seoul during a series of North Korean military provocations and supporting Seoul's ambitions to play a leadership role on global issues, President Obama has strengthened a critical U.S. alliance in China's northeast periphery.[61] His administration has also looked to China's south and made a concerted effort to improve American ties with the ten-member Association of Southeast Asian Nations

(ASEAN). Since Obama came to office, the United States has signed the ASEAN Treaty of Amity and Cooperation and joined the East Asian Summit, an annual pan-Asian gathering of which ASEAN remains the core. Publicly affirming the need for peaceful resolution of territorial disputes in the South China Sea has won America favor among Southeast Asian claimants nervous about Beijing's maritime ambitions. Bilaterally, the United States has negotiated a comprehensive strategic partnership with Indonesia and elevated ties with Vietnam.[62]

Military hedging has continued under Obama's presidency. The Pentagon has worked to flesh out an Air-Sea Battle concept focused on preserving American power projection in the Western Pacific as China develops increasingly accurate long-range strike capabilities.[63] U.S. hedging on the military side is also evident in cyberspace, a domain Chinese strategists see as key to fighting wars.[64] In June 2009, the Pentagon established a new cyber command. Media reporting at the time suggested that the organization's mandate transcended the protection of U.S. military networks and included preparing for offensive operations against potential foes.[65]

The "pivot" to Asia, which the Obama administration unveiled in a series of policy statements during the fall of 2011, constitutes a regional strategy, not a China strategy, but some of its major elements advance U.S. hedging against China's rise. On the diplomatic side, the "pivot" emphasizes further bolstering American alliances in the Asia-Pacific region and building closer partnerships with key emerging powers such as India and Indonesia. The economic side of the "pivot" is America's championing of the Trans-Pacific Partnership talks, negotiations which aim to create a free trade zone among commercially "likeminded" nations spanning the Pacific basin. On the military side, the "pivot" includes rotation of U.S. marines through Darwin, Australia, deployment of littoral combat ships to Singapore, and a pledge to sustain and strengthen American forces in the region despite cuts to the top-line U.S. defense budget.[66]

Autocracy Overhangs China's Rise

Consecutive U.S. administrations have coupled integration with hedging because a rising China remains a one-party dictatorship. The opacity of decision-making in Beijing, the enigma of Chinese intentions, and a lack of access opportunities have compelled the past three American presidents to prepare for a future in which China may not smoothly join the existing global order.

Kremlinology with Chinese Characteristics

Autocracy creates an undercurrent of uncertainty in U.S. interactions with China. Although American officials do not anticipate a discontinuous change in China's overarching foreign policy orientation, they are sometimes at a loss to explain specific Chinese actions. Accounting for this is the character of China's domestic institutions.

In the absence of a free press that pries open Beijing's internal deliberations, American officials must piece together rumors and inferences in what amounts to Kremlinology with Chinese characteristics. Open sources provide an inadequate basis for tracking deliberations among the country's top leadership. So affirm past and current U.S. officials. In interviews, they typically describe Chinese open sources in the following terms. Because China's media no longer languish in a Maoist straitjacket, open sources have value. By monitoring debates in the Chinese press, American diplomats and intelligence analysts can make inferences about what sorts of discussions are occurring inside the Chinese government. However, open sources are not sufficient for definitive judgments. Prior to the government's announcement of a decision, there is no way to ascertain whether opinions aired in a newspaper are actually representative of thinking within the Chinese leadership. Moreover, open sources can, at best, only shed light on the broadest contours of decision-making in Beijing. The specific details—the individuals involved and their positions in the debate—remain unknown.[67]

Uncertainty therefore accompanies American interactions with China. As one State Department official involved in China affairs puts it: "We have no clarity about decision-making at the top levels. Across any issue—from the military to the environment—we do not know who authorized the policy at the top level or even whether the policy was authorized at all."[68] Officials who worked under the Bush and Clinton administrations came away with a similar sense of their constrained vantage point. James Kelly, an assistant secretary of state from 2001 to 2005, recollects: "We would often wonder what was the position of Zhongnanhai [the leadership compound of the CCP]. Aside from top officials, we never adequately knew whether any official outside of the Foreign Ministry was handling a given issue."[69] Robert Suettinger, national intelligence officer for East Asia in 1998, recounts: "In the case of China, there were many areas that were a black box—leadership decisions, internal party affairs, the military, and anything related to intelligence."[70]

Another attribute of authoritarian rule—a dearth of checks and balances— also imparts a degree of uncertainty to U.S. interactions with China. The PLA is more than a national military; it is one arm of the Communist Party, and thereby part of the country's dominant power structure. This renders civil-military relations in China a potentially significant factor in its external behavior. And like China's decision-making process as a whole, its civil-military relations are opaque, both because of widespread censorship, and because of the PLA's status as a party army. American officials report they have little understanding of how the PLA interfaces with China's civilian leadership. They regard its internal role as a major source of unpredictability, above all in instances where China might consider the use of force.[71] Some see how the PLA executes top-level directives together with how it disseminates information to civilian leaders as producing "slippage" in Chinese policies—outcomes unforeseen in Washington and even Beijing.[72]

Diplomatic and military incidents have underscored the inherent limits of Kremlinology with Chinese characteristics. When a Chinese fighter jet collided with an American EP-3 spy plane in April 2001, forcing it to land on Hainan Island, American officials were at a loss to understand what was transpiring in Beijing. "Among the questions that had to be answered was who was in charge in China. Throughout the incident, there was a question of who was calling the shots. China's initial demands were not clear, as was who was speaking for the government and where demands came from."[73] China's 2007 test of an antisatellite (ASAT) weapon served as another reminder of America's constrained vantage point. Inside the U.S. government, "there were a lot of questions about who authorized the ASAT test, how directly the Politburo approved, whether President Hu approved the specific launch or just a broader ASAT program." U.S. authorities were sufficiently baffled to commission studies that, among other issues, assessed the potential for rogue PLA operations.[74] The challenge of deciphering China's opaque decision-making process was highlighted yet again in 2010 when Beijing took a more assertive position on a series of territorial disputes in the East and South China Seas. Observers in Washington remain unsure whether this reflected the PLA's initiative, the leadership succession of 2012, the influence of China's nationalistic netizens, or some other factor.[75] A similar degree of uncertainty has surrounded Beijing's late 2013 declaration of an Air Defense Identification Zone over much of the East China Sea—a unilateral move that surprised many in Washington.[76]

Power for What Purpose?

Authoritarian characteristics such as pervasive state secrecy and a muzzled press have obscured the scope of Beijing's ambitions. Will China accept a position of leadership within the existing international order? Will it instead seek regional dominance or global hegemony? Or will China pursue some third course that contemporary observers have yet to envision? Although a definitive answer remains beyond reach, American officials since 1997 have made assessments about China based on the limited information available to them. With Beijing's deliberations walled off from outside view, they have little choice but to treat Chinese behavior as a primary indicator of intentions.

Unsurprisingly then, the PLA's modernization program has become a major catalyst for American mistrust of China. By the late 1990s, the PLA's growing strength had already produced unease about China at the top level of the Clinton administration. One senior diplomat at the time recalls: "Given the absence of transparency, blatant lying about budgetary figures, and China's pursuit of area denial capabilities, you could not feel good."[77] The view at the Pentagon was similar. Walter Slocombe, then under secretary of defense for policy, remembers: "China's military budget was concerning because they were planning to be able to shoot us. From a military point of view, the question was what could they do, not what would they like to do."[78] American officials began conflating China's ambitions and military capabilities virtually as soon as it emerged as a rising power.

Even as the Bush administration focused on the Middle East and Central Asia in the wake of the September 11 attacks, China's military buildup remained a lightning rod for mistrust. This was evident in the Pentagon's annual report to Congress on the PLA, which year after year, called into question the purpose behind Chinese power.

> The outside world has little knowledge of Chinese motivations and decision-making or of key capabilities supporting PLA modernization. This lack of transparency prompts others to ask . . . Why this growing investment? Why these continuing large and expanding arms purchases? Why these continuing robust deployments?[79]

The PLA's burgeoning capabilities likewise explained why State Department officials appointed by President Bush doubted China's commitment to a "peaceful rise." Deputy Secretary of State Robert Zoellick noted in 2005: "China's rapid military modernization and increases in capabilities raise questions about the purposes of this buildup."[80] Writing in *Foreign Affairs* several years later, Secretary of State Condoleezza Rice observed: "We understand that as countries develop, they will modernize their armed forces. But China's lack of transparency about its military spending and doctrine and its strategic goals increases mistrust and suspicion."[81]

When the Obama administration took power, some within were relatively optimistic about Chinese ambitions. It was no accident that the Pentagon report on the PLA released in 2009 contained softer language, simply warning that "limited transparency in China's military and security affairs poses risks to stability by creating uncertainty."[82] An early call for the United States and China to engage in "strategic reassurance" issued by then Deputy Secretary of State James Steinberg, though apparently never enshrined as administration policy, also spoke to a more generous view of Chinese intentions.[83]

This initial optimism soon faded, however, because the Obama administration, like its predecessors, had little recourse but to take behavior as a primary indicator of Chinese ambitions. The year 2010 proved a watershed. Beijing's more assertive rhetoric in territorial disputes ranging from the South China Sea to the Senkaku/Diaoyu Islands, its use of pressure tactics such as large-scale military exercises and the suspension of critical mineral exports to Japan, and its refusal to condemn North Korean military attacks against South Korea—all occurring against the backdrop of a steady increase in PLA strength—raised fundamental questions within the Obama administration about the purpose behind Chinese power.[84]

A Paucity of Access

An authoritarian system limits opportunities to shape China's strategic behavior. With basic information about China's decision-making process obscured under a closed regime, it is difficult for outsiders to influence Chinese policies by capitalizing on internal disagreements. Robert Suettinger describes the weak vantage point of U.S. officials: "We knew of differences among China's leaders, but not how they fell out. There was nothing we could do to take advantage of this because we simply did not know enough."[85]

The institution in China the United States can most easily engage—the Ministry of Foreign Affairs (MFA)—has no capacity to function as a point of access. To start, it has limited voice within the Chinese government; preeminent authority rests with the Politburo. It also cannot afford to appear overly solicitous of American interests. MFA needs to constantly prove its patriotic bona fides to other elements of the Chinese government because authoritarian rule, in putting a premium on domestic secrecy, promotes suspicion of foreigners and the bureaucracy responsible for managing relations with them.[86]

The PLA, which appears to exercise significant authority over foreign policy decision making, remains protected from outside influence.[87] China shields much of the PLA from interaction with foreigners. Former Under Secretary of Defense Slocombe recalls: "One of the problems dealing with the PLA was that they had a large 'barbarian handling' operation—officers who spent their careers dealing with foreigners. We did not usually talk with people on the operational side."[88] Contacts between the PLA and foreign militaries that do occur are subject to strict legal regulation. This has a chilling effect on American engagement of the PLA. "The Chinese system is so constraining that it is almost impossible to get to know PLA officers," reports a now-retired U.S. military officer.[89] U.S.-China military ties will continue to wax and wane depending on the state of the overall relationship, but America is unlikely to develop meaningful inroads into the PLA.

Societal actors in China's authoritarian system lack the influence to become points of access. China's private sector has distinct foreign policy interests. Yet despite economic liberalization, major domestic corporations remain dependent on the Chinese government.[90] American officials see little point in lobbying a private sector incapable of independent political action.[91] Nor can the United States bypass the Chinese government through appealing to the domestic media, and by extension, the Chinese people. Beijing continues to regulate what Chinese journalists can publish and broadcast. Messages America may want to convey must pass through a filter Beijing controls. Thus, one American official observes: "We usually talk to the media to reach the government, not the Chinese."[92]

With few points of access inside or outside the government in Beijing, opportunities for shaping China's future course are comparatively slim. This further exacerbates American concerns about China's rise.[93]

Economic Interdependence and U.S. Strategy

Both the scholarship on economic interdependence and some observers rooted in the U.S. policymaking community point to commercial ties as a factor shaping American strategy toward China. In the popular narrative, trade and investment linkages serve as ballast in U.S.-China relations. When tensions flare, business groups lobby the U.S. government to change course, or at the least, not to escalate.[94] It is also said that Beijing's immense holdings of Treasury bonds constrain U.S. strategy. In disputes with America's largest foreign banker, strong pressure reputedly exists for accommodation and a return to business as usual.

There are many problems with this narrative. America and a rising China are economically entangled: U.S.-China trade as a share of American GDP has expanded from 0.9 percent in 1997 to about 3.3 percent by the end of 2013.[95] U.S. foreign direct investment in China has also surged from $5 billion in 1997 to more than $50 billion by the close of 2012.[96] Meanwhile, China has accumulated more than $1.3 trillion in Treasury bonds, making it the largest foreign holder of American sovereign debt.[97] Chinese foreign direct investment in the United States remains low, but rapid growth in recent years suggests an incipient takeoff.[98]

In contrast to predictions made by scholars and observers within the policy community, business lobbies today exert little influence on American strategy toward China. Corporations profiting from the Chinese market are largely interested in specific policies directly affecting their bottom line.[99] The main focal point for their lobbying is export controls. Their achievements are modest—the sale of a particular product.[100] The ballast role attributed to business lobbies appears overstated. Corporations generally refrain from addressing the security side of the U.S.-China relationship. They are hesitant to voice opinions for fear of triggering accusations of selling out U.S. interests.[101]

Insofar as business lobbies have stabilized American relations with China, their influence appears set to decline. Some elements of the U.S. business community have become disenchanted with the Chinese market for reasons ranging from widespread theft of intellectual property to nontariff barriers on foreign firms. What was once a relatively monolithic supporter of cordial and cooperative relations with Beijing now shows signs of fragmenting.[102]

Claims that indebtedness to China constrains U.S. strategy appear unfounded. Although Chinese ownership of Treasury bonds has sharply increased since the late 1990s, the United States has continued to integrate and hedge. Growing indebtedness has not brought about greater American accommodation of China's rise. Moreover, such claims overlook the nature of Treasury bonds. U.S. debt is far from fungible. China cannot threaten to sell off Treasury bonds without risking a run on the market that would devalue its remaining holdings and wreak mutual economic destruction.[103] Owner-ship of American sovereign debt may entangle China more than the United States. This asymmetry would explain Beijing's inability to move away from Treasury bonds after Washington lost its AAA credit rating in August 2011.[104] More generally, as the smaller economy, China should disproportionately ex-perience the constraints imposed by commercial interdependence with the United States.

Conclusion

Speaking in 1997 as China's ascent became clearly visible, President Clin-ton observed: "China is big, it is growing, and it will influence the world in the years ahead. For the United States and the world, the essential question is—how will China use its influence?"[105] Today that question remains unan-swered. China's system of one-party rule casts a pall of uncertainty over its ambitions and at the same time closes off opportunities for the shaping of strategic behavior. Against a backdrop of limited information and minimal access, Beijing's deliberate opacity in the military sphere has generated larger concerns about the veracity of its professed commitment to a peaceful rise. For this reason, U.S. officials have for almost two decades fixated on greater transparency in China's military decision-making and spending as a key confidence-building measure. China's autocratic system continues to exacer-bate tensions that in the best of circumstances would attend the emergence of a new superpower. Barring a political opening in Beijing, the best China's leadership can hope for is that America will continue to integrate and hedge as China's ascendancy continues.

Chapter 7

Neighboring Titan

The United States is not the only democratic nation experiencing a fateful transition as China rises. America's ally and China's neighbor, Japan, confronts a much sharper power shift. Once Asia's largest economy and leading voice, Japan has in recent years fallen behind China, its fading dynamism accelerating the relative decline brought about by China's rapidly expanding economy and growing military prowess. Japan's response to the rise of China parallels that of the United States. Since China's ascendance became apparent in the late 1990s, the Japanese government has opted to integrate and hedge. What induced Washington to embrace this approach has likewise influenced Tokyo's strategic choices. Because China's authoritarian regime has produced uncertainty and mistrust and circumscribed opportunities to shape strategic behavior, Japanese leaders, like their American counterparts, have looked to integrate China into international institutions while preparing for any eventuality.

Japan's response to the rise of China lends particular weight to the argument advanced in the book. Every other case has featured either Great Britain or the United States. They share a common linguistic, cultural, and political heritage. It is possible that Great Britain and the United States share a geopolitical outlook too—one that inclines them to mistrust autocracies for purely ideological reasons.[1] That China's domestic institutions have shaped the choices of Japan, an Asian country outside the Anglo-American tradition, suggests that during power transitions, the linkage between regime type and strategy applies to a broader set of democratic states.

The Balance of Power

Much of China's rise has coincided with a period of economic malaise and political paralysis in Japan. This has brought about a transformation in the balance of power. China has surpassed Japan on all the major indicators of national capability. Looking forward, the power disparity will continue to widen unless China's ascent falters or Japan successfully manages the difficult task of national renewal.

Gross Domestic Product

Japan's economic preeminence in Asia has ended with China's rise. At the start of the 1980s, China's GDP was equivalent to only 25 percent of what Japan produced. The economic takeoff engineered by Deng and sustained by successive generations of Beijing leadership enabled China to achieve growth rates averaging 10 percent annually across three decades.[2] Japan's relative economic performance over this period pales in comparison. The asset bubble that underpinned Japanese economic expansion during the late 1980s burst at the decade's end, resulting in ten years of economic stagnation. Anemic GDP growth resumed in the early 2000s, but the global financial crisis that erupted in 2008 did enormous damage to Japan's export-driven economy.[3] China, in contrast, weathered the crisis relatively unscathed. The difference in Chinese and Japanese growth rates has overturned the economic balance of power. By the end of 2012, China's economy was about 2.7 times as large as Japan's.[4]

International Trade

Once Asia's largest trading power, Japan is now overshadowed by China's commercial prowess. In 1980, just before China began to embrace the global economy, its international trade was only 14 percent that of Japan. With China's market opening, the elixir of cheap labor and high-quality infrastructure proved irresistible to foreign corporations looking for overseas production facilities. Exports surged as China became the world's workshop; imports also increased as multinationals brought in components for end-stage production and China required ever larger quantities of energy and raw materials to sustain its booming economy. Japanese trade also grew over the intervening period, but because of factors ranging from a strong yen to residual nontariff barriers, the rate of expansion was much less than China's. Trade conducted by China in 2012 was equivalent to about 2.3 times that of Japan.[5]

Military Expenditures

The wealth generated by a burgeoning economy has allowed China to eclipse Japan in the military sphere. Lined up against the Japan Self-Defense Forces (JSDF) in 1990, the People's Liberation Army was resource poor: its budget was only one-third of what the JSDF received. China has since embarked on a large-scale military modernization effort: declared PLA budgets have expanded at double-digit rates for more than twenty years. Japan, trapped in a fiscal climate characterized by spiraling pension and health care costs and a flat revenue base, has from 1997 onward struggled to sustain military budgets at the previous year's level. Mid-range estimates of PLA budgets show that China surpassed Japan on military expenditures in 2005 and by 2012 spent more than 2.5 times as much on armaments. The main fruits of China's superior military investment—new maritime and air capabilities—directly offset the JSDF's traditional strengths. Recent but modest increases in Japanese military spending will not prevent the JSDF from falling farther behind the PLA as the gap in resources steadily widens.[6]

R&D Spending

Aspirations to become a world leader in science and technology have led China to overtake Japan in research and development spending. China has come from far behind: in 1991 R&D expenditures in China were only 10 percent of those in Japan. Since then, the Chinese government has made a concerted effort to boost domestic R&D spending. Between 1991 and 2006, R&D expenditures in China expanded 15.1 percent annually. Japan managed to grow domestic R&D spending by only 2 percent per year across this period, in part because of its prolonged economic malaise.[7] In the aftermath of the global financial crisis, China has continued to ramp up R&D expenditures in a bid to seize the commanding heights of twenty-first century industry. Whether China's bid will succeed remains uncertain, but its determination to become an innovation powerhouse has overturned Japan's earlier lead in R&D spending. By the close of 2012, R&D expenditures in China were 158 percent those of Japan.[8] Given China's commitment to grow R&D spending to 2.5 percent of a GDP that is already the world's second largest, Japan's relative position on this indicator of national power will continue to erode.[9] Table 9 summarizes how an ascendant China has overturned Japan's earlier predominance.

Table 9: Japan-China Balance of Power (%)

	GDP		International trade		Military expenditures		R&D spending*	
	1980	2012	1980	2012	1990	2012	1991	2013
China	25	273	14	229	33	266	10	158

* This comparison uses two different datasets measuring R&D spending in purchasing power parity terms.

The Balance of Perceptions

The rise of China began to penetrate the consciousness of Japanese elites in the late 1990s. Perceptions of a power transition first centered on China's economic eclipse of Japan and by the turn of the century, extended to the maritime domain, where China was regarded as ascendant. The juxtaposition of China's remarkable economic performance and the period of political dysfunction in Tokyo that lasted from 2007 to 2013 has further reinforced a sense of national decline among Japanese elites.

Economic Leader to Laggard

Although the Japanese economy stagnated during the first half of the 1990s, China's many internal problems tempered concerns about a diminishment of Japan's relative economic standing. Following the Tiananmen Square protests, Japanese elites deemed China politically unstable.[10] Its economic prospects appeared uncertain. Even as the possibility of another Tiananmen-like uprising receded, observers in Japan identified other obstacles to China's continued economic growth. *Yomiuri Shimbun*, a moderately conservative newspaper and barometer for mainstream opinion in Japan's foreign policy establishment, editorialized that income inequality, regional disparities, and public discontent generated by high inflation might impede China's transition to a market economy.[11] Rather than projecting China's double-digit growth rates into the future, Japanese leaders at first viewed the country's economic takeoff as fragile and potentially subject to severe setbacks.[12]

This view changed in the late 1990s as China's economic ascent continued and Japan remained mired in the wreckage of the bubble economy. One indicator of a shift in Japanese perceptions was a report published by the

Foreign Affairs Commission of the Liberal Democratic Party (LDP), which at the time held the reins of government in Tokyo. Released in 1997, the report noted: "It is highly likely that China will catch up to and overtake Japan economically by around the year 2010," and categorized China as "an emerging economic Great Power."[13] China's advancing position in the global economy also attracted the attention of *Yomiuri*, which observed: "With the restoration of Hong Kong, the Chinese economy will, both in terms of GDP and trade, become the third largest in the Asia-Pacific region after the United States and Japan."[14] The robustness of the Chinese economy in the face of the Asian financial crisis that erupted in mid-1997 fully catalyzed Japanese perceptions of relative economic decline. China's capacity to weather the crisis more or less unscathed suggested that despite a host of internal problems, it would continue to experience GDP growth that far outpaced Japan's.[15]

Japanese concerns about waning economic prowess initially focused on China's expanding national output but have since come to encompass less-quantifiable indicators of economic power such as competitiveness in high technology. The evolution of the Japanese government's Science and Technology Basic Plan underscores this shift. The Basic Plans released in 1996 and 2001 did not pinpoint China as posing a challenge for innovation leadership. However, the third Basic Plan published in 2008 singled out China as one of the main competitors for Japanese domestic industry.[16]

In the following years, Japanese elites generally became even more pessimistic about their country's relative economic trajectory. Although long anticipated, China displacing Japan as the world's number two economy in 2010 was still keenly felt.[17] The juxtaposition of Beijing's competent economic management during and after the global financial crisis and Tokyo's political paralysis and policy failures further accentuated Japanese perceptions of flagging economic competitiveness. Recent, all-out efforts by the Shinzo Abe administration to revitalize Japan's economy attest to the palpable sense in Tokyo that even longstanding areas of comparative advantage can no longer be taken for granted.

Contested Waters

Another area where Japanese elites see their country's strength in eclipse is sea power. Japanese views of the maritime balance of power have changed markedly since the early 1990s, when the Japanese Maritime Self-Defense Forces (JMSDF) greatly outclassed the coastal navy China deployed. In a belittling assessment at the time, the Japanese government characterized China's fleet as a collection of small, obsolete vessels.[18] While acknowledging Chinese intentions to construct a modern fleet, defense officials in Tokyo expected that PLA efforts to build a blue-water navy would confront grave difficulties. Skepticism of China's maritime ambitions appeared warranted in Japanese eyes, for the Soviet Union, though a military superpower, had nonetheless failed to develop a functioning blue-water navy.[19]

Within a decade of these assessments, Japanese faith in the longevity of the JMSDF's dominance began to fade. Chinese purchases of advanced Russian weaponry such as Kilo submarines and Sovremenny destroyers were seen as "surprising and impressive" by military planners in Tokyo. Defense officials initially considered these procurements more a factor complicating Taiwan contingencies than a challenge to the JMSDF's supremacy.[20] But as China's naval modernization moved beyond Russian imports to include domestic production of more sophisticated surface vessels and submarines, concerns about a shift in the maritime balance of power emerged. The JMSDF began taking the Chinese navy as a benchmark for its future force requirements, a sure sign that military planners in Tokyo viewed East Asia's waterways as increasingly contested.[21]

Multiple developments have subsequently reinforced Japanese perceptions of China's maritime ascendance. One of these developments is the growth of PLA Navy activities in the waters surrounding Japan.[22] Another development is the sea trial of China's first aircraft carrier. This new capability, when mature, is expected to impose constraints on the JMSDF's freedom of operation.[23]

Japan's Enduring China Strategies

Like the United States, Japan since the late 1990s has responded to China's rise by pursuing a course of integration and hedging. This choice of strategies has persisted across a tumultuous period in Japan's domestic politics marked by the fall of the long-governing LDP, the rise and decline of the Democratic Party of Japan (DPJ), and the LDP resurgence and return to power.

The LDP Approach

Starting in the late 1990s under LDP rule, Japan embraced a two-pronged approach to China's ascendance that outlasted the party's grip on political power. The early centerpiece of Japan's integration strategy was Chinese accession to the WTO. A leading advocate for China's admission, the Japanese government viewed the WTO as a way to enmesh China in a rules-based trading system that would curb its more problematic commercial practices. Japan completed market access agreements with China before the United States or the EU did. In 1997 it concluded an agreement on industrial goods and two years later negotiated a second agreement on services. Japanese backing for China's membership in the WTO also included advocacy; the government in Tokyo lobbied foreign counterparts to support China's accession.[24]

For Japan, integrating China had an environmental dimension as well. The Kyoto Protocol adopted in December 1997 included China as a signatory. However, this accord exempted developing countries—a category encompassing China—from mandatory greenhouse emissions cuts.[25] In the decade after the Kyoto Protocol, China's contribution to global warming rapidly increased: the country became the world's largest producer of carbon dioxide.[26] Consequently, Japan sought to enlist China's participation in a new global agreement on the emission of greenhouse gases.[27] However, Japanese efforts to explain why China should support a new climate accord met with only an equivocal response.[28]

Japan's integration strategy relied on bilateral institutions in addition to multilateral regimes such as the WTO and a successor to the Kyoto Protocol. This was the case in the East China Sea, where Japanese and Chinese sovereignty claims conflicted because of differing interpretations of maritime law.[29] Looking to institute a maritime regime regulating each side's behavior, the Japanese government in August 2000 began negotiations with China on a prior-notification mechanism for research activities in the disputed area. The agreement Japan achieved in February 2001 required two months' advance notice before entering the other side's exclusive economic zone.[30] When tensions flared in early 2005 as China stepped up gas exploration alongside the median line boundary, Japan proposed a new maritime regime: codevelopment of undersea resources on both sides of the line. Negotiations with China proved fruitless at first, but in June 2008, Japan secured an agreement for a "joint development zone" spanning the disputed area.[31]

While seeking to embed China within diverse international institutions, Japan under LDP rule simultaneously hedged. The cornerstone of this hedging strategy was deepening Japan's alliance with the United States. In 1997, Washington and Tokyo agreed on new guidelines for defense cooperation stipulating that Japan would provide rear-area support for U.S. forces in "situations in areas surrounding Japan," a deliberately opaque term that raised the possibility of alliance intervention against China during a regional contingency.[32] A few years later Japan concluded an agreement with the United States authorizing joint research on a next generation missile interceptor.[33]

As China's rise became more pronounced after 2000, Japan took further steps to consolidate security ties with the United States. It contributed JMSDF vessels to American-led operations in the Indian Ocean following the September 11, 2001, terrorist attacks—a move above all intended to demonstrate alliance solidarity to Washington that also sent an unmistakable signal to Beijing. In December 2003, the Japanese government announced that it would purchase missile defense off-the-shelf from the United States rather than wait for the next generation of technology to mature, a decision that delivered an additional boost to its American alliance.[34] Shortly thereafter, Japan deployed troops to Iraq to support postwar reconstruction, an action that while motivated by a genuine urge to make an international contribution, had the added benefit of generating significant U.S. goodwill.[35] Capping off these initiatives, Japan and the United States in late 2005 unveiled a comprehensive set of common strategic objectives.[36] Seen from Beijing, the subtext was clear: the two allies remained in lockstep.

Japanese hedging against China also took the form of building partnerships with other Asian powers. Assiduously courting the Association of Southeast Asian Nations, Japan in 2002 proposed a comprehensive economic partnership that came to fruition during the twilight of LDP rule in December 2008.[37] In the intervening period, Japan concluded bilateral trade accords with five ASEAN member states and became a signatory to the Treaty of Amity and Cooperation.[38] Whereas Japan's engagement of Southeast Asia was predominantly economic, its efforts to forge closer ties with Australia and India were multifaceted. Japan pursued economic partnership agreements with both Indo-Pacific powers, though tortuous trade negotiations failed to conclude before the LDP was swept from power in August 2009.[39] Japanese strategic outreach advanced much more rapidly. In 2002, Japan, Australia, and the United States began a "Trilateral Strategic Dialogue" at the subcabinet level that in 2005 became a regular gathering for foreign ministers. Bilaterally, Japan and Australia issued a joint declaration in 2007 announcing a new strategic partnership. In practice, this meant expanded military cooperation and intelligence sharing.[40] With India, Japan ratcheted up security contacts in the form of defense exchanges and military exercises. The two countries formalized security cooperation by establishing a "Strategic and Global Partnership" in 2008.[41]

The DPJ Approach

The DPJ came to power from the opposition; until September 2009 it had never held the reins of government. As a conglomeration of former socialists, LDP defectors, and technocratic young politicians, the DPJ lacked a unified outlook, with a multiplicity of policy ideas on China coexisting inside the party. Within the DPJ, the instinct that initially prevailed was to rebalance Japan's approach toward China by deemphasizing hedging. Embodying this instinct was the party's first prime minister, Yukio Hatoyama, who at the start of his tenure advocated an East Asian Community excluding the United States and publicly called on Japan to focus more on Asia and rely less on its American ally.[42] In another move away from hedging, Hatoyama undermined Japan's relationship with the United States by reopening an agreement governing the relocation of an American military base on the island of Okinawa. Not only did the dispute over Marine Corps Air Station Futenma antagonize Washington; it also crowded out the larger alliance agenda.[43]

However, the DPJ's deemphasis of hedging proved fleeting. In what amounted to a reverse course, Tokyo in May 2010 decided to reaffirm the earlier agreement on Futenma, tabling if not resolving a major point of friction with Washington.[44] The DPJ's recommitment to hedging was further manifested in the new National Defense Program Guidelines unveiled in December 2010. This strategic planning document called for the redeployment of military forces to Japan's southwestern maritime frontier with China and the procurement of submarines and other equipment relevant to a range of scenarios involving the PLA.[45] Under the new guidelines, Japan's defense posture became increasingly China-centric.

The DPJ never retreated from one element of hedging: regional outreach. In May 2010, Japan and Australia signed an acquisition and cross servicing agreement. The accord enabled the two countries to engage in new forms of military cooperation such as sharing food, fuel, and logistics support.[46] Under the DPJ, Japan boosted military relations with South Korea. During the latter half of 2010, Tokyo dispatched observers to participate in U.S.-South Korea exercises in the Yellow Sea and hosted South Korean observers at large-scale military drills with the United States.[47] These seemingly modest steps were actually landmark developments because a maritime dispute and the legacy of Japanese colonialism has traditionally precluded strategic cooperation between Tokyo and Seoul. Even as Japan struggled to recover from the devastating effects of the March 2011 tsunami, it continued to consolidate ties with other Asian powers. Within less than a month of this natural catastrophe, Japan and India agreed to create a trilateral dialogue with the United States to discuss "regional and global issues of shared interest."[48]

While the DPJ took about a year to fully adopt hedging as a strategy for managing China's rise, it was never reluctant to embrace integration. Prime Minister Hatoyama's concept for an East Asian Community, though inadequately defined and unwelcome in Washington, was an attempt to embed China in a new regional framework that might constrain its behavior. When the East Asian Community failed to gain traction, Japan switched to supporting ASEAN's efforts to strengthen the web of regional institutions in which China participates. Under DPJ rule, Japan also attempted to integrate China through bilateral regimes. The DPJ tried to build on the 2008 agreement committing Tokyo and Beijing to joint resource development in disputed areas of the East China Sea. However, its efforts to implement the agreement met with Chinese resistance.[49]

The LDP Approach

Since the LDP regained control of government in late 2012, integration and hedging have continued under a party that still includes many of the political leaders responsible for charting Japan's initial approach toward China. Recent efforts to tie Beijing into international institutions have taken the form of a growing push for a trilateral Japan-China-South Korea Free Trade Agreement. In March 2013, the three countries launched the first round of negotiations; Japanese leaders appear to believe that a successful trade deal, in addition to offering greater access to a lucrative export market, will serve to stabilize relations with Beijing.[50] A restored LDP has also sought to hedge against a widening imbalance of power with China. The government of Prime Minister Shinzo Abe has committed Japan to joining the Trans-Pacific Partnership, boosted Japan's defense budget for the first time in eleven years, and worked to build out Japan's strategic partnership with India.[51]

Autocracy Overhangs China's Rise

The consistency of Japanese strategy across periods of LDP and DPJ rule points to the influence of regime type in the ongoing Japan-China power transition. By putting a black box at the core of Chinese decision-making, obscuring long-term Chinese intentions, and closing off access opportunities, the one-party system in Beijing induced the LDP to pair integration with hedging. The same byproducts of China's regime type later compelled the DPJ, once in office, to prepare for the possibility of a nonpeaceful rise.

Undercurrents of Uncertainty

A degree of uncertainty characterizes Japanese interactions with China. The broadest contours of China's foreign policy can be anticipated in the near term, but the potential for unwelcome surprises overhangs narrower issue areas. The nature of China's domestic institutions accounts for this.

Like their American counterparts, Japanese officials can only decipher Beijing's internal deliberations through a process resembling the Kremlinology of an earlier era. The absence of a free press within China limits efforts to understand high-level decision-making. Japanese diplomats posted to Beijing report that publicly available information sheds light on China's current policies, yet with the Chinese media heavily censored, open sources remain of limited utility.[52] Information concerning deliberations within the Chinese government remains closely held. As one Japanese official who served in Beijing puts it:

> Fundamentally, the only information we can obtain is the result of a decision. We cannot observe what occurred prior, what debates unfolded within the Chinese government, who advocated and opposed the decision, etc. At best, we can try to trace the decision-making process backward from the result.[53]

Media controls that lie at the heart of autocratic rule have eliminated a potential window on the Chinese government's inner workings.

A dearth of checks and balances within China lends additional uncertainty to interactions between Tokyo and Beijing. Lines of authority are murky in a system without a well-defined separation of powers backed by rule of law. Japanese policymakers at a variety of levels testify to the challenge of mapping China's internal dynamics. One mid-ranking official observes:

> Within the Chinese government, "human control" prevails rather than legal control. It is very difficult to understand a system based on human relationships. Who is close to whom? Who has influence?

Because "human control" characterizes the Chinese government, pre-diction is especially challenging.[54]

This viewpoint is echoed at the highest levels in Tokyo. Shigeru Ishiba, a two-time defense minister and LDP politician, notes: "My impression is that China's decision-making is unpredictable. . . . I have dealt with China for a long time. Rule of law does not exist in that country. Rather, relationships are paramount."[55]

The character of China's civil-military relations exacerbates the undercurrent of uncertainty in Japanese interactions with China. With state secrecy pervasive and checks and balances lacking, the PLA's role in Chinese foreign policy remains opaque. Military incidents sparked by China have therefore generated intense questioning in Tokyo about the extent to which civilian leaders in Beijing control the PLA. The November 2004 discovery of a Chinese submarine submerged in the waters off Okinawa left Japanese officials wondering whether the incursion had been ordered by the PLA without prior civilian authorization.[56] Within the Japanese government, China's testing of an antisatellite weapon in 2007 again raised questions about the PLA's potential autonomy.

It was possible the PLA never informed the civilian leadership prior to the test. Or the civilian leadership was briefed but failed to understand the international implications. Either way, the test led us to question political-military relations in China. We began to worry that the PLA might cause another incident in the future.[57]

The DPJ as a ruling party could not avoid confronting the uncertainty stemming from China's autocratic system. The party's watershed moment was a collision between a Chinese fishing trawler and the Japanese Coast Guard that occurred near the disputed Senkaku/Diaoyu islands in September 2010. The aftermath of the incident was an exercise in Kremlinology with Chinese characteristics. Was the trawler captain actually a PLA officer? Did the Chinese government encourage the fishing ship to enter the disputed area, and if so, was the action motivated by the PLA alone or the civilian leadership? Did the trawler captain independently decide to ram two Japanese Coast Guard vessels?[58] By demonstrating Japan's limited understanding of the decision-making process in Beijing, the collision underscored the peril of relying entirely on international institutions to manage China's rise. For a critical mass within the DPJ, the logic of hedging became irresistible.

The Rise and Rebirth of Mistrust

The purpose behind Chinese power remains an enigma. Does China truly aspire to "peaceful development" as its leaders have proclaimed? Will China seek to dominate neighboring countries and remake global order as it continues to rise? Or will China follow a path uncharted by previous ascendant states? Without a free press capable of illuminating leadership debates in Beijing, the answer remains unknowable. This has not prevented Japanese officials from evaluating the intentions China harbors. Because Beijing's internal deliberations remain shrouded in secrecy, observers in Japan have turned to the only indicator they can easily monitor: Chinese behavior.

The PLA's growing strength has therefore generated considerable mistrust in Japan. Doubts about the purpose behind Chinese power emerged early as the modernization of the PLA gathered steam. At the end of the 1990s, defense officials in Tokyo took note that China's military buildup had proceeded more rapidly than anticipated and was quality-centric. To them, both developments suggested questionable intentions.[59] After 2000, the acceleration of China's military buildup set off additional alarm bells in Tokyo. The Japanese defense establishment viewed China's rapidly expanding military power as a harbinger of future antagonism. In 2001, Japan's annual Defense White Paper for the first time asked whether China's military modernization had exceeded the requirements for self-defense.[60] The tone of the Defense White Paper became increasingly critical in subsequent years:

> Until now, China has not concretely made clear the current disposition of its equipment, the pace of maintenance, the composition of military units, the results of major exercises and training, and the amount and breakdown of its defense budget. . . . In order to reduce concerns about China, it is imperative that China improve the transparency of its defense policy and military capabilities.[61]

Because the Defense White Paper was intended for an international audience, it actually understated the extent to which mistrust of China had permeated Japan's defense establishment. In fact, defense officials in Tokyo became primed to infer the worst possible intentions from Chinese behavior.

When a Chinese submarine was detected in the waters off Okinawa in November 2004, Japanese military planners regarded the incursion as a mali-
cious probe. "The point was to test our will and ability to respond. . . . We
reacted well by chasing down the submarine. If we had not responded vigor-
ously, China would have been emboldened and behaved more adventurously
in the future."[62] The PLA's successful targeting of an aging Chinese weather
satellite in January 2007 was interpreted in an even harsher light. For Japan's
defense establishment, the test raised fundamental questions about China's
willingness to uphold the existing global order.

> Our greatest concern stemming from the ASAT test was that it went
> directly against China's ostensive role as a responsible stakeholder.
> The ASAT test was a very unpredictable move, and not a policy choice
> a responsible stakeholder would pursue. Also, China's obfuscating re-
> sponse to inquiries about the ASAT test was not representative of a
> responsible stakeholder.[63]

By the twilight of LDP rule in 2009, perhaps a majority of civilian defense
officials and senior JSDF officers believed that China would emerge as an
adversary over the medium to long term.[64]

Like the defense establishment it presided over, the LDP became increasingly wary of Chinese intentions. During the late 1990s, mistrust of
China started to coalesce inside the party.[65] As the PLA's strength became
increasingly evident after 2000, anxiety about Chinese ambitions became a
fixture within the LDP. Hard-line LDP lawmakers such as Taro Aso bluntly
expressed their misgivings about China. Speaking to reporters in December 2005 as Japan's foreign minister, Aso pointed to China's rising military
spending and averred: "It is beginning to be a considerable threat."[66] Senior
LDP politicians known for less hawkish views also harbored doubts about
Chinese intentions due to the PLA's advancing modernization. During an
interview with the author in early 2009, Nobutaka Machimura, a two-time
foreign minister, speculated: "Why is China's defense spending so large?
Until now, why China continues to expand its defense budget at so rapid a
pace has been uncertain."[67] In another author interview at the time, a former
minister of finance, Sadakazu Tanigaki, was troubled by the prospect of a
Chinese aircraft carrier. "In the absence of external transparency, we are left
wondering what sort of intentions the aircraft carrier signals. It will create
a sense of threat."[68] One-party rule in Beijing meant that LDP hardliners

and moderates alike had little choice but to conflate Chinese ambitions and military capabilities.

The DPJ that came to power in September 2009 featured diverse and conflicting views of China. While younger politicians such as Seiji Maehara and Aki Nagashima evinced mistrust of Beijing, the group of lawmakers that initially held the upper hand inside the party were optimistic about Chinese intentions. Prime Minister Hatoyama and Ichiro Ozawa—the orchestrator of the DPJ's sweeping victory—regarded China as a pivotal partner in the making, not a potential adversary. When assessing Beijing's ambitions, the DPJ's early leadership ignored the military dimension of China's rise. American officials on multiple occasions actually warned Hatoyama's government to take the PLA's modernization seriously.[69] Having dismissed the possibility of a confrontation with China, DPJ leaders in the fall of 2009 perceived most elements of hedging as unnecessarily antagonistic.

Once the DPJ took over responsibility for managing Japan's relationship with China, however, this optimistic perspective started to sour. Like their LDP counterparts who had controlled the reins of government in Tokyo, DPJ lawmakers had no other option than to treat Chinese behavior as a primary indicator of intentions. The April 2010 buzzing of JMSDF ships by a Chinese naval helicopter raised doubts about the benevolence of Beijing, but what ultimately transformed the balance of views within the DPJ was the aftermath of the September 2010 boat collision. When Japanese authorities took the trawler captain into custody, Beijing attempted to pressure Tokyo into releasing him. Using extralegal measures, China detained Japanese nationals and cut off exports of strategic minerals vital to the health of the Japanese economy.[70] These actions shocked the DPJ and fueled mistrust of Chinese intentions. Although some remnants inside the party continued to regard China's rise as entirely benign, the optimism that existed in fall 2009 no longer prevailed.

Access Denied

The centralization of power and ubiquitous secrecy associated with authoritarian rule have frustrated Japanese efforts to influence China's trajectory. As China emerged on the global scene, Japan supposedly benefited from a cohort of LDP politicians with extensive networks in Beijing. Referred to as "pipes," these politicians nonetheless failed to achieve anything akin to access. Reflecting on their role, a former high-ranking diplomat recounts: "I did not consider pipes to be effective. China might take note of their advice, but its policy would remain unchanged. Pipes acted as a back channel for transmitting information and nothing more."[71] This cohort of LDP politicians also proved irreplaceable when its members either died or retired from politics. The next generation of leading Japanese politicians has not filled the void. It is telling that in an author interview, a China expert at Japan's Ministry of Foreign Affairs could not name even a single politician serving as a conduit with Beijing.[72] Japanese parliamentarians continue to visit China, but their trips are more for publicity than for real relationship building.[73]

Structurally, the Chinese system contains few points of access for Japan. China's Ministry of Foreign Affairs has little capacity to modify national policies detrimental to Japanese interests. In a regime that concentrates authority at the apex of the Communist Party, Chinese diplomats exercise little clout. Moreover, as representatives of an authoritarian regime, they are tightly constrained when interacting with foreigners. One retired Japanese diplomat reports:

> While at the Ministry of Foreign Affairs, I became close to a handful of senior Chinese officials and party leaders. I thought they could never be fully open to me, but believed I should be perfectly open with them. Sometimes, in private conversations, they would repeat official positions, but as we became closer, they were more frank. Still, it was pretty much a one-way street in terms of information exchange.[74]

The PLA, an important player in China's foreign policy, offers no foothold for access. To start, the PLA is probably more hostile to Japan than any other organ of the Chinese government for reasons ranging from the simmering dispute in the East China Sea to nationalistic military education. Legal barriers imposed by Beijing to minimize outward information flows also restrict Japanese engagement of the PLA. It is difficult for JSDF officers to simply develop relationships with their Chinese counterparts. A mid-ranking JSDF officer observes:

> I have no real contacts among officers in the Chinese navy. Even if we get acquainted with them at a reception, they will never provide an e-mail address or contact information. Because it is impossible to develop relationships with mid-level officers and officials, there is no way to monitor China's policy process.[75]

In a regime where authority remains centralized, engaging societal actors fails to translate into access opportunities. Segments of Chinese society that might otherwise influence foreign policy decisions are either co-opted by the government—the business community—or subject to state controls—the media. Consequently, Japanese officials have written off "American-style lobbying" as a tool for shaping China's strategic behavior.[76] This lack of access compounds Japanese anxiety about the growth of Chinese power.

Other Influences on Japanese Strategy

One-party rule in Beijing has decisively shaped the context in which Tokyo formulates a response to China's rise. However, additional factors such as Japan's alliance with the United States and economic interdependence with China may also have influenced Tokyo's choices.

American Fingerprints

It is possible that Japan's approach toward China reflects the desires of a third party—the United States. Under the terms of the U.S.-Japan alliance, Tokyo relies on Washington for extended nuclear deterrence and power projection capability. Since the late 1990s, this security dependence has intensified as Japan's economy has stagnated while the rise of China and the advent of a nuclear-armed North Korea have transformed the strategic landscape. Because of Japan's asymmetric dependence on the United States, some argue that Japan's approach toward China is not entirely independent. In this narrative, Washington exercises a de facto veto over Tokyo's choice of strategies. When Japan diverges from the preferred American approach toward China, it experiences severe diplomatic pressure to change course.

This perspective contains some truth. The strategies adopted by Japan and the United States are closely intertwined because the two countries are allies. It would be surprising if Japan's approach toward China did not take the United States into account. Tokyo's one-sided dependence on Washington also limits the strategies it can independently adopt. Even if Japan wished to contain China, self-imposed military restrictions coupled with growing resource constraints would make the transition to containment contingent on a similar decision by the United States. The recent past has also demonstrated that Washington reacts strongly if Tokyo attempts to deemphasize hedging.

It is impossible to explain the DPJ's about-face without pointing to the public and private pressure the U.S. government applied.[77]

However, going a step farther—claiming that Japanese strategy toward China is "made in Washington"—would be an exaggeration. During the period of LDP rule that ended in late 2009, Japan settled on integration and hedging because this combination of strategies promised to mitigate the potential downside of a rising autocracy. This choice was not dictated by the United States. Looking at the recent past, it would be wrong to read too much into the DPJ's turnaround. Although initially motivated by American displeasure, the DPJ's reversal was fully catalyzed by the September 2010 boat collision, which because China lacked domestic transparency, loomed large as an indicator of intentions. Even if Washington had remained silent, a critical mass of the DPJ would have ultimately come to regard hedging as a necessity. Last, the LDP after returning to power in December 2012 has embraced the two-pronged approach toward China that it earlier pioneered without American prompting.

Economic Interdependence

The constraining role of economic interdependence may also shed light on Japan's strategic choices given its extensive commercial links with China. Between 1997 and the end of 2012, Japan-China trade increased from about 1.5 to 5.6 percent of Japan's GDP.[78] Japanese foreign direct investment in China has more than quadrupled, from $21 billion in 1997 to approximately $93 billion by the close of 2012.[79] Although still a marginal proportion of Japan's total national debt, Chinese purchases of Japanese government bonds appear to be increasing.[80]

Japan's economic entanglement with China is a reality but thus far not a constraint on its strategic choices. Despite a pecuniary interest in stable relations with China, the Japanese private sector remains wary of Beijing's geopolitical ambitions. Business lobbies in Tokyo have never opposed consolidation of the U.S.-Japan alliance or called on the Japanese government to refrain from forging strategic ties with other Asian powers. On the contrary, corporate leaders in Tokyo have quietly supported the Japanese government's hedging strategy.[81]

The only time Japanese business groups have aggressively lobbied for greater accommodation of China was on a matter of symbolism rather than substance: the Yasukuni Shrine. Commemorating Japan's war dead, including a handful of "Class A" war criminals convicted by the Allied tribunal after World War II, the shrine became a point of contention between Tokyo and Beijing because of Prime Minister Junichiro Koizumi's repeat visits there. Seeking in January 2004 to keep Japan-China relations on an even keel, a nationwide business association, Nippon Keidanren, cautioned that prime ministerial visits to the shrine could jeopardize commercial deals with China. This warning went unheeded and Japanese ties with China became strained. In May 2006, Japan's other apex business organization, Keizai Doyukai, issued a public document critiquing Koizumi's continued visits to Yasukuni. Such remonstrations were brushed aside by Koizumi, who insisted that "business and politics are two separate matters."[82] The private sector's multiyear failure to manage an issue that poisoned relations between Tokyo and Beijing demonstrates that even if they wished to, business groups would have little capacity to constrain Japanese strategic choices.

The 2012 flare-up of tensions between Japan and China over the Senkaku/ Diaoyu islands underscored the limited restraints imposed by significant economic ties. The bilateral dispute directly affected the Japanese business community, which at the time suffered from a boycott by Chinese consumers and a shift by Chinese factories toward South Korean suppliers. By some estimates, intensifying tensions trimmed Japan's GDP growth by a percentage point in the last quarter of 2012.[83] Yet Japanese companies responded by trying to diversify their export markets and production networks rather than calling on the government to back down in the face of Chinese pressure.

Conclusion

Japan's response to the ascendancy of China doubly affirms the book's argument. Despite a linguistic, cultural, and political heritage vastly different from that of either Great Britain or the United States, Japan has charted the same course when confronting an autocracy's rise. This has a significant implication: in power transitions featuring a nondemocracy, the root of mistrust is not perceptions grounded in a particular Anglo-American outlook, but the way in which centralized authority and a lack of transparency deprive outsiders of information about intentions and limit opportunities for access. The DPJ's reemphasis of hedging before its 2012 defeat lends further backing to the book's argument. Once in office and compelled to interpret China's behavior through the lens afforded by its domestic institutions, a critical mass of the DPJ came to perceive Beijing as a threat, and gravitated toward the two-pronged approach favored by the LDP. This convergence, together with the LDP's consistent fidelity to pairing integration with hedging, testifies to how regime type frames the strategic choices of democratic leaders as they respond to power shifts.

Chapter 8

Implications for the Twenty-First Century

Regime type is key to understanding the dynamics of fateful transitions. Autocracies sow mistrust as they gain in power while democracies can rise and reassure. In power shifts ranging from the British response to the emergence of the United States and Germany in the late nineteenth century to China's recent arrival on the international stage and the American and Japanese reactions, this dynamic holds true. Across time and geopolitical traditions, regime type sets the boundaries for the way democratic leaders manage a new power's rise.

Implications for Theory

This book set out to demonstrate that a state's domestic institutions shape the external reaction to its ascendance. The power shifts surveyed not only reinforce this argument but also point to new theoretical refinements and directions for future research.

The Democratic Peace

Although the role of regime type in power transitions affirms the democratic peace, the case studies call for rethinking why pacific relations prevail among democracies. At each juncture, institutions underpinning democracy clarified the rising state's intentions and provided outsiders with opportunities to engage domestic actors involved in foreign policymaking. Reassurance rested on a combination of transparency and access. Normative accounts of the democratic peace, which emphasize shared values and practices, and some institutional explanations, which focus on domestic constraints to military mobilization, fail to capture these sources of reassurance. The broader democratic peace surely reflects a multitude of factors, but transparency and access may carry greater weight than currently recognized.

This finding indicates that democratic peace scholars should devote greater attention to measuring the impact of transparency and access. The case studies confirm both byproducts of regime type as sources of reassurance, but only a large-scale survey can provide a basis for claims that extend beyond this book. Statistical work on the democratic peace might benefit from taking a more granular approach than the Polity IV dataset permits. Future academic work could productively leverage the World Bank's Database of Political Institutions and the Freedom House Freedom of the Press survey. Using data from each, scholars can begin to distinguish the relative contributions of transparency and access to the conflict-reducing role of shared democracy among states.

Power Transitions

The book's main argument and the supporting historical evidence reveal an oversight in the literature on power transitions. Recent scholarship has observed that mistrust does not inevitably accompany a state's ascendancy: relations between established and emerging powers can range from cooperation to competition. Yet explanations put forward to account for variation in the security dilemma overlook a critical factor: the new power's regime type. The insecurity experienced by democratic leaders during power shifts depends on whether they can accurately gauge a rising state's ambitions and influence its foreign policy from within. Democratic institutions in a new power mitigate the security dilemma, while autocratic government has the opposite effect. Consequently a dictatorship's ascendance will be more prone to instability and more likely to culminate in war, though military conflict is not preordained.

In light of the book's findings, academic work on power transitions should address a new set of questions. Can rising autocracies compensate for their internal handicaps and find ways to reassure? Do transparency and access similarly influence the strategy formation of autocracies experiencing unfavorable power shifts? Are there constraints on the degree to which dictatorships can engage domestic actors within a rising democracy? The answers to these questions will help to chart future relations between today's established and emerging powers.

Economic Interdependence

In each of the case studies, economic linkages exerted at most an ephemeral influence on the democratic power's strategy. Groups benefiting from commercial ties with the ascendant state sometimes lobbied against confrontational policies but never succeeded in preventing democratic leaders from pursuing their preferred course. Moreover, regardless of whether significant trade and investment ties existed, democratic leaders always approached containment as a last resort. Rather than illuminating the strategy formation of democratic powers, economic interdependence may better explain the choices of rising states. At the outset of a transition, a new power disproportionately experiences the constraints imposed by commercial ties because of its smaller economy. These constraints become increasingly brittle as the state's economy expands and trade with the democratic power declines as a share of GDP. The pacific benefit of economic interdependence may decrease throughout power transitions, placing a premium on another source of restraint: the democratic power's integration strategy.

The book points to several areas of new research on economic interdependence. Much of the scholarship on the commercial peace has focused on trade, yet in the case studies, other meaningful economic entanglements existed. In fact, the strongest example of economic interdependence constraining democratic leaders was the standstill agreement between Great Britain and Germany during the interwar period. Scholars should more systematically investigate nontrade linkages. The power shifts in this book sometimes featured interest groups lobbying democratic governments to accommodate a rising state. However, such efforts never prevented democratic leaders from implementing their preferred strategy. Work on the interplay of economic interdependence and foreign policy needs to more precisely assess the conditions under which trade and investment ties produce politically influential lobbies.

Implications for Policy

The findings in this book also contain insights for contemporary policymakers. First, the leadership in Beijing has made a risky bet against history by assuming that economic modernization would assure the world of China's benign intentions without requiring changes to one-party rule at home. Second, to short-circuit the cycle of mistrust, reaction, and counterreaction that increasingly defines relations between Washington and Beijing, the United States should encourage gradual political liberalization in China. Third, India's democratic government will translate into a strategic advantage as its rise continues. Fourth, and last, rising democracies such as India, Brazil, and Indonesia present

America with the best opportunity to strengthen the international order that has advanced peace, prosperity, and freedom for more than six decades.[1]

China's Losing Bet Against History

In 1991, Deng Xiaoping famously explained that in order to reassure the world of its peaceful intentions, China should "cope with affairs calmly; hide our capacities and bide our time; be good at maintaining a low profile; and never claim leadership."[2] Since then, China's reassurance strategy has evolved as its economic clout and military capabilities have become impossible to mask, and its participation in global governance has become unavoidable. Rather than maintaining a low profile, China has gone on the offensive to combat perceptions that its growing strength constitutes a threat, initially vowing a "peaceful rise," and more recently, reiterating its commitment to "peaceful development." China has also engaged in confidence-building dialogues with its neighbors and the United States, both at the official and Track Two levels. Although China's reassurance strategy has changed, the nature of its gamble has not. The Chinese government has consistently wagered that alleviating mistrust abroad will not require political reform at home.

For China's leadership, this bet against history has always held considerable appeal. It leaves unchallenged the consensus against political liberalization that emerged after the Tiananmen Square protests and the collapse of the world's first communist state, the Soviet Union.[3] It also permits the Chinese government to believe that political reform can be postponed indefinitely without incurring international blowback. Above all, it keeps open the option that Beijing might use its growing economic power to dilute aspects of the rules-based international order that have threatened to change China's own domestic political institutions.

But China's bet is unraveling. Despite a concerted effort to put a friendly face on its rise, China has failed to quell growing doubts about its future course. These doubts exist not only in the United States and Japan, as Chapters 6 and 7 documented; concerns about Chinese intentions have surged across much of Asia as well. In 2009, the Center for Strategic and International Studies published an opinion survey of strategic elites in the Asia-Pacific region. When asked what nation would constitute the greatest threat to regional peace and security in ten years' time, respondents from Australia, India, Indonesia, and South Korea in addition to Japan all listed China as the most likely country.[4] In the wake of Beijing's more recent assertiveness toward Japan, South Korea, Vietnam, and the Philippines, public attitudes toward China have deteriorated further, and identification of China as a potential threat has increased again.

The mistrust of China that overhangs Washington and many Asian capitals stems from the nature of China's domestic institutions, not simply from its behavior on the world stage. China's system of one-party rule has magnified anxieties that, in the best of circumstances, would attend the emergence of a new superpower. There is no small irony in China's situation today. Its leadership has demonstrated an admirable determination to learn from the mistakes of past rising powers, going so far as to sanction a television miniseries tracing the ascent of nine states.[5] And yet, Beijing has overlooked the way in which regime type frames power transitions. History suggests that autocracies cannot rise and indefinitely reassure. Betting against history is like betting against the house; history usually wins.

China's lack of domestic political reform is now becoming a strategic liability. No matter how many times a rising China reiterates its commitment to "peaceful development," no matter how many confidence-building dialogues a rising China participates in or free trade agreements it signs, the anxieties generated by its authoritarian system will remain. Rightly or wrongly, China will be mistrusted and even feared. Wary of China's growing power, the United States, Japan, India, South Korea, Australia, and others will behave in ways that harm China's interests. Although China will not face a unified alliance as the Soviet Union did during the Cold War, it will confront an international landscape that is increasingly unwelcoming.

China's flawed bet against history will result in more than quasi encirclement—over the long term, a system of one-party rule will prevent China from realizing a level of political and economic influence commensurate with its objective strength. Widespread mistrust of China's ambitions will constrict its ability to take a leadership role in the international community. The opacity of basic economic decisions such as the setting of interest rates and currency values will limit China's ability to become the linchpin of the global financial order. In this sense, an authoritarian system will ultimately deprive China of the fruits of its rise. The next generation of leaders in Beijing would do well to consider this problem as they chart their nation's future course.

Political Liberalization as Strategy

If the United States is to forestall a repeat of historic rivalries with rising authoritarian states, it will be critical to develop a strategy to encourage gradual political liberalization within China.

To start, Americans have to understand the limits of integration and hedging as tools of foreign policy. Until today, the United States and China have kept tensions in check and avoided falling into an enduring rivalry. This was possible because China, though rising and autocratic, was still weak. But as China's strength mounts, the uncertainty surrounding its ascendance compels the United States to place greater emphasis on hedging. The delicate balance between integration and hedging, which has permitted the United States and China to cooperate while managing mistrust, is at risk of breaking down. What will replace it is unmitigated competition.

Beyond integration and hedging, a third strategy toward China is necessary—a strategy that has no real historical parallel but nonetheless holds the potential to short-circuit the cycle of mistrust, reaction, and counterreaction that all too often causes an autocracy's rise to culminate in acute rivalry if not military conflict. This strategy would focus on political reform within China as an indispensable dimension of building better U.S.-China relations.

America's third strategy toward China will require presidential ownership to be effective. To give some concrete examples, the president of the United States should regularly meet with the Dalai Lama and accord sufficient access and attention to legitimate Chinese dissidents. It will be essential that the leadership in Beijing consistently hears from the president and his or her senior foreign policy team about the importance to the United States of specific issues of democratic governance in China. Values discourse with China should not be relegated to the "human rights" dialogue by the assistant secretary of state for democracy, human rights, and labor. It is not enough to simply find "dialogues" that check the box for American human rights advocacy groups.

Presidential ownership of this strategy will help to ensure that it does not devolve into a self-defeating crusade against China. The leadership in Beijing will always be suspicious of American strategies for "peaceful evolution" in China, but they will engage more productively if it is clear that the American president is not interested in weakening China's economic development. Whoever sits in the Oval Office should explain to his or her Chinese counterpart that improvement in governance, rule of law, religious freedom, and civil society would all help China to become stronger—not weaker. Consistent presidential attention to necessary changes within China will also help to prevent sudden explosions in the relationship. Vacillating between deference and overassertion on human rights and democracy will do more damage to American ties with China than an unwavering position that contains no surprises for Beijing.

The United States should support efforts that help Chinese officials strengthen their own institutions. Today, for example, Georgetown University sity engages in a dialogue with the Party School on religious freedom; the Supreme Court works with Chinese jurists on questions of jurisprudence; nongovernmental organizations like the Asia Foundation seek partnerships with local Chinese organizations and universities seeking to be more effective in meeting citizens' needs. These efforts at institution building take place within the parameters of China's own constitution. The results will be gradual, but the resources should be increased. Meanwhile, there is no contradiction between encouraging this slower insider strategy of reform in China and more direct efforts by organizations like the National Endowment for Democracy or Freedom House to spotlight human rights and democracy failures that may be more embarrassing for Beijing. The U.S. government should support both.

It is critical to realize that despite the sometimes tone-deaf nature of Chinese foreign policy toward Asia, Chinese leaders are not impervious to the opinions of their neighbors. As Asia's web of formal institutions and informal networks continues to evolve and strengthen, the United States should actively promote an agenda that moves the region away from the idea of "non-interference in internal affairs" and toward respect for individual rights within member states. The momentum regionally is with the United States on this question, but there is no single view of what constitutes universal norms. Washington will therefore have to pursue a differentiated approach toward advancing democratic norms in Asia, one that reflects the diversity of the region and its international institutions. That may mean partnering with advanced economies like Japan, South Korea, Australia, and the European Union on a caucus to advance transparent development assistance and good governance in the region, while working with Indonesia to encourage ASEAN to strengthen the human rights commission in its charter. The United States will also want to increase coordination with other likeminded states so that Beijing hears as unified a message as possible on domestic Chinese practices that deny human rights or obstruct the development of transparent and accountable institutions.

And last, despite the limited nature of confidence-building measures that fall short of political liberalization, the United States should increase regional and international pressure on Beijing to reduce the opaqueness around its foreign and national security decision-making processes. The PLA will resist, since that same opaqueness is seen by the military leadership in China as a strategic asset. So the answer will be to hold civilian leaders responsible for the actions of the PLA. There is no doubt that the Central Military Commission of the Communist Party exerts control over the PLA from the top, but there are few checks and balances or sources of information or operational guidance below that. Setting expectations that China's civilian leaders will be pressed by their Japanese, South Korean, Indian, Vietnamese, and other counterparts on PLA activities will condition the civilian leadership in Beijing to do their homework and establish and strengthen their own independent levers to adjust PLA operations, rhetoric, and planning so that these do not undermine larger Chinese foreign policy interests.

While embracing a third strategy of political liberalization, the United States needs to recognize that pressing for rapid democratization would actually make a U.S.-China rivalry more likely. The leadership in Beijing would regard a push for overnight elections as a deeply hostile act. The target should be rule of law, good governance, and greater accountability—political reforms that do not inherently threaten the Communist Party, and may even help to boost its flagging legitimacy. Ultimately, the United States cannot democratize China. But what it can do is shape the environment in which Beijing's leadership debates political liberalization. Without this third strategy in place, there is a strong likelihood that integration and hedging will fail to avert enduring competition.

India's Democratic Advantage

Although they may regard China's rise as well ahead of their own, India's ruling elites should recognize that influence comes not only from wealth and military power but from the capacity to reassure. India's long-standing democratic institutions endow it with a geopolitical advantage overlooked by many outside observers who see rough and tumble parliamentary politics and popular protests as a potential challenge to sustaining high rates of economic growth. In the short term, the pessimists may be right about the complications democracy introduces to national development. But over the long term, India will successfully manage these complications and derive increasing strategic benefit from its status as a rising democratic power.

Constitutional safeguards on freedom of expression ensure a degree of domestic transparency that extends to India's external objectives. No great question mark overhangs India's ambitions abroad. Outsiders can turn to India's independent newspapers, which mirror or even anticipate discussions within the government. Major strategic decisions inevitably play out in the public domain—an example is the ongoing debate over whether and to what degree India should align itself with the United States. In addition, foreign observers can engage in free and open discussions with key figures in the ruling elite. Like every government, India's has its sensitive information, but there is no wall of secrecy that stifles interactions between officials and outsiders. Indeed, the senior leadership in New Delhi appear keen to explain India's outlook to foreigners, and in past years, have given a number of candid speeches on this topic.[6] An overabundance of information may at times bewilder observers, but the outlines of Indian intentions are clear for the world to see.

Another way India's open political system reassures is through creating opportunities for outsiders to influence the direction of its rise. Characteristics of democratic rule such as decentralization of authority empower groups outside the Indian government. As a 2011 study by the Lowy Institute notes, India's internationally minded business community and vibrant news media have become major forces in the making of its diplomacy.[7] These domestic groups provide points of entry for external powers looking to shape India's foreign policy from within. It would be a mistake to exaggerate the impact of foreign efforts to cultivate powerful constituencies inside India, but these efforts reassure outsiders that their perspective will at least receive a fair hearing.

By functioning as a source of reassurance in the ways outlined above, democratic government facilitates India's ascent. Despite India's testing of nuclear weapons in the late 1990s and accelerating military buildup, mistrust of its intentions remains low. In the 2009 survey of Asian and American strategic elites conducted by the Center for Strategic and International Studies in Washington, less than 5 percent of all respondents listed India as the greatest threat to regional peace and security in ten years' time. China, by contrast, was cited as a future threat by 38 percent of all respondents.[8]

The strategic advantage conveyed by democratic rule is particularly evident in the case of India's relationship with the United States. While the world's sole superpower has hedged against the rise of China, it has accommodated India's emergence through policies ranging from modifying nuclear export regimes to championing India's permanent membership in a reformed United Nations Security Council. Concerns about China have informed America's approach toward India. However, the United States has embraced India's emergence without residual misgivings because of the multiple reassurances that democratic rule conveys.

Democratic institutions have allowed New Delhi to circumvent the cycle of mistrust, reaction, and counterreaction that ordinarily accompanies a new power's rise. A case in point is the growth of the Indian Navy. Given India's geographic position, its new maritime capabilities directly affect the many countries that rely on the sea lines of communication linking the Persian Gulf to the Strait of Malacca. Conceivably, India could one day utilize its expanding navy to disrupt freedom of navigation in this vital stretch of ocean, yet observers have sufficient insight into New Delhi's thinking to dismiss such a scenario as implausible. Again, the contrast with China is instructive. Foreign analysts have interpreted Beijing's naval buildup and aggressive rhetoric in the South China Sea as a harbinger of expansionist ambitions because an autocratic system obscures information that might provide a more nuanced perspective on Chinese actions.

The way is clear for India to rise into a position of global leadership. Trusting India's intentions, the world's established powers are ready to welcome it as a coequal partner in sustaining the rules-based system that has underpinned international peace and prosperity for more than sixty years. If India decides to fully cast off old frames of reference with regard to the West and the rest, it can attain a level of influence that China, with its current political system, will never equal.

Rising Democracies as Pivotal Partners

The book's final insight relates to the role of rising democracies in American foreign policy.

For more than six decades, the United States has worked with its allies in Europe and Asia to maintain an interlocking web of rules, institutions, norms, and relationships.[9] While by no means banishing war, this international order has facilitated the longest period of peace among great powers in modern times. Because of the economic stability and openness engendered by the global order, the world has experienced a dramatic increase in trade and investment and a rise in per capita incomes unknown to an earlier age.[10] Moreover, democracy has taken root in new areas of the world, including regions where dictatorship had long prevailed, enabling more than half of humanity to live under democratically elected governments.[11]

Today the international order confronts numerous challenges. Some of these challenges largely relate to the rise of China, such as outsized maritime claims and the bypassing of international financial institutions. Other challenges involve a weakened global financial architecture, the nuclear ambitions of North Korea and Iran, and a retrenchment of democracy in some parts of the world. At the same time, a combination of fiscal and political pressures constrains the role of traditional supporters of the global order such as the United States and Europe. Although no single nation or grouping possesses the power or ambition to construct a rival system, the global order now trends toward fragmentation, a trajectory inimical to all countries that depend on an open and stable world for their security and prosperity.

The United States must seize the opportunity to strengthen and adapt the international order by enlarging its circle of supporters. The book's findings about the role of regime type during power transitions indicate that rising democracies hold great promise in this endeavor. Because these new powers feature domestic transparency, Washington can work with them in an environment devoid of the type of mistrust that limits the scope of U.S.-China cooperation. At the same time, rising democracies present American leaders with a plethora of access opportunities. They have vibrant civil societies, business lobbies, and foreign policy processes encompassing diverse individuals with a multiplicity of perspectives.

Transparency and access provide no guarantee that rising democracies will come to bolster today's international order. Countries such as Brazil, India, and Indonesia remain skeptical of elements of the existing system. On top of this, domestic challenges in these countries will compete for the resources and attention that a larger global role demands. America's engagement with rising democracies is critical. The choices they make—about whether to take on new global responsibilities, passively benefit from the efforts of established powers, or complicate the solving of key challenges—may, together, decisively influence the trajectory of the current international order.

Conclusion

Since the eclipse of Pax Britannica at the turn of the twentieth century, fateful transitions have usually culminated in rivalry or war. History does not perfectly repeat, but the impact of regime type on power shifts transcends any given period. Transparent ambitions and opportunities for access enable democracies to reassure as they ascend while autocracies generate mistrust as they rise because their domestic institutions obscure intentions and keep out foreign influence. If leaders in today's established and emerging powers can fully grasp this, they can forge a more successful path than their predecessors.

Appendix 1: Omitted Cases

This book explains how democratic powers navigate the rise of other states; it does not attempt to illuminate the strategic choices that all democratic countries, large and small, make. Thus, the number of power transitions relevant to this study is small. Even then, a number of potential cases were considered but ultimately omitted. In all these cases, at least one of the following conditions obtained.

(1) Failure to rise: the distribution of capabilities did not shift along multiple dimensions, including at least one enduring indicator of national power.
(2) Failure to perceive: democratic leaders never fully perceived another state's ascendancy.

The first omitted case is Great Britain's strategy toward czarist Russia during the latter half of the nineteenth century. This case differs from a fateful transition on both material and perceptual grounds. Between 1870 and 1900, Russian GDP as a share of British national wealth remained static at 83 percent. The value of Russia's trade peaked in 1879 at 32 percent of Great Britain's, and by 1900 was down to 26 percent. Russian military spending was superior to that of Great Britain at the start of this period, but from the mid-1880s on, generally fell below British expenditures.[1] Russia's commercial and maritime weakness meant that it was never seen as a threat to British primacy. Instead, British leaders perceived Russia as a rival for influence in the Dardanelles, Central Asia, and the Far East.

The second case excluded is the British response to Japan's emergence during the late nineteenth and early twentieth centuries. Both power and perceptions disqualify this case. The establishment of a modern state under the Meiji Emperor and the importation of Western technology and military techniques improved Japan's position relative to Great Britain, but the gap on key dimensions of national power remained significant. Between 1870 and 1913, Japan's GDP grew from 25.3 to 31.9 percent of British GDP, a modest shift for a period spanning four decades. At the same time, Japan's international trade never surpassed 13 percent of British global commerce. During the Russo-Japanese War of 1904–1905, Japan's spending on armaments exceeded Great Britain's, but this was due to the material demands of the conflict. From 1870 to 1913, Japan's peacetime military expenditures grew significantly in relative terms, but only in three years did they surpass one-third of British military outlays; the overall disparity in military spending thus remained large. British elites never perceived an emerging Japan as having the potential to surpass their nation in raw economic and military power. Rather, they viewed Japan as a rising state in a narrowly defined region, the Far East, in which Great Britain was simply one of several competing European powers. Such perceptions of Japan were significantly different from the way that London interpreted the growth of American and German power.[2]

The third omitted case is U.S. strategy toward Japan during the interwar period. Japan's actual and perceived material inferiority distinguish this case from those considered in the book. Between 1919 and 1940, Japan's GDP remained less than one quarter of U.S. output. Until 1937, its military expenditures were less than half those of the United States. Thereafter, Japanese arms spending surged past U.S. military allocations. However, this apparent shift in the balance of power reflected Japan's invasion of China. Resources expended on what soon became a quagmire did little to augment Japanese military capabilities vis-à-vis the United States. While Japan's trade increased in relative terms, the value of U.S. commerce remained more than twice as high. Furthermore, Japan's material weakness was the lens through which U.S. leaders interpreted its actions. The occupation of Manchuria in 1931 and Japan's all-out invasion of China in 1937 were deemed threats to a treaty-based international order but did not generate concerns about waning U.S. primacy. Notably, during the run-up to Pearl Harbor, American officials regarded a Japanese attack as unlikely due to what they perceived as the manifest predominance of the United States.[3]

The fourth omitted case—also from the interwar period—is Great Britain's strategy toward the Soviet Union. Evaluating relative changes in the distribution of capabilities fails to disqualify this case: the USSR experienced sustained increases on two enduring indicators of national power. Between 1928 and 1938, Stalin's forced industrialization program boosted Soviet GDP from 95 percent of British output to 136 percent. Moreover, annual Soviet military outlays dwarfed those of Great Britain, sometimes by as much as eight times. The situation was reversed for the value of each state's international trade. Yet despite marked changes in the balance of power, British leaders did not perceive a loss of primacy. Rather, they viewed the Soviet Union largely as an ideological challenge. Communist subversion was considered a menace to the domestic stability of Great Britain and its far-flung Asian interests. Soviet military prowess was in fact dismissed, particularly after Stalin purged the Red Army's officer corps.[4] Consequently, British perceptions of the USSR rule out this case.

The fifth omitted case is the U.S. approach toward Japan during the 1980s and early 1990s. The reason for excluding this case is that Japan's ascendance was truncated by internal economic problems. When the financial bubble underpinning Japan's post-1985 prosperity burst in 1990, the country went on to experience a "lost decade" of economic growth. Even at the high-water mark of Japanese relative power, its GDP and international trade never surpassed 60 percent those of the United States, and spending on armaments peaked at 18 percent of U.S. military expenditures.[5]

Appendix 2: Coding Checks and Balances

The World Bank Database of Political Institutions codes the number of checks and balances (referred to as "checks") using the following criteria.[1]

•• Checks equal one if either the executive branch or the legislative branch is not competitively elected.
•• If both the executive branch and the legislative branch are competitively elected:
  - The existence of a chief executive equals one check.
  - Competitive election of the chief executive equals one check.
  - Opposition control of the legislature equals one check.
  - In a presidential system:
    • Each chamber of the legislature equals one check unless the president's party controls the lower house and there is a closed list system.
    • Each party allied with the president's party that is ideologically closer to the primary opposition party equals one check.
  - In a parliamentary system:
    • Each party that enables the ruling coalition to retain a majority equals one check.
    • Each party in the ruling coalition that is closer to the primary opposition party on economic issues equals one check.
    • The prime minister's party does not equal one check if a closed rule exists.

Appendix 3: Measuring Freedom of the Press

Chapter 3: Pax Britannica Eclipsed

1. Does the constitution contain provisions designed to protect freedom of the press? (Y=0; N=1)

   The U.S. constitution did not originally guarantee freedom of the press. However, the first amendment to the constitution—part of the Bill of Rights ratified in 1791—provides that "Congress shall make no law . . . abridging the freedom of speech, or of the press."[1] The constitution of Germany never enshrined journalistic freedom. Instead, the Reich Press Law of 1874 protected freedom of the press and abolished the most intrusive forms of censorship. Even so, because freedom of the press fell short of a constitutional right, parliament could empower the German government to control the media.[2] (United States=0; Germany=1)

2. Do the penal code, security laws, or any other laws restrict reporting and are journalists punished under these laws? (Y=1; N=0)

   The United States had libel laws under which journalists could be prosecuted for criticizing public officials. But by the end of the nineteenth century, protection of journalists from libel suits had substantially expanded. In many, though not all states, judges came to recognize that even false statements against public officials could be defended if made in good faith.[3] In Germany, provisions of the Reich Press Law and the Imperial Criminal Code allowed prosecutors to confiscate and, subject to court approval, destroy written work for libel, slander, or lèse-majesté. These charges were used to convict and punish left-leaning journalists.[4] (United States=0; Germany=1)

3. Are media outlets' news and information content significantly determined by the government or a particular partisan interest? (Y=1; N=0)
High-circulation U.S. newspapers in the mid-1890s were independent.
Changes in the revenue structure of newspapers—the rise of commercial advertising—freed editors from dependence on political parties. At
the turn of the century, independent newspapers predominated, particularly in large urban areas.[5] By contrast, government authorities and
partisan interest groups were responsible for a significant amount of
media content in Germany. The Press Bureau within the Ministry of
Foreign Affairs issued editorial guidance to "inspired" newspapers. Another effort undertaken by the German government was heavy subsidi-
zation of the Christian Journal Society, an organization that distributed
proestablishment newspapers and other propaganda material. Partisan
interest groups in Germany also wielded substantial editorial authority.
Many newspapers were financially bound to a particular political party
or economic group. This did not always ensure progovernment content, as evidenced by the rapid growth of the Social Democratic press.[6]
A diversity of viewpoints existed, but Germany lacked truly independent news outlets. (United States=0; Germany=1)

4. Is there official censorship? (Y=1; N=0)
The First Amendment precluded the U.S. government from using official censorship. In Germany, the Reich Press Law did not. The German government systematically wielded charges of slander, libel, and
lèse-majesté against publications that it found objectionable. Moreover, local authorities sometimes exercised preventive censorship. In
exchange for financial guarantees, local papers gave officials the right
to block publication of articles judged inimical to the central government.[7] (United States=0; Germany=1)

5. Are journalists or media outlets subject to extralegal intimidation or
physical violence by state authorities? (Y=1; N=0)
Violence against media outlets occurred sporadically within the United
States at the turn of the century. However, the perpetrators were racist
mobs, not government authorities. Censorship in Germany took the
form of legal pressure and restrictive ordinances rather than physical
coercion. The German government's constant concern to find ways of

invoking the law against the left-leaning press testifies to its eschewal of extralegal intimidation.[8] (United States=0; Germany=0)

6. Are significant portions of the media owned or controlled by the government? (Y=1; N=0)
American newspapers at the end of the nineteenth century were financially independent. Boosted by advertising revenues, they had become powerful business operations, and sometimes generated fortunes for their owners.[9] In Germany, the government did not own a significant proportion of the media. The newspaper industry was large and highly fragmented, with 3,452 newspapers in 1901 and more than 4,000 in 1912.[10] (United States=0; Germany=0)

Scores: United States=0; Free Press
Germany=4; Unfree Press

Chapter 4: Germany Resurgent

1. Does the constitution contain provisions designed to protect freedom of the press? (Y=0; N=1)
The constitution of the Weimar Republic guaranteed the right of self-expression. This right was taken to encompass freedom of the press.[11] However, after the Reichstag fire of February 27, 1933, Hitler secured a decree suspending seven sections of the constitution covering individual and civil liberties. Journalistic freedom in Germany was thereby deprived of constitutional safeguards.[12] (Germany=1)

2. Do the penal code, security laws, or any other laws restrict reporting and are journalists punished under these laws? (Y=1; N=0)
The Reich Press Law of October 1933 allowed the Nazi regime to prosecute journalists for any reporting that "tends to weaken the strength of the German Reich . . . or offends the honor and dignity of Germany."[13] This law was used to close down left-leaning and Jewish-run newspapers and bar individual journalists—1,300 within Hitler's first two years as chancellor—from practicing their profession.[14] (Germany=1)

3. Are media outlets' news and information content significantly determined by the government or a particular partisan interest? (Y=1; N=0)
Under the Nazi regime, the German media quickly became a mouthpiece for government propaganda. The Reich Press Law of 1933 effectively transformed journalists into representatives of the state. They were required to "regulate their work in accordance with National Socialism as a philosophy of life and as a conception of government."[15] To ensure that journalists toed the Nazi line, the Ministry of Propaganda issued daily directives to all editorial desks on what news to print and what to suppress. The Nazis also co-opted radio, the new mass media of the 1930s. Radio broadcasting had been a state monopoly during the Weimar Republic. Hitler's ascension to the chancellorship thus gave the Nazis absolute control over what was broadcast over the airwaves.[16] (Germany=1)

4. Is there official censorship? (Y=1; N=0)
Official censorship was a hallmark of the Third Reich. The Nazis exercised censorship in various forms. One was the Reich Press Law's requirement that all journalists accord the Nazi regime favorable coverage. Another was the daily press directive originating from the Ministry of Propaganda. Supplementing such mechanisms of preventive censorship was the repression of alternative media outlets. Hitler moved against communist and socialist newspapers in early February 1933. The Catholic press lingered on, but was banned in 1935.[17] (Germany=1)

5. Are journalists or media outlets subject to extralegal intimidation or physical violence by state authorities? (Y=1; N=0)
Extralegal intimidation and violence against journalists was a common feature of Nazi rule. Upon attaining power, the Nazi leadership threatened the Ullsteins, the Jewish owners of Germany's largest publishing house. When attempts to placate the Nazis failed, the Ullsteins sold their publishing empire for a pittance. During March and April 1933, storm troops were unleashed against the left-wing press. In one notable case, they invaded the offices of Germany's most prestigious paper, the *Frankfurter Zeitung*.[18] Last, journalists who challenged the Nazi regime could be interned in concentration camps, where they,

like other political prisoners, experienced physical deprivation, torture, and death. (Germany=1)

6. Are significant portions of the media owned or controlled by the government? (Y=1; N=0)
Nazi ownership of media outlets was significant as early as 1933. With radio broadcasting a state monopoly, the party gained instant control over the airwaves when it took power. Then in December 1933, Germany's two press agencies came into the Nazi orbit and were merged into the German News Office. Acquisition and elimination gave the Nazi party an ever-larger share of newspaper circulation. Having already bought out the Ullsteins, Nazi publisher Max Amann leveraged an April 1935 ordinance to purchase or close down some five to six hundred newspapers over the course of eighteen months. An agent of the Nazi regime, Amann by 1939 controlled over two-thirds of German newspapers and magazines.[19] (Germany=1)

Score: Germany=6; Unfree Press

Chapter 5: Red Star Rising

1. Does the constitution contain provisions designed to protect freedom? (Y=0; N=1)
The Soviet constitution of 1936 contained a provision that gave lip service to freedom of the press—Article 125. However, Article 125 in fact established a constitutional basis for censorship. It guaranteed freedom of the press only "in conformity with the interests of the workers and for the purposes of strengthening the socialist system."[20] The ultimate arbiter of what information met these criteria was the Soviet government. (USSR=1)

2. Do the penal code, security laws, or any other laws restrict reporting and are journalists punished under these laws? (Y=1; N=0)
Clause 10 of Article 58 of the Soviet criminal code created a legal framework for restricting reporting. It criminalized "propaganda or agitation containing an appeal to overthrow, undermine or weaken

the Soviet authority or to commit individual counter-revolutionary crimes." What information constituted anti-Soviet agitation and propaganda was left to the discretion of the state. Potential punishments under Clause 10 ranged from six months' incarceration to death by shooting.[21] Clause 10 was used to persecute numerous Soviet citizens. Given the secrecy that accompanied political trials, whether this group included journalists is uncertain.[22] (USSR=0/1)

3. Are media outlets' news and information content significantly determined by the government or a particular partisan interest? (Y=1; N=0)
Through 1950, the Soviet press played the role Stalin had prescribed for it: the "prime instrument through which the Party speaks daily, hourly, with the working class in its own indispensable language."[23] As head of the Communist Party, Stalin exercised substantial control over media content. At every administrative level of the USSR, party committees worked closely with editorial staff to offer political guidance. With newspaper and magazine editors appointed by the party, and with many themselves party members, this guidance did not go unheeded.[24] Pervasive censorship, which is detailed below, further cemented Stalin's ability to determine media content. (USSR=1)

4. Is there official censorship? (Y=1; N=0)
By 1943, a system of censorship was already well established inside the Soviet Union. During the 1930s, the Soviet government set up the *Glavlit*, a censorship office. It was tasked with pre- and postpublication censorship over all information pertaining to the USSR's political, economic, and military security. Guiding the *Glavlit's* activities was the *perechen*, a list of information that constituted state secrets. The central *Glavlit* in Moscow was replicated at lower administrative levels: *Glavlit* agents were posted to media outlets across the Soviet Union. The formidable censorship apparatus developed over the 1930s was tightened during World War II, and remained in place until Stalin's death.[25] (USSR=1)

5. Are journalists or media outlets subject to extralegal intimidation or physical violence by state authorities? (Y=1; N=0)
Glavlit agents routinely reported what they censored to the Soviet secret police.[26] This amounted to extralegal intimidation of the media by state authorities. (USSR=1)

6. Are significant portions of the media owned or controlled by the government? (Y=1; N=0)
The Soviet government exercised total economic control over the media. It owned all newspapers, magazines, telegraphic agencies, and broadcasting studios. Moreover, state ownership extended to the inputs and infrastructure required for the media to operate—printing plants, newsprint, cables, telegraph lines, railroads, and so on.[27] (USSR=1)

Score: USSR=5/6; Unfree Press

Chapter 6: Emerging Superpower

1. Does the constitution protect freedom of the press? (Y=0; N=1)
China's constitution contains a provision safeguarding freedom of the press—Article 35. But subsequent constitutional provisions undermine this right. Article 53 requires citizens to keep state secrets, while Article 54 demands that citizens protect the "honour and interests of the motherland."[28] Collectively, these two articles create a constitutional basis for censorship. (China=1)

2. Do the penal code, security laws, or any other laws restrict reporting and are journalists punished under these laws? (Y=1; N=0)
Article 105 of China's Criminal Law and Article 4 of China's State Security Law provide a foundation for suppressing the media. The former law criminalizes "incitement to subvert the political power of the state and overthrow the socialist system by spreading rumors, slander or other means." The latter law outlaws "stealing, secretly gathering, buying, or unlawfully providing State secrets."[29] In effect, both laws restrict any reporting the Chinese government deems detrimental to its interests. Journalists who challenge the legitimacy of Communist Party rule or publish investigative pieces unfavorable to the state can be charged with "revealing state secrets" or "inciting subversion." In 2012, at least twenty-seven reporters imprisoned in China were incarcerated for such antistate crimes.[30] (China=1)

3. Are media outlets' news and information content significantly determined by the government or a particular partisan interest? (Y=1; N=0)

Chinese authorities exercise substantial control over media content. The Communist Party's Central Propaganda Department oversees all news outlets. It can order journalists to drop coverage of an issue, run a particular story, or skew reporting in ways sympathetic to the government. At the subnational level, branches of the Communist Party contain propaganda organs that provide "guidance" for reporting on local news.[31]

The Chinese government also influences media content through more subtle economic inducements. Typically, Chinese journalists receive a low base salary along with bonuses for reports they publish or broadcast. This creates a financial incentive to avoid topics likely to run afoul of the government. Salary schemes thus encourage journalists to engage in self-censorship.[32]

Last, the Chinese government actively shapes online content—an increasingly significant medium given China's more than 590 million web users.[33] Starting in 2005, the Chinese Communist Party has paid individual citizens to post progovernment comments on websites and messaging boards. This army of Internet commentators reportedly numbers over 200,000 strong.[34] (China=1)

4. Is there official censorship? (Y=1; N=0)

All Chinese media outlets are subject to regulations delineating inappropriate types of content. Information unfit for public consumption includes anything that "disrupts the social order or undermines social stability" or is "detrimental to social morality or to the finer cultural traditions of the nation."[35] In practice, this means topics like the PLA, the Communist Party's internal dynamics, ethnic unrest in Tibet and Xinjiang, Taiwanese independence, and the Falun Gong are off-limits to journalists. The Chinese government also constrains media coverage on a case by case basis.[36]

China has perfected methods of online censorship. Government regulation requires Internet service providers to block websites featuring content deemed politically subversive. At the government's behest, providers filter searches to direct Chinese web users away from locations containing politically sensitive information. Providers also delete postings critical of the authorities. In extreme cases, the Chinese government has temporarily ordered the shutdown of Internet data centers hosting problematic websites.[37] (China=1)

5. Are journalists or media outlets subject to extralegal intimidation or physical violence by state authorities? (Y=1; N=0)

Physical violence against Chinese journalists is a common occurrence outside Beijing. Local officials use the police or hired thugs to assault reporters pursuing unflattering stories. Another violent form of suppression utilized by Chinese authorities is coerced hospitalization. This tactic was employed against at least one journalist. Finally, the Central Propaganda Department can intimidate reporters by publicly denouncing them and stripping them of media accreditation.[38] (China=1)

6. Are significant portions of the media owned or controlled by the government? (Y=1; N=0)

The Chinese government maintains direct control over a considerable swath of the domestic media. Xinhua, China Radio International, China Central Television, *Guangming Daily*, and *People's Daily*—all major national media outlets—constitute extensions of the state. They are run by high-ranking Communist Party cadres and tasked with conveying the official line to the public. Below the national level, provincial and municipal authorities exercise direct control over numerous local newspapers and television stations. Economic reforms have produced an extensive commercial press dependent on advertising revenue rather than government subsidies. However, privatization of ownership has not accompanied commercialization. As a result, the Chinese government retains effective economic control over all media outlets, not just ones that are state run.[39] (China=1)

Score: China=6; Unfree Press

Notes

Chapter 1. Fateful Transitions

1. Zeev Maoz and Bruce Russett, "Normative and Structural Causes of the Democratic Peace, 1946–1986," *American Political Science Review* 87, 3 (September 1993): 624.

2. On normative arguments, see Bruce Russett, *Grasping the Democratic Peace: Principles for a Post-Cold War World* (Princeton, N.J.: Princeton University Press, 1993), 31–35; William J. Dixon, "Democracy and Peaceful Settlement of International Conflict," *American Political Science Review* 88, 1 (March 1994): 15–18; Spencer R. Weart, *Never at War: Why Democracies Will Not Fight One Another* (New Haven, Conn.: Yale University Press, 1998), 77–87, 87–93; Sebastian Rosato, "The Flawed Logic of Democratic Peace Theory," *American Political Science Review* 97, 4 (November 2003): 586.

3. Russett, 38–39; Michael W. Doyle, "Kant, Liberal Legacies, and Foreign Affairs," in Michael E. Brown, Sean M. Lynn-Jones, and Steven E. Miller, eds., *Debating the Democratic Peace* (Cambridge, Mass.: MIT Press, 1997), 24–25.

4. Maoz and Russett, 625–26; Rosato, 587; Bruce Bueno de Mesquita and David Lalman, *War and Reason: Domestic and International Imperatives* (New Haven, Conn.: Yale University Press, 1992), 155–56.

5. Bruce Bueno de Mesquita, James D. Morrow, Randolph M. Siverson, and Alastair Smith, "An Institutional Explanation of the Democratic Peace," *American Political Science Review* 93, 4 (December 1999): 791–807; Bruce Bueno de Mesquita, James D. Morrow, Randolph M. Siverson, and Alastair Smith, *The Logic of Political Survival* (Cambridge, Mass.: MIT Press, 2003).

6. Joanne Gowa, *Ballots and Bullets: The Elusive Democratic Peace* (Princeton, N.J.: Princeton University Press, 1999), 62–63, 113.

7. David E. Spiro, "The Insignificance of the Liberal Peace," *International Security* 19, 2 (Fall 1994): 60–62.

8. Christopher Layne, "Kant or Cant: The Myth of the Democratic Peace," *International Security* 19, 2 (Fall 1994): 38.

9. Rosato, 587–99.

10. Edward D. Mansfield and Jack Snyder, "Democratization and the Danger of War," *International Security* 20, 1 (Summer 1995): 5–38; Edward D. Mansfield and Jack

Snyder, "Democratic Transitions, Institutional Strength, and War," *International Security* 56, 2 (Spring 2002): 297–337; Edward D. Mansfield and Jack Snyder, *Electing to Fight: Why Emerging Democracies Go to War* (Cambridge, Mass.: MIT Press, 2007).

11. John R. Oneal and Bruce Russett, "The Kantian Peace: The Pacific Benefits of Democracy, Interdependence, and International Organizations," *World Politics* 52, 1 (October 1999): 34.

12. John M. Owen, *Liberal Peace, Liberal War: American Politics and International Security* (Ithaca, N.Y.: Cornell University Press, 1997), 22–59, 158–72.

13. Charles Lipson, *Reliable Partners: How Democracies Have Made a Separate Peace* (Princeton, N.J.: Princeton University Press, 2003), 14, 150–52.

14. David Kinsella, "No Rest for the Democratic Peace," *American Political Science Review* 99, 3 (August 2005): 453–57.

15. Branislav L. Slantchev, Anna Alexandrova, and Erik Gartzke, "Probabilistic Causality, Selection Bias, and the Logic of the Democratic Peace," *American Political Science Review* 99, 3 (August 2005): 459–62.

16. Michael W. Doyle, "Three Pillars of the Liberal Peace," *American Political Science Review* 99, 3 (August 2005): 463, italics removed.

17. John R. Oneal, Bruce Russett, and Michael L. Berbaum, "Causes of Peace: Democracy, Interdependence, and International Organizations," *International Studies Quarterly* 47, 3 (September 2003): 384.

18. Vipin Narang and Rebecca M. Nelson, "Who Are These Belligerent Democratizers? Reassessing the Impact of Democratization on War," *International Organization* 63, 2 (Spring 2009): 357–79. For an earlier and less systematic critique of the democratization and war hypothesis, see Michael McFaul, "Are New Democracies War-Prone?" *Journal of Democracy* 18, 2 (2007): 160–67.

19. In the language of social science, the argument faces a "least-likely" test. See Harry Eckstein, "Case Study and Theory in Political Science," in Fred I. Greenstein and Nelson W. Polsby, eds., *Handbook of Political Science*, vol. 1, *Political Science: Scope and Theory* (Reading, Mass.: Addison-Wesley, 1975); also see Gary King, Robert O. Keohane, and Sidney Verba, *Designing Social Inquiry: Scientific Inference in Qualitative Research* (Princeton, N.J.: Princeton University Press, 1994), 209.

20. Paul Kennedy, *The Rise and Fall of the Great Powers: Economic Change and Military Conflict from 1500 to 2000* (New York: Random House, 1987), xv.

21. Robert Gilpin, *War and Change in World Politics* (New York: Cambridge University Press, 1981), 42–43.

22. Ibid., 186–87, 197–98. For a similar argument, see George Modelski, *Long Cycles in World Politics* (Seattle: University of Washington Press, 1987).

23. A. F. K. Organski, *World Politics* (New York: Knopf, 1958), 299–338.

24. Organski, 333; A. F. K. Organski and Jacek Kugler, *The War Ledger* (Chicago: University of Chicago Press, 1980), 59–60.

25. Douglas Lemke and Jacek Kugler, "The Evolution of the Power Transitions Perspective," in Douglas Lemke and Jacek Kugler, eds., *Parity and War: Evaluations and*

Extensions of the War Ledger (Ann Arbor: University of Michigan Press, 1996), 12; Robert Powell, *In the Shadow of Power: States and Strategies in International Politics* (Princeton, N.J.: Princeton University Press, 1999), 142.

26. On the effects of the nuclear revolution, see John Lewis Gaddis, "The Long Peace: Elements of Stability in the Postwar International System," *International Security* 10, 4 (Spring 1986): 120–23; and Stephen Van Evera, "Primed for Peace: Europe After the Cold War," *International Security* 15, 3 (Winter 1990–1991): 12–14. Gilpin recognizes that nuclear weapons render the cost of total war prohibitive, but argues that a series of limited wars may still displace the dominant state. See Gilpin, 216.

27. Woosang Kim and James D. Morrow, "When Do Power Shifts Lead to War?" *American Journal of Political Science* 36, 4 (November 1992): 897n1.

28. Stephen R. Rock, *When Peace Breaks Out: Great Power Rapprochement in Historical Perspective* (Chapel Hill: University of North Carolina Press, 1989).

29. Randall L. Schweller, "Domestic Structure and Preventive War: Are Democracies More Pacific?" *World Politics* 44, 2 (January 1992): 248–51.

30. Dale Copeland, *The Origins of Major Wars* (Ithaca, N.Y.: Cornell University Press, 2000).

31. Randall L. Schweller, "Managing the Rise of Great Powers: History and Theory," in Alastair Iain Johnston and Robert S. Ross, eds., *Engaging China: The Management of an Emerging Power* (New York: Routledge, 1999), 7–18.

32. David M. Edelstein, "Managing Uncertainty: Beliefs About Intentions and the Rise of Great Powers," *Security Studies* 12, 1 (Autumn 2002): 1–40.

33. Paul K. MacDonald and Joseph M. Parent, "Graceful Decline? The Surprising Success of Great Power Retrenchment," *International Security* 35, 4 (Spring 2011): 28.

34. G. John Ikenberry, "The Rise of China and the West: Can the Liberal System Survive?" *Foreign Affairs* 81, 1 (January/February 2008): 23–37. Parts of this paragraph were first published in Michael J. Green and Daniel M. Kliman, "China's Hard Power and the Potential for Conflict in Asia," *SERI Quarterly* 4, 2 (April 2011): 33–41, used here with coauthor permission.

35. Charles A. Kupchan, *How Enemies Become Friends: The Sources of Stable Peace* (Princeton, N.J.: Princeton University Press, 2010), 7.

36. Robert Art, "The United States and the Rise of China: Implications for the Long Haul," *Political Science Quarterly* 125, 3 (Fall 2010): 369–70.

37. Charles Glaser, "Will China's Rise Lead to War? Why Realism Does Not Mean Pessimism," *Foreign Affairs* 90, 2 (March/April 2011). An extended version of this argument is made in Charles L. Glaser, *Rational Theory of International Politics: The Logic of Competition and Cooperation* (Princeton, N.J.: Princeton University Press, 2010).

38. William C. Wohlforth, "Unipolarity, Status Competition, and Great Power War," *World Politics* 61, 1 (2009): 30.

39. A famous articulation of this argument is Norman Angell, *The Great Illusion: A Study of the Relation of Military Power in Nations to Their Economic and Social Advantage* (London: Putnam's, 1911).

40. Richard Rosecrance, *The Rise of the Trading State: Commerce and Conquest in the Modern World* (New York: Basic Books, 1986); Oneal and Russett, "The Kantian Peace." On the general construction of identity, see Alexander Wendt, *Social Theory of International Politics* (New York: Cambridge University Press, 1999).

41. This formulation is the "spirit of commerce" identified by Kant. Bruce Russett and John R. Oneal, *Triangulating Peace: Democracy, Interdependence, and International Organizations* (New York: Norton, 2001).

42. James D. Morrow, "How Could Trade Affect Conflict?" *Journal of Peace Research* 36, 4 (July 1999): 481–89; Erik Gartzke, Quan Li, and Charles Boehmer, "Investing in the Peace: The Impact of Economics on International Conflict," *International Organization* 55, 2 (Spring 2001): 392, 418; Havard Hegre, John R. Oneal, and Bruce Russett, "Trade Does Promote Peace: New Simultaneous Estimates of the Reciprocal Effects of Trade and Conflict," *Journal of Peace Research* 47, 6 (November 2010): 763–74.

43. Oneal and Russett, "The Kantian Peace," 34. Similar results are reported by Edward Mansfield, *Power, Trade, and War* (Princeton, N.J.: Princeton University Press, 1994); Rafael Reuveny and Heejoon Kang, "International Trade, Political Conflict/Cooperation, and Granger Causality," *American Journal of Political Science* 40, 3 (August 1996): 943–70; John R. Oneal and James Lee Ray, "New Tests of the Democratic Peace Controlling for Economic Interdependence, 1950–1985," *Political Research Quarterly* 5, 4 (December 1997): 751–75; Erik Gartzke, "Kant We All Just Get Along? Opportunity, Willingness, and the Origins of the Democratic Peace," *American Journal of Political Science* 42, 1 (January 1998): 1–27; John R. Oneal and Bruce Russett, "Assessing the Liberal Peace with Alternative Specifications: Trade Still Reduces Conflict," *Journal of Peace Research* 36, 4 (1999): 423–42.

44. Russett and Oneal, *Triangulating Peace*.

45. Katherine Barbieri, "Economic Interdependence: A Path to Peace or Source of Interstate Conflict?" *Journal of Peace Research* 33, 1 (February 1996): 29–49.

46. Dale C. Copeland, "Economic Interdependence and War: A Theory of Trade Expectations," *International Security* 20, 4 (Spring 1996): 7.

47. Gartzke, Li, and Boehmer, "Investing in the Peace," 395; John R. Oneal, Frances H. Oneal, Zeev Maoz, and Bruce Russett, "The Liberal Peace: Interdependence, Democracy, and International Conflict, 1950–1985," *Journal of Peace Research* 33, 1 (February 1996): 11–28; Oneal and Russet, "Assessing the Liberal Peace."

48. Oneal, Russett, and Berbaum, "Causes of Peace," 384–85.

49. Joanne Gowa and Edward D. Mansfield, "Power Politics and International Trade," *American Political Science Review* 87, 2 (June 1993): 408–20. Also see Joanne Gowa, *Allies, Adversaries, and International Trade* (Princeton, N.J.: Princeton University Press, 1995); Edward D. Mansfield and Rachel Bronson, "Alliances, Preferential Trading Arrangements, and International Trade Patterns," *American Political Science Review* 91, 1 (March 1997): 94–107.

50. Omar M. G. Keshk, Brian M. Pollins, and Rafael Reuveny, "Trade Still Follows the Flag: The Primacy of Politics in a Simultaneous Model of Interdependence and

Armed Conflict," *Journal of Politics* 66, 4 (November 2004): 1155–79; Hyung Min Kim and David L. Rousseau, "The Classical Liberals Were Half Right (or Half Wrong): New Tests of the 'Liberal Peace,' 1960–88," *Journal of Peace Research* 42, 5 (September 2005): 523–43.

51. Soo Yeon Kim, "Ties That Bind: The Role of Trade in International Conflict Processes, 1950–1992" (Ph.D. Dissertation, Yale University, 1998).

52. Oneal, Russett, and Berbaum in "Causes of Peace" control for joint democracy and joint membership in international governmental organizations. A similar finding on alliances is made by James D. Morrow, Randolph M. Siverson, and Tressa E. Tabares, "The Political Determinants of International Trade: The Major Powers, 1907–90," *American Political Science Review* 92, 3 (September 1998): 649–61.

53. Hegre, Oneal, and Russett, "Trade Does Promote Peace," 764.

54. Paul A. Papayoanou, "Interdependence, Institutions, and the Balance of Power: Britain, Germany, and World War I," *International Security* 20, 4 (Spring 1996): 42–76. Also see Paul A. Papayoanou, *Power Ties: Economic Interdependence, Balancing, and War* (Ann Arbor: University of Michigan Press, 1999).

55. Kevin Narizny, "The Political Economy of Alignment: Great Britain's Commitments to Europe, 1905–39," *International Security* 27, 4 (Spring 2003): 184–219. For a more complex version of this argument, see Kevin Narizny, *The Political Economy of Grand Strategy* (Ithaca, N.Y.: Cornell University Press, 2007).

Chapter 2. Power Shifts and Strategy

1. A. F. K. Organski and Jacek Kugler, *The War Ledger* (Chicago: University of Chicago Press, 1980), 33–34.

2. Indra de Soysa, John R. Oneal, and Yong-Hee Park, "Testing Power-Transition Theory Using Alternative Measures of National Capabilities," *Journal of Conflict Resolution* 41, 4 (August 1997): 509–28; Douglas Lemke and Suzanne Werner, "Power Parity, Commitment to Change, and War," *International Studies Quarterly* 40, 2 (June 1996): 235–60.

3. Fareed Zakaria, *From Wealth to Power: The Unusual Origins of America's World Role* (Princeton, N.J.: Princeton University Press, 1998).

4. Paul Kennedy also makes this argument in *The Rise and Fall of the Great Powers: Economic Change and Military Conflict from 1500 to 2000* (New York: Random House, 1987).

5. In 1870, China's economy was still nearly twice the size of Great Britain's. Angus Maddison, *The World Economy: A Millennial Perspective* (Paris: OECD, 2001), 261.

6. The disparity between Japan's economic and military capabilities has been widely noted by foreign policy analysts and scholars. See Yoichi Funabashi, "Japan and the New World Order," *Foreign Affairs* 70, 5 (Winter 1991/1992): 58–74; Joseph S. Nye, Jr., "The Changing Nature of World Power," *Political Science Quarterly* 102, 2 (Summer 1990): 182, 187; Peter J. Katzenstein, *Cultural Norms and National Security: Police and Military in Postwar Japan* (Ithaca, N.Y.: Cornell University Press, 1996).

7. To derive a single measure of national capabilities, the Correlates of War composite index divides a state's share of each indicator over the world total and computes the average of these scores. de Soysa, Oneal, and Park, 517.

8. For more information on omitted cases, see Appendix 1 to this volume.

9. Domestic costs in a democracy may rule out preventive war against a rising state. Crushing an emerging power when it remains too weak to pose a challenge will enjoy little popular support—the public will resist sacrificing blood and treasure for a conflict that appears solely motivated by a desire for continued national preeminence. For one account of why democracies do not wage preventive war, see Randall L. Schweller, "Domestic Structure and Preventive War: Are Democracies More Pacific?" *World Politics* 44, 2 (January 1992): 235–69.

10. Paul Kennedy, "The Tradition of Appeasement in British Foreign Policy, 1865–1939," in Paul Kennedy, *Strategy and Diplomacy, 1870–1945* (London: Allen and Unwin, 1983), 16.

11. Emphasis omitted. Stephen R. Rock, *Appeasement in International Politics* (Lexington: University Press of Kentucky, 2000), 12.

12. Paul W. Schroeder, "Alliances, 1815–1945: Weapons of Power and Tools of Management," in Klaus Knorr, ed., *Historical Dimensions of National Security Problems* (Lawrence: University Press of Kansas, 1975), 227–62.

13. G. John Ikenberry, *After Victory: Institutions, Strategic Restraint, and the Rebuilding of Order After Major Wars* (Princeton, N.J.: Princeton University Press, 2001), 40–42, 64.

14. Randall L. Schweller, "Managing the Rise of Great Powers: History and Theory," in Alastair Iain Johnston and Robert S. Ross, eds., *Engaging China: The Management of an Emerging Power* (New York: Routledge, 1999), 13.

15. The paucity of international governmental organizations during the nineteenth and first half of the twentieth centuries is noted in Bruce Russett, John R. Oneal, and David R. Davis, "The Third Leg of the Kantian Tripod for Peace: International Organizations and Militarized Disputes," *International Organization* 52, 3 (Summer 1998): 442–43.

16. Schweller, "Managing the Rise of Great Powers," 15.

17. Rock, *Appeasement in International Politics*, 12.

18. Evan S. Medeiros, "Strategic Hedging and the Future of Asia-Pacific Stability," *Washington Quarterly* 29, 1 (Winter 2005–2006): 145.

19. When discussing alliances in the abstract, I use Stephen Walt's expansive definition: a "formal or informal arrangement for security cooperation between two or more sovereign states." Stephen Walt, *The Origins of Alliances* (Ithaca, N.Y.: Cornell University Press, 1987), 12.

20. George Kennan introduced the term "containment" in July 1947. See John Lewis Gaddis, *Strategies of Containment: A Critical Appraisal of Postwar American National Security Policy* (Oxford: Oxford University Press, 1982), 4.

21. The linkage between a nation's military capabilities and attractiveness as an ally is not always recognized. For example, James Morrow argues that arms and allies are perfect substitutes. See James D. Morrow, "Arms Versus Allies: Trade-Offs in the Search for Security," *International Organization* 47, 2 (Spring 1993): 207–33.

22. My definition of transparency draws on Charles Lipson, *Reliable Partners: How Democracies Have Made a Separate Peace* (Princeton, N.J.: Princeton University Press, 2003), 6–7; Ikenberry, *After Victory*, 76.

23. Kurt Taylor Gaubatz, "Democratic States and Commitment in International Relations," *International Organization* 50, 1 (Winter 1996): 122.

24. Lipson, 11.

25. This concept of access draws on work by Albert Hirschman, *Exit, Voice, and Loyalty: Responses to Decline in Firms, Organizations, and States* (Cambridge, Mass.: Harvard University Press, 1970); Ikenberry, *After Victory*, 77; Michael Mastanduno, "The United States Political System and International Leadership: A 'Decidedly Inferior' Form of Government?" in G. John Ikenberry, ed., *American Foreign Policy: Theoretical Essays*, 2nd ed. (New York: HarperCollins, 1996), 336, 343.

26. Exploiting internal divisions is a tactic used by foreign governments in what is arguably the world's most open political system—that of the United States. See Mastanduno, 336. On the use of access by the United States, see Leonard J. Schoppa, "Two-Level Games and Bargaining Outcomes: Why Gaiatsu Succeeds in Japan in Some Cases But Not Others," *International Organization* 37, 43 (Summer 1993): 353–86.

27. Normally, states consider capabilities and intentions to be coterminous. Most military capabilities can be used for offensive or defensive purposes. Without an alternative source of information about a state's intentions, other states will therefore infer expansionist ambitions from an increase in military strength. Robert Jervis, *Perceptions and Misperceptions in International Politics* (Princeton, N.J.: Princeton University Press, 1976), 64–65, 68. On the difficulty of differentiating between offensive and defensive weapons, see Robert Jervis, "Cooperation Under the Security Dilemma," *World Politics* 30, 2 (January 1978): 199–206.

28. Lipson, 79–80, 87–90.

29. This assessment of how international institutions impose constraints over time draws on Robert O. Keohane, *After Hegemony: Cooperation and Discord in the World Economy* (Princeton, N.J.: Princeton University Press, 1984), 101–4; Ikenberry, *After Victory*, 69–70.

30. Perceptions of regime type may hinge on the behavior of a rising state. For example, Americans during World War II came to believe their Soviet ally was becoming less autocratic, but as tensions with Moscow increased after the conflict's end, this perception reversed. In reality, the Soviet Union remained a totalitarian state throughout this period. On how democratic states may subjectively perceive regime type, see Ido Oren, "The Subjectivity of the 'Democratic' Peace: Changing U.S. Perceptions of Imperial Germany," *International Security* 20, 2 (Fall 1995): 147–84.

31. The Polity IV codebook recognizes the limitations of polity scores in the middle of the scale. See Monty G. Marshall, Keith Jaggers, and Ted Robert Gurr, *Polity IV Project: Dataset Users' Manual*, November 2010, 17.

32. Thorsten Beck, George Clarke, Alberto Groff, Philip Keefer, and Patrick Walsh, "New Tools in Comparative Political Economy: The Database of Political Institutions," *World Bank Economic Review* 15, 1 (September 2001): 165–76; Philip Keefer and David Stasavage, "The Limits of Delegation: Veto Players, Central Bank Independence, and the Credibility of Monetary Policy," *American Political Science Review* 77, 3 (August 2003): 407–23.

33. These democracies include Austria (1976–1983), Finland (1996–1999), Greece (1986–2004), Iceland (1998–2004), Japan (1987–1993; 2001–2004), New Zealand (1976–1992), Norway (1975–1981), and Switzerland (1975–1995).

34. On this coding procedure, see Appendix 2 to this volume. Also see Philip Keefer, *Database of Political Institutions: Changes and Variable Definitions*, World Bank Research Group, December 2007, 19–20.

35. Some of these questions have been modified from the original format. They are taken from recent surveys, including Freedom House, *Freedom of the Press 2013: Middle East Volatility Amidst Global Decline* (Washington, D.C.: Freedom House, 2013), 37–38.

Chapter 3. Pax Britannica Eclipsed

1. D. J. Coppock, "The Causes of the Great Depression, 1873–1896," *Manchester School of Economic and Social Studies* 29, 3 (1961): 227.

2. Calculations based on GDP figures from Angus Maddison, *Historical Statistics for the World Economy: 1–2003 AD*, table 2, last updated August 2007, http://www.ggdc .net/maddison/.

3. Bradford Perkins, *The Great Rapprochement: England and the United States, 1895–1914* (New York: Atheneum, 1968), 126–27; Ross J. S. Hoffman, *Great Britain and the German Trade Rivalry, 1875–1914* (Philadelphia: University of Pennsylvania Press, 1933), 114–48, 168–97.

4. Calculations based on trade figures from Katherine Barbieri, Omar Keshk, and Brian Pollins, *Correlates of War Project* (hereafter cited as COW) *Trade Data, Version 2.01*, 2008, http://correlatesofwar.org.

5. On the growth of British military spending, see Aaron L. Friedberg, *The Weary Titan: Britain and the Experience of Relative Decline, 1895–1905* (Princeton, N.J.: Princeton University Press, 1988), 97–98. For a description of U.S. demobilization, see Kenneth Bourne, *Britain and the Balance of Power in North America, 1815–1908* (Berkeley: University of California Press, 1967), 336.

6. Calculations based on military expenditure figures from the COW *National Material Capabilities dataset, Version 3.02*, http://correlatesofwar.org.

7. Calculation based on steel production figures from the COW *National Material Capabilities dataset*. Note that before 1900, COW figures are estimates based on crude pig iron output.

8. Bourne, 308, 336–37.

9. Calculations based on warship tonnage figures from Table 20 in Paul Kennedy, *The Rise and Fall of the Great Powers: Economic Change and Military Conflict from 1500 to 2000* (New York: Random House, 1987), 203.

10. Bourne, 337–38; Arthur J. Marder, *The Anatomy of British Sea Power: A History of British Naval Policy in the Pre-Dreadnought Era, 1880–1905* (New York: Knopf, 1940), 442.

11. Paul Kennedy, *The Rise of the Anglo-German Antagonism, 1860–1914* (London: Allen and Unwin, 1980), 286, 451; Zara S. Steiner, *Britain and the Origins of the First World War* (London: Macmillan, 1977), 49; Marder, 289–90, 460.

12. One far-sighted intellectual was John Seeley, who predicted in 1882 that Russia and the United States would "surpass in power the states now called great as much as the great country-states of the sixteenth century surpassed Florence," quoted in Friedberg, 32–33.

13. Friedberg, 44.

14. Ibid., 80–81.

15. "Royal Commission on the Depression of Trade and Industry: Final Report," quoted in ibid., 39–40.

16. Ibid., 41; Hoffman, 230.

17. Quote from a *Times* article published on October 6, 1891. Cited in Hoffman, 227n6. The *Times* had intimate ties to the British political establishment, and was thus representative of elite opinion. Perkins, 7.

18. Hoffman, 231, 234, 239–40; 239, 240 include the excerpts from "Decay of the Iron Industry."

19. Ibid., 230–32.

20. Friedberg, 45.

21. "Board of Trade Memorandum on the Comparative Statistics of Population, Industry and Commerce in the United Kingdom and Some Leading Foreign Countries," quoted in ibid., 49–50.

22. Ibid., 139.

23. Bourne, 310.

24. "Reinforcements of Colonial Garrisons in Time of Anticipated War," quoted in Friedberg, 162.

25. Bourne, 336.

26. Lord Selborne quoted in George Monger, *The End of Isolation: British Foreign Policy, 1900–1907* (London: Thomas Nelson, 1963), 72n1.

27. Marder, 442–43.

28. Ibid., 288, 294–95.

29. Reginald Custance quoted in ibid., 463.

30. Kennedy, *The Rise of the Anglo-German Antagonism*, 252.

31. Friedberg, 179, 190–91.

32. Data from Center for Systemic Peace, Polity IV Annual Time-Series, 1800–2012, http://www.systemicpeace.org/inscr/inscr.htm.

33. Kennedy, *The Rise of the Anglo-German Antagonism*, 403.

34. Keith Werhan, *Freedom of Speech: A Reference Guide to the United States Constitution* (Westport, Conn.: Praeger, 2004), 9.

35. During the 1890s, independent newspapers dominated the twenty-five largest U.S. cities. Ted C. Smythe, *The Gilded Age Press, 1865–1900* (Westport, Conn.: Praeger, 2003), 17–18, 56, 206.

36. Gary D. Stark, "Trials and Tribulations: Authors' Responses to Censorship in Imperial Germany, 1885–1914," *German Studies Review* 12, 3 (October 1989): 448; Alex Hall, "The War of Words: Anti-Socialist Offensives and Counter-Propaganda in Wilhelmine Germany 1890–1914," *Journal of Contemporary History* 11, 2/3 (July 1976): 20. For a detailed analysis of media freedom in the United States and Germany, see Appendix 3 to this book.

37. Perkins, 15–16; Charles S. Campbell, *Anglo-American Understanding, 1898–1903* (Baltimore: Johns Hopkins University Press, 1957), 11–15; Ernest R. May, *Imperial Democracy: The Emergence of America as a Great Power* (New York: Harcourt, Brace, 1961), 45; Marshall Bertram, *The Birth of Anglo-American Friendship: The Prime Facet of the Venezuelan Boundary Dispute: A Study of the Interreaction of Diplomacy and Public Opinion* (Lanham, Md.: University Press of America, 1992), 34–35.

38. Grover Cleveland, "President Cleveland's Message on the Venezuelan Question," *New York Times*, December 18, 1895.

39. Bertram, 84; Stephen R. Rock, *Appeasement in International Politics* (Lexington: University Press of Kentucky, 2000), 27.

40. Campbell, 27–29; May, 50–51.

41. Rock, *Appeasement in International Politics*, 27–28; Perkins, 174–76; Campbell, 48, 51.

42. Perkins, 175, 178–81, 183; Campbell, 66–71.

43. Perkins, 162–65; Campbell, 50, 90–91.

44. This agreement was heavily skewed toward the U.S. position. Perkins, 164–65.

45. Ibid., 167.

46. Ibid., 168–71; Campbell, 109, 114, 116.

47. Rock, *Appeasement in International Politics*, 30; Campbell, 38.

48. Perkins, 164.

49. Spring-Rice to Ferguson in Stephen Gwynn, ed., *The Letters and Friendships of Sir Cecil Spring-Rice, a Record*, vol. 1 (Boston: Houghton Mifflin, 1929), 119.

50. Spring-Rice to Villiers in ibid., 175.

51. Spring-Rice to Ferguson in ibid., 57–58.

52. Spring-Rice to Stephen and Spring-Rice to Daisy in ibid., 72–73, 76.

53. Spring-Rice quoted in ibid., 51.

54. Bertram, 39–40.

55. J. A. S. Grenville, *Lord Salisbury and Foreign Policy: The Close of the Nineteenth Century* (London: Athlone, 1970), 67; Chamberlain quoted in May, 48.

56. Bertram, 67.

57. Historians have yet to confirm whether Gray was in fact speaking for Cleveland. Ibid., 68, 96.

58. Quote from *New York Journal of Commerce*, then a leading financial journal. Ibid., 62.

59. Ibid., 63; John M. Owen, "How Liberalism Produces Democratic Peace," *International Security* 19, 2 (Fall 1994): 117.

60. Salisbury to Victoria in George Earle Buckle, ed., *The Letters of Queen Victoria, Third Series: A Selection from Her Majesty's Correspondence and Journal Between the Years 1886 and 1901*, vol. 3 (New York: Longmans, Green, 1932), 14. Also see May, 49.

61. Salisbury quoted in Andrew Roberts, *Salisbury: Victorian Titan* (London: Weidenfeld and Nicolson, 1999), 617, 632; David Steele, *Lord Salisbury: A Political Biography* (London: UCL Press, 1999), 332.

62. Campbell, 43.

63. Chamberlain to Victoria in Buckle, *The Letters of Queen Victoria*, 75.

64. Campbell, 44–45.

65. Ibid., 41–42; Perkins, 41–46.

66. Balfour to Carnegie quoted in Perkins, 161.

67. Balfour before the House of Commons quoted in Bourne, 350.

68. Marder, 450. After 1904 the War Office continued to draft contingency plans for an Anglo-American conflict, but military planners regarded such scenarios as improbable. See Bourne, 394, and Grenville, 389. Moreover, the War Office was not representative of mainstream opinion within the British government. According to Grenville, it was a "lunatic fringe."

69. Grenville, 153–57.

70. Ibid., 317, 331.

71. D. W. Sweet, "Great Britain and Germany, 1905–1911," in F. H. Hinsley, ed., *British Foreign Policy Under Sir Edward Grey* (Cambridge: Cambridge University Press, 1977), 216, 218; and Steiner, 49. The British viewed limiting Germany's naval buildup as essential to preserving cordial relations. David Lloyd George, *War Memoirs of David Lloyd George, 1914–1915* (Boston: Little, Brown, 1933), 17.

72. Sweet, "Great Britain and Germany, 1905–1911," 218, 222–23; Lloyd George, 21.

73. Steiner, 54–57; Sweet, "Great Britain and Germany, 1905–1911," 228–29, 233.

74. Friedberg, 181–90, 194–95; Steiner, 31–32.

75. Fisher quoted in Kennedy, *The Rise of the Anglo-German Antagonism*, 420.

76. On the advent of the dreadnought class of battleships, see Marder, 515–45. Shipbuilding figures are from Friedberg, 153; Steiner, 49, 52–54, 57; and Sweet, "Great Britain and Germany, 1905–1911," 232.

77. Monger, 108, 134–35; Steiner, 29. Although segments of the British government perceived the Anglo-French entente as anti-German from its inception, key members like Lansdowne and Balfour did not. Kennedy, *The Rise of the Anglo-German Antagonism*, 266–67.

78. From December 1905 to May 1906, Great Britain and France undertook military

talks to explore the concept of a British expeditionary force. However, the entente remained far from a formal alliance. Monger, 190–92; Steiner, 194; Kennedy, *The Rise of the Anglo-German Antagonism*, 283.

79. Grey quoted in Monger, 281–82; Kennedy, *The Rise of the Anglo-German Antagonism*, 441.

80. Spring-Rice to Strachey in Kennedy, *The Rise of the Anglo-German Antagonism*, 431.

81. Eyre Crow, "Memorandum on the Present State of British Relations with France and Germany," in G. P. Gooch and Harold Temperley, eds., *British Documents on the Origins of the War, 1898–1914*, vol. 3, *The Testing of the Entente, 1904–1906* (London: HMSO, 1928), 407.

82. Kennedy, *The Rise of the Anglo-German Antagonism*, 316–17.

83. Ibid., 254–55, 269.

84. Sweet, "Great Britain and Germany, 1905–1911," 227–28; Steiner, 63; Lloyd George, 12.

85. Marder, 459; Steiner, 175.

86. Kennedy, *The Rise of the Anglo-German Antagonism*, 269; Sweet, "Great Britain and Germany, 1905–1911," 216.

87. Selborne quoted in Steiner, 31; Marder, 464.

88. Kennedy, *The Rise of the Anglo-German Antagonism*, 444; Steiner, 57; and Sweet, "Great Britain and Germany, 1905–1911," 218, 227.

89. Kennedy, *The Rise of the Anglo-German Antagonism*, 219.

90. Salisbury quoted in ibid., 219–20.

91. Grenville, 98–103; and Spring-Rice to Francis and Spring-Rice to Villiers in Gwynn, *The Letters and Friendships of Sir Cecil Spring-Rice*, 188–89, 195–96.

92. Grenville, 163.

93. Salisbury quoted in ibid., 277. For an exhaustive treatment of the Samoan dispute, see Paul Kennedy, *The Samoan Tangle: A Study in Anglo-German-American Relations, 1878–1900* (New York: Barnes and Noble, 1974).

94. Lansdowne quoted in Thomas Wodehouse Newton, *Lord Lansdowne: A Biography* (London: Macmillan, 1929), 338.

95. Kennedy, *The Rise of the Anglo-German Antagonism*, 409.

96. Spring-Rice to Villiers in Gwynn, *The Letters and Friendships of Sir Cecil Spring-Rice*, 243.

97. Lascelles quoted in Newton, *Lord Lansdowne*, 331.

98. Lansdowne quoted in ibid., 332.

99. Kennedy, *The Rise of the Anglo-German Antagonism*, 398.

100. Lloyd George, 30. On Lloyd George's view of Germany, also see Kenneth O. Morgan, "Lloyd George and Germany," *Historical Journal* 39, 3 (September 1996): 758.

101. M. L. Dockrill, "British Policy During the Agadir Crisis of 1911," in F. H. Hinsley, ed., *British Foreign Policy Under Sir Edward Grey* (Cambridge: Cambridge University Press, 1977), 270–73.

102. Ibid., 284; Kennedy, *The Rise of the Anglo-German Antagonism*, 449.

103. Asquith quoted in Dockrill, "British Policy During the Agadir Crisis of 1911," 281; Bentley B. Gilbert, "Pacifist to Interventionist: David Lloyd George in 1911 and 1914. Was Belgium an Issue?" *Historical Journal* 28, 4 (December 1985): 871; Steiner, 73–74, 200.

104. Gilbert, "Pacifist to Interventionist," 866–68; Steiner, 140; Dockrill, "British Policy During the Agadir Crisis of 1911," 278; Kennedy, *The Rise of the Anglo-German Antagonism*, 448–49.

105. Lloyd George quoted in Gilbert, "Pacifist to Interventionist," 875.

106. Dockrill, "British Policy During the Agadir Crisis of 1911," 282–83.

107. Steiner, 95–97; Richard T. B. Langhorne, "Great Britain and Germany, 1911–1914," in Hinsley, ed., *British Foreign Policy Under Sir Edward Grey*, 290; Richard Langhorne, "The Naval Question in Anglo-German Relations, 1912–1914," *Historical Journal* 14, 2 (June 1971): 359, 363, 366.

108. Grey quoted in Langhorne, "The Naval Question in Anglo-German Relations," 367.

109. Kennedy, *The Rise of the Anglo-German Antagonism*, 449, 452; Steiner, 200.

110. Steiner, 104, 209.

111. Great Britain submitted a similar query to the French government, which responded affirmatively. Michael G. Ekstein and Zara Steiner, "The Sarajevo Crisis," in Hinsley, ed., *British Foreign Policy Under Sir Edward Grey*, 406–7.

112. Ibid., 408; Steiner, 237.

113. Grey quoted in Steiner, 239.

114. Arthur Marsden, "The Blockade," in Hinsley, ed., *British Foreign Policy Under Sir Edward Grey*, 488.

115. Gilbert, "Pacifist to Interventionist," 879–85.

116. Ekstein and Steiner, "The Sarajevo Crisis," 407–9; Gilbert, "Pacifist to Interventionist," 865; Trevor Wilson, "Britain's Moral Commitment to France in August, 1914," *History* 64, 212 (October 1979): 385–86, 390.

117. Trade to GDP percentage figures are based on data from Bruce Russett and John R. Oneal, *Triangulating Peace: Democracy, Interdependence, and International Organizations* (New York: Norton, 2001). Available at http://pantheon.yale/edu/~brusset/PeaceStata.zip. Figures on British investment in the United States cited in Perkins, 122, 124. In the pre–World War I period, *all* of Europe took less than 10 percent of British foreign investments. Kennedy, *The Rise of the Anglo-German Antagonism*, 293–95; Steiner, 62.

118. Bertram, 59–60, 95–96; Steele, 331.

119. Lloyd George, 61; Steiner, 234; and Kennedy, *The Rise of the Anglo-German Antagonism*, 304, 459.

120. John J. Mearsheimer, *The Tragedy of Great Power Politics* (New York: Norton, 2001), 44.

121. Great Britain's capacity to oppose French colonial expansion at Fashoda in 1898 indicates that until the Boer War, resource constraints did not preclude a confrontational

approach toward other powers. For a general survey of the Fashoda crisis, see Darrell Bates, *The Fashoda Incident of 1898: Encounter on the Nile* (New York: Oxford University Press, 1984).

122. Campbell, 195–96.

123. Perkins, 313.

124. Kennedy, *The Rise of the Anglo-German Antagonism*, 386, 388–89.

Chapter 4. Germany Resurgent

1. Versions of the appeasement narrative include Winston S. Churchill, *The Second World War*, vol. 1, *The Gathering Storm* (Boston: Houghton Mifflin, 1948); Robert Vansittart, *The Mist Procession* (London: Hutchinson, 1958); and Martin Gilbert and Richard Gott, *The Appeasers* (Boston: Houghton Mifflin, 1963). More contemporary historians benefiting from unfettered access to official archives have debunked the appeasement narrative. I draw on their work in this chapter.

2. On Germany and the Treaty of Versailles, see Margaret Macmillan, *Paris 1919: Six Months That Changed the World* (New York: Random House, 2003), 167–203. Between 1929 and 1932, industrial production in Germany declined by a considerably greater percentage than in Great Britain. Peter Temin, *Lessons from the Great Depression* (Cambridge, Mass.: MIT Press, 1989), 2.

3. On the recovery of the German economy under Hitler, see Richard Grunberger, *The 12-Year Reich: A Social History of Nazi Germany, 1933–1945* (New York: Holt, Rinehart and Winston, 1971), 19, 29; and William L. Shirer, *The Rise and Fall of the Third Reich: A History of Nazi Germany* (New York: Simon and Schuster, 1960), 258–59.

4. Calculations based on GDP figures from Angus Maddison, *Historical Statistics for the World Economy: 1–2003 AD*, table 2, last updated August 2007, http://www.ggdc .net/maddison/. For a definitive treatment of the German economy under Hitler, see Adam Tooze, *The Wages of Destruction: The Making and Breaking of the Nazi Economy* (London: Allen Lane, 2006).

5. The British share of world trade in 1932 was 13.4 percent. While Great Britain remained by far the world's largest importer, its total exports trailed those of the United States and Germany. Walter A. Morton, *British Finance, 1930–1940* (Madison: University of Wisconsin Press, 1943), 202, table 5; League of Nations, *World Economic Survey 1932–1933* (Geneva: Economic Intelligence Service, 1933), 218.

6. William Carr, *Arms, Autarky and Aggression: A Study in German Foreign Policy, 1933–1939* (London: Edward Arnold, 1972), 49–65, 105. A classic account of German economic policy toward Southeastern Europe can be found in Albert O. Hirschman, *National Power and the Structure of Foreign Trade* (Berkeley: University of California Press, 1945), 34–40. All trade figures are based on data from Katherine Barbieri, Omar Keshk, and Brian Pollins, *COW Project Trade Data, Version 2.01*, 2008, http://correlatesofwar.org.

7. James P. Levy, *Appeasement and Rearmament: Britain, 1936–1939* (Lanham, Md.: Rowman and Littlefield, 2006), 51; Wesley K. Wark, *The Ultimate Enemy: British Intelligence and Nazi Germany, 1933–1939* (Ithaca, N.Y.: Cornell University Press, 1985), 18.

8. Calculations based on military expenditure figures from the COW *National Material Capabilities dataset, Version 3.02*, http://correlatesofwar.org.

9. Calculations based on steel production figures from the COW *National Material Capabilities dataset*.

10. Wark, 127, 248; Levy, 80–81.

11. Wark, 35.

12. Calculations of relative strength in first-line aircraft are based on data from Wark, 244; and H. Montgomery Hyde, *British Air Policy Between the Wars, 1918–1939* (London: Heinemann, 1976), 334, 502.

13. Wark, 35.

14. Uri Bialer, *The Shadow of the Bomber: The Fear of Air Attack and British Politics, 1932–1939* (London: Royal Historical Society, 1980), 23.

15. Ibid., 20.

16. Ibid., 49–50, 69–70; John Rugierro, *Neville Chamberlain and British Rearmament: Pride, Prejudice, and Politics* (Westport, Conn.: Greenwood Press, 1999), 29.

17. Bialer, 70–73.

18. Ibid., 60; Donald Cameron Watt, "British Intelligence and the Coming of the Second World War in Europe," in Ernest R. May, ed., *Knowing One's Enemies: Intelligence Assessment Before the Two World Wars* (Princeton, N.J.: Princeton University Press, 1984), 256.

19. Foreign Office report quoted in Bialer, 24.

20. Ibid., 56, 61, 68–69, 71–74; Wark, 37–42; Watt, "British Intelligence and the Coming of the Second World War in Europe," 255–57.

21. Center for Systemic Peace, Polity IV Annual Time-Series, 1800–2012, http://www.systemicpeace.org/inscr/inscr.htm.

22. Shirer, 194–96, 198–201, 229–30; Richard J. Evans, *The Third Reich in Power, 1933–1939* (New York: Penguin, 2005), 13, 109–13, 637.

23. Peter J. Fliess, *Freedom of the Press in the German Republic, 1918–1933* (Baton Rouge: Louisiana State University Press, 1955), 9–15.

24. Reich Press Law quoted in Shirer, 245.

25. Ibid., 190, 194, 245–46; Grunberger, 393; Oron J. Hale, *The Captive Press in the Third Reich* (Princeton, N.J.: Princeton University Press, 1964), 86, 131, 137–38, 144, 151; Evans, 133, 144, 146. For a detailed analysis of media freedom in Nazi Germany, see Appendix 3 to this volume.

26. See Churchill, *The Second World War*, vol. 1; Vansittart, *The Mist Procession*.

27. Anthony R. Peters, *Anthony Eden at the Foreign Office, 1931–1938* (New York: St. Martin's, 1986), 43–44, 54; Bialer, 77–78.

28. Peters, 84; Gaines Post, Jr., *Dilemmas of Appeasement: British Deterrence and Defense, 1934–1937* (Ithaca, NY: Cornell University Press, 1993), 42–43; Joseph A. Maiolo, *The Royal Navy and Nazi Germany, 1933–1939: A Study in Appeasement and the Origins of the Second World War* (New York: St. Martin's, 1998), 34–38.

29. Peters, 223; Post, 250; Stephen R. Rock, *Appeasement in International Politics*

(Lexington: University Press of Kentucky, 2000), 56–58; Peter Neville, *Hitler and Appeasement: The British Attempt to Prevent the Second World War* (London: Hambledon, 2006), 76; Andrew J. Crozier, *Appeasement and Germany's Last Bid for Colonies* (Basingstoke: Macmillan, 1988), 196–97; Andrew Roberts, *"The Holy Fox": A Biography of Lord Halifax* (London: Weidenfeld and Nicolson, 1991), 70–73.

30. Vansittart's memorandum of February 3, 1936, quoted in Peters, 172.

31. Neville, 70–71; Post, 203; Maiolo, 46.

32. Neville, 74; Post, 270; Peters, 304–5; Halifax quoted in Rock, *Appeasement in International Politics*, 57.

33. Defence Requirements Committee report of February 28, 1934, quoted in Post, 32.

34. Levy, 57; Neville, 26, 123; Post, 37; Wark, 57.

35. Wark, 57; Levy, 108.

36. Levy, 57. Figures on military spending are from the COW *National Material Capabilities dataset, Version 3.02.*

37. Levy, 58, 83, 95; Neville, 37; Post, 233; N. J. Crowson, *Facing Fascism: The Conservative Party and the European Dictators, 1935–1940* (London: Routledge, 1997), 128–29.

38. On the dearth of intelligence sources in Nazi Germany, see Baldwin's recollections in "14 October 1938 Hinchingbrooke Note," in Philip Williamson and Edward Baldwin, eds., *Baldwin Papers: A Conservative Statesman, 1908–1947* (Cambridge: Cambridge University Press, 2004), 458–59.

39. Peters, 192–93; Rock, *Appeasement*, 52; note by Hankey quoted in Neville, 201.

40. Baldwin quoted in "12 June 1934 W. P. Crozier Interview Note," in Williamson and Baldwin, *Baldwin Papers*, 322.

41. Winston S. Churchill, *Great Contemporaries* (London: Thornton Butterworth, 1937), 261.

42. Rock, *Appeasement in International Politics*, 52; Crowson, 41–43.

43. To assess how these Cabinet members viewed Hitler, I have drawn on Robert Self, *Neville Chamberlain: A Biography* (Aldershot: Ashgate, 2006), 278–79; Graham Stewart, *Burying Caesar: Churchill, Chamberlain and the Battle for the Tory Party* (London: Weidenfeld and Nicolson, 1999), 290–91; David Dutton, *Simon: A Political Biography of Sir John Simon* (London: Aurum Press, 1993), 169–70, 255; Roberts, *"The Holy Fox"*, 47–48; and David Carlton, *Anthony Eden: A Biography* (London: Allen Lane, 1981), 124.

44. Neville, 146–48.

45. Vansittart quoted in Ian Colvin, *Vansittart in Office: An Historical Survey on the Origins of the Second World War Based on the Papers of Sir Robert Vansittart* (London: Gollancz, 1965), 23.

46. Vansittart was made chief diplomatic adviser to the government. Peters, 98; Neville, 140; Colvin, 171–74.

47. In his remarks to parliament after the occupation of the Rhineland, Churchill argued Germany would soon confront a choice between halting rearmament and going to war. He intimated Hitler would choose the latter option. Although Churchill in October 1937 published a more conciliatory article about Germany in the *Evening Standard*,

this was not reflective of his actual attitude. Privately, he retained grave misgivings about German aims, as evident in his letter to Lord Londonderry that same month. R. A. C. Parker, *Churchill and Appeasement* (London: Macmillan, 2000), 84; Martin Gilbert, *Churchill: A Life* (London: Heinemann, 1991), 581.

48. Parker, *Churchill and Appeasement*, 132, 143–44; Norman Rose, *Churchill: An Unruly Life* (London: Simon and Schuster, 1994): 241; R. A. C. Parker, *Chamberlain and Appeasement: British Policy and the Coming of the Second World War* (Basingstoke: Macmillan, 1993), 323, 325; Frank McDonough, *Neville Chamberlain, Appeasement, and the British Road to War* (New York: Manchester University Press, 1998), 102–12.

49. Alan Bullock, *Hitler: A Study in Tyranny* (New York: HarperPerennial, 1991), 149.

50. Rumbold to Simon, quoted in Neville, 146–47.

51. "28 July 1936: Reply to a Deputation of Conservative Peers and MPs," in Williamson and Baldwin, *Baldwin Papers*, 378.

52. Watt, "British Intelligence and the Coming of the Second World War in Europe," 249; Rock, *Appeasement in International Politics*, 53.

53. C. A. MacDonald, "Economic Appeasement and the German 'Moderates' 1937–1939. An Introductory Essay," *Past and Present* 56, 1 (August 1972): 105, 107.

54. Watt, "British Intelligence and the Coming of the Second World War in Europe," 250; Neville, 149; Roberts, *"The Holy Fox"*, 73.

55. Letter to Ida, September 3, 1938, in Robert Self, ed., *The Neville Chamberlain Diary Letters*, vol. 4, *The Downing Street Years, 1934–1940* (Aldershot: Ashgate, 2005), 342.

56. Letter to Ida, September 6, 1938, in ibid., 342.

57. Henderson quoted in Neville, 90.

58. Letter to Ida, September 3, 1938 in Self, *The Neville Chamberlain Diary Letters*, 342.

59. Letter to Ida, September 11, 1938, in ibid., 344.

60. For this reason the British government eschewed an official demarche on the Sudetenland until September 27. Parker, *Chamberlain and Appeasement*, 159; Neville, 90, 106.

61. Hitler quoted in Parker, *Chamberlain and Appeasement*, 163.

62. Robert Kee, *Munich: The Eleventh Hour* (London: Hamilton, 1988), 172–74.

63. Text of the Munich Agreement in ibid., 215.

64. Parker, *Chamberlain and Appeasement*, 180; Levy, 123.

65. Wark, 33; Post, 25, 37, 249; Peters, 277; Letters to Ida, July 4, November 26, 1937, 259, 286.

66. Levy, 119; Parker, *Chamberlain and Appeasement*, 177–78; Stewart, 306.

67. Letter to Ida, October 15, 1938, in Self, *The Neville Chamberlain Diary Letters*, 355.

68. Quote from Self, *The Neville Chamberlain Diary Letters*, 318–19; Parker, *Chamberlain and Appeasement*, 170–72; Roberts, *"The Holy Fox"*, 112–22.

69. Neville, 102; quote from Alec Douglas-Home, *The Way the Wind Blows: An Autobiography* (New York: Quadrangle/New York Times, 1976), 66.

70. Letter to Ida, September 11, 1938, in Self, *The Neville Chamberlain Diary Letters*, 348.

71. Kee, 216. Text of the Anglo-German declaration quoted in Parker, *Chamberlain and Appeasement*, 180.

72. Cabinet minutes of March 18, 1939, quoted in Parker, *Chamberlain and Appeasement*, 204.

73. Crowson, 39.

74. Cadogan's diary quoted in Neville, 145.

75. Levy, 74, 129, 132; Parker, *Chamberlain and Appeasement*, 192; Neville, 126, 156. Figures on military spending are from the COW *National Material Capabilities dataset, Version 3.02*.

76. Levy, 129, 131; Neville, 169, 171; Post, 341; Maiolo, 159, 177.

77. Neville, 175–78; Michael J. Carley, *1939: The Alliance That Never Was and the Coming of World War II* (Chicago: Ivan Dee, 1999), 144–212; Alan Bullock, *Hitler and Stalin: Parallel Lives* (London: HarperCollins, 1991), 684.

78. The Admiralty hoped to convince Germany to ratify a 40,000-ton limitation on battleships and join a global mechanism for disseminating warship details. Maiolo, 177, 179–82.

79. Parker, *Chamberlain and Appeasement*, 264–76; Neville, 186.

80. Correlli Barnett, *Engage the Enemy More Closely: The Royal Navy in the Second World War* (London: Hodder and Stoughton, 1991), 67–68.

81. Scott Newton, *Profits of Peace: The Political Economy of Anglo-German Appeasement* (New York: Oxford University Press, 1996), 145.

82. Letter to Hilda, September 10, 1939, in Self, *The Neville Chamberlain Diary Letters*, 445.

83. Trade to GDP percentage figures are based on data from Bruce Russett and John R. Oneal, *Triangulating Peace: Democracy, Interdependence, and International Organizations* (New York: Norton, 2001), available at http://pantheon.yale/edu/~brusset/PeaceStata.zip.

84. Neil Forbes, "London Banks, the German Standstill Agreements, and 'Economic Appeasement' in the 1930s," *Economic History Review* n.s. 40, 4 (November 1987): 573, 575; Newton, *Profits of Peace*, 58–59.

85. G. C. Peden, *British Rearmament and the Treasury: 1932–1939* (Edinburgh: Scottish Academic Press, 1979), 67–105. On the Treasury's struggle with the service departments, see Robert Shay, Jr., *British Rearmament in the Thirties: Politics and Profits* (Princeton, N.J.: Princeton University Press, 1977); and Dutton, 243–54.

86. Newton, *Profits of Peace*, 69–70; Peden, 64–67; Dutton, 252.

87. Newton, *Profits of Peace*, 91–92.

88. MacDonald, 121, 127.

Chapter 5. Red Star Rising

1. Calculations based on GDP figures from Angus Maddison, *Historical Statistics for the World Economy: 1–2003 AD*, table 2, http://www.ggdc.net/maddison.

2. Calculations based on trade figures from Katherine Barbieri, Omar Keshk, and Brian Pollins, *COW Trade Data, Version 2.01*, 2008, http://correlatesofwar.org.

3. Calculations based on military expenditure figures from COW *National Material Capabilities dataset, Version 3.02*, http://correlatesofwar.org.

4. David Holloway, *Stalin and the Bomb: The Soviet Union and Atomic Energy, 1939–1956* (New Haven, Conn.: Yale University Press, 1994), 88–105, 127–33, 172–95, 213–17; Robert S. Norris and William M. Arkin, "NRDC Nuclear Notebook: Global Nuclear Stockpiles, 1945–1997," *Bulletin of the Atomic Scientists* 53, 6 (November/December 1997): 67.

5. Roosevelt quoted in George C. Herring, Jr., *Aid to Russia, 1941–1946: Strategy, Diplomacy, the Origins of the Cold War* (New York: Columbia University Press, 1973), 104.

6. "Admiral William Leahy to Secretary of State Hull," in Lynn Etheridge Davis, *The Cold War Begins: Soviet-American Conflict over Eastern Europe* (Princeton, N.J.: Princeton University Press, 1974), 142.

7. Maurice Matloff, *Strategic Planning for Coalition Warfare, 1943–1944* (Washington, D.C.: Office of the Chief of Military History, Department of the Army, 1959), 292–93, 523.

8. "Russia—Seven Years Later," in George F. Kennan, *Memoirs: 1925–1950* (Boston: Little, Brown, 1967), 506.

9. Walter Millis, ed., *The Forrestal Diaries* (New York: Viking, 1951), 24.

10. Melvyn P. Leffler, "National Security and U.S. Foreign Policy," in Melvyn P. Leffler and David S. Painter, eds., *Origins of the Cold War: An International History* (London: Routledge, 1994), 30.

11. "American Relations with the Soviet Union: A Report to the President by the Special Counsel to the President, September 24, 1946," in Thomas H. Etzold and John Lewis Gaddis, eds., *Containment: Documents on American Policy and Strategy, 1945–1950* (New York: Columbia University Press, 1978), 65. This document is generally referred to as the Clifford-Elsey Report.

12. "NSC 7: The Position of the United States with Respect to Soviet-Directed World Communism, March 30, 1948," in Etzold and Gaddis, *Containment*, 165.

13. Data from Center for Systemic Peace, *Polity IV Annual Time-Series, 1800–2012*, http://www.systemicpeace.org/inscr/inscr.htm.

14. Yoram Gorlizki and Oleg Khlevniuk, *Cold Peace: Stalin and the Soviet Ruling Circle, 1945–1953* (Oxford: Oxford University Press, 2004), 7, 19–45, 51–52, 74–95.

15. Mark W. Hopkins, *Mass Media in the Soviet Union* (New York: Pegasus, 1970), 100; James W. Markham, *Voices of the Red Giants: Communications in Russia and China* (Ames: Iowa State University Press, 1967), 105.

16. Markham, 125–26; Hopkins, 95, 128.

17. Stalin quoted in Markham, 100.

18. Adam B. Ulam, *The Rivals: America and Russia Since World War II* (New York: Viking, 1971), 17; Wilson D. Miscamble, *From Roosevelt to Truman: Potsdam, Hiroshima, and the Cold War* (New York: Cambridge University Press, 2007), 63.

19. "American Relations with the Soviet Union: A Report to the President by the Special Counsel to the President, September 1946," in Arthur Krock, *Memoirs: Sixty*

Years on the Firing Line (New York: Funk and Wagnalls, 1968), 438; W. Averell Harriman and Elie Abel, *Special Envoy to Churchill and Stalin, 1941–1946* (New York: Random House, 1975), 237.

20. "American Relations with the Soviet Union," in Krock, 440; John Lewis Gaddis, *The United States and the Origins of the Cold War, 1941–1947* (New York: Columbia University Press, 1972), 28. For a detailed treatment of the Dumbarton Oaks negotiations, see Robert C. Hilderbrand, *Dumbarton Oaks: The Origins of the United Nations and the Search for Postwar Security* (Chapel Hill: University of North Carolina Press, 1990).

21. Ulam, 54; "American Relations with the Soviet Union," in Krock, 441; Gaddis, *Origins of the Cold War*, 235; Daniel Yergin, *Shattered Peace: The Origins of the Cold War and the National Security State* (Boston: Houghton Mifflin, 1977), 103; Robert J. Donovan, *Conflict and Crisis: The Presidency of Harry S. Truman, 1945–1948* (New York: Norton, 1977), 57.

22. Gaddis, *Origins of the Cold War*, 22–23; Thomas G. Paterson, *Soviet-American Confrontation: Postwar Reconstruction and the Origins of the Cold War* (Baltimore: Johns Hopkins University Press, 1973), 148. On U.S.-Soviet negotiations during the Bretton Woods Conference, see Armand Van Dormael, *Bretton Woods: Birth of a Monetary System* (New York: Holmes and Meier, 1978), 191–97; Miscamble, 41–42.

23. Donovan, 135; Gaddis, *Origins of the Cold War*, 271–72; Yergin, 149; Harriman and Abel, 525–26.

24. The Soviet Union would receive reparation payments from Germany in kind rather than in cash; though still subject to future negotiations, the baseline figure for German reparations was set at $20 billion. Gaddis, *Origins of the Cold War*, 102; Yergin, 64–65; Ulam, 53–54.

25. Under the new formula, each power would exact reparations from its zone in Germany. Beyond that, the Soviets would receive 25 percent of industrial equipment removed from the Western zones. "American Relations with the Soviet Union," in Krock, 441–42; Ulam, 74–75; Yergin, 96–97, 114, 117–18.

26. At its peak in May 1945, the Red Army numbered 11,365,000 troops, whereas the U.S. military, at its largest, had twelve million. Yergin, 270; and John Lewis Gaddis, *Strategies of Containment: A Critical Appraisal of Postwar American National Security Policy* (New York: Oxford University Press, 1982), 23.

27. Office of Strategic Services Report, May 19, 1943, cited in Davis, 64.

28. "USSR Situation, Capabilities and Intentions (as of 20 August 1943)," cited in Davis, 69.

29. Yergin, 18–35; Davis, 65–66; Martin Weil, *A Pretty Good Club: The Founding Fathers of the U.S. Foreign Service* (New York: Norton, 1978), 160.

30. Harriman and Abel, 218.

31. Ibid., 244.

32. Harriman and Abel, 317, 343–44; Harriman to Stettinius, April 6, 1945, in U.S. Department of State, *Foreign Relations of the United States: Diplomatic Papers, 1945*, vol. 5, *Europe* (Washington, D.C.: Government Printing Office, 1945), 194, 821. Stalin's

failure to come to the aid of the Warsaw uprising particularly influenced Harriman's views. John Lewis Gaddis, *George F. Kennan* (New York: Penguin, 2011), 183; Miscamble, 58, 82-83.

33. Herring, 138-39; John R. Deane, *The Strange Alliance: The Story of our Efforts at Wartime Co-Operation with Russia* (New York: Viking, 1946), 84-86; Melvyn P. Leffler, *A Preponderance of Power: National Security, the Truman Administration, and the Cold War* (Stanford, Calif.: Stanford University Press, 1992), 31.

34. Weil, 152-55; Harriman and Abel, 345.

35. Millis, *Forrestal Diaries*, 14; Yergin, 206.

36. Stimson diaries quoted in Gaddis, *Origins of the Cold War*, 93.

37. Roosevelt quoted in Gaddis, *Strategies of Containment*, 9. For a detailed treatment of Roosevelt's enduring optimism about Soviet intentions, see Miscamble, 51-56, 59.

38. "Doc. 531: Roosevelt to Churchill, March 29, 1945," in Francis L. Loewenheim, Harold D. Langley, and Manfred Jonas, eds., *Roosevelt and Churchill: Their Secret Wartime Correspondence* (New York: Dutton, 1975), 689; Miscamble, 69-70; Leffler, *A Preponderance of Power*, 25.

39. Roosevelt quoted in Harriman and Abel, 444.

40. Harry S. Truman, *Memoirs*, vol. 1, *Year of Decisions* (Garden City, N.Y.: Doubleday, 1955), 70-72; Harriman and Abel, 448-49; Gaddis, *Origins of the Cold War*, 202; Millis, *Forrestal Diaries*, 49-50; Gaddis, *George F. Kennan*, 192; Miscamble, 110-11, 163; Leffler, *A Preponderance of Power*, 31.

41. Yergin, 118.

42. Truman, *Year of Decisions*, 412.

43. Ibid., 523.

44. Charles R. Shrader, *The Withered Vine: Logistics and the Communist Insurgency in Greece, 1945-1949* (Westport, Conn.: Praeger, 1999), 165-72.

45. Yergin, 160; Gaddis, *Origins of the Cold War*, 288-89; quote from Truman, *Year of Decisions*, 552.

46. Gaddis, *Origins of the Cold War*, 300-301; Millis, *Forrestal Diaries*, 134-35.

47. "Russia—Seven Years Later," in Kennan, *Memoirs*, 528. Kennan also underscored the inability of Stalin's advisers to understand foreign views. Gaddis, *George F. Kennan*, 185-86.

48. Harriman and Abel, 344-45.

49. Stettinius quoted in Yergin, 101; for a similar quote, see Miscamble, 97.

50. Ulam, 72; Truman, *Year of Decisions*, 386.

51. Truman quoted in Weil, 252; also see Leffler, *A Preponderance of Power*, 52-53.

52. Weil, 251; Ulam, 67.

53. Miscamble, 279-80.

54. Long Telegram in Kennan, *Memoirs*, 557.

55. Gaddis, *Origins of the Cold War*, 309-12; Bruce Kuniholm, *The Origins of the Cold War in the Near East: Great Power Conflict and Diplomacy in Iran, Turkey, and Greece* (Princeton, N.J.: Princeton University Press, 1980), 317-32; Yergin, 187-90.

186 Notes to Pages 92–96

57. Truman quoted in Harriman and Abel, 550.

58. Yergin, 188.

59. Ibid., 190; Weil, 264; Gaddis, *Origins of the Cold War*, 318.

60. Donovan, 196; Paterson, 155.

61. Yergin, 266; Donovan, 206.

62. Paterson, 254.

63. Yergin, 236; John S. Hill, "American Efforts to Aid French Reconstruction Between Lend-Lease and the Marshall Plan," *Journal of Modern History* 64, 3 (September 1992): 521–22.

64. Gaddis, *Strategies of Containment*, 23.

65. Yergin, 233–35; Gaddis, *Origins of the Cold War*, 336; Kuniholm, 359–64, 371–73.

66. Weil, 264; Millis, *Forrestal Diaries*, 192; Harry S. Truman, *Memoirs*, vol. 2, *Years of Trial and Hope* (Garden City, N.Y.: Doubleday, 1956), 265; Miscamble, 294–96; Leffler, *A Preponderance of Power*, 123–24.

67. On August 22, Forrestal tasked the vice-chief of naval operations to prepare a brief on naval capabilities "in the event of trouble in Europe." The next day, Forrestal and Acheson agreed to request a review of U.S. capabilities that could be deployed in the event of a European war. Millis, *Forrestal Diaries*, 196–97; Dean Acheson, *Present at the Creation: My Years in the State Department* (New York: Norton, 1969), 195–96; Kuniholm, 361–62.

68. "American Relations with the Soviet Union," in Etzold and Gaddis, 66.

69. "American Relations with the Soviet Union," in Krock, 425.

70. "American Relations with the Soviet Union," in Etzold and Gaddis, 69; Miscamble, 301; Leffler, *A Preponderance of Power*, 131–32.

71. Donovan, 196; Paterson, 155.

72. Yergin, 266; Donovan, 206, 252.

73. Acheson, 217–19; Yergin, 280–84; Miscamble, 309–10.

74. Kennan, *Memoirs*, 325–53; Paterson, 208–13, 325; Yergin, 309–10, 314, 320, 326–29, 357; Ulam, 127–29, 134–36; Donovan, 288–90; Miscamble, 311–12.

75. Leffler, *A Preponderance of Power*, 203.

76. Lawrence S. Kaplan, *NATO 1948: The Birth of the Transatlantic Alliance* (Lanham, Md.: Rowman and Littlefield, 2007), 105–32; "Washington Exploratory Conversations on Security, September 9, 1948," in Etzold and Gaddis, 144; Ulam, 151. On the origins of the Mutual Defense Assistance Program, see Acheson, 308–13. The amount allocated to NATO is specified in "United States: Mutual Defense Assistance Act of 1949," *American Journal of International Law* 44, 1, Supplement: Official Documents (January 1950): 30–31; Miscamble, 313–14.

77. Gaddis, *Origins of the Cold War*, 327–31; Paterson, 257; Yergin, 376, 395; Miscamble, 312–13.

78. Yergin, 387–88; Ulam, 149–51; Truman, *Years of Trial and Hope*, 122–31. For a

detailed history of the Berlin airlift, see Andrei Cherny, *The Candy Bombers: The Untold Story of the Berlin Airlift and America's Finest Hour* (New York: Putnam, 2008).

79. John W. Dower, *Embracing Defeat: Japan in the Wake of World War II* (New York: Norton, 1999), 525–26, 528–33; Michael Schaller, *The American Occupation of Japan: The Origins of the Cold War in Asia* (New York: Oxford University Press, 1985), 109–40; Miscamble, 317.

80. Yergin, 236; Paterson, 68–69.

81. Paterson, 71–72.

82. Michael Mastanduno, *Economic Containment: CoCom and the Politics of East-West Trade* (Ithaca, N.Y.: Cornell University Press, 1992), 78–80.

83. Gaddis, *Origins of the Cold War*, 341; Yergin, 357; Donovan, 200.

84. Yergin, 266; Norris and Arkin, "NRDC Nuclear Notebook"; Leffler, "National Security and U.S. Foreign Policy," 33.

85. Dale Copeland, *The Origins of Major Wars* (Ithaca, N.Y.: Cornell University Press, 2000).

86. Gaddis, *Origins of the Cold War*, 341.

Chapter 6. Emerging Superpower

1. Quote from James Kynge, *China Shakes the World: A Titan's Troubled Rise—and the Challenge for America* (Boston: Houghton Mifflin, 2007), xiv.

2. China's potential to equal or surpass the United States remains contested, and it is important not to ignore challenges China confronts, such as environmental degradation and endemic corruption. For skeptical views of China's future trajectory, see Minxin Pei, *China's Trapped Transition: The Limits of Developmental Autocracy* (Cambridge, Mass.: Harvard University Press, 2008); and Michael Beckley, "China's Century? Why America's Edge Will Endure," *International Security* 36, 3 (Winter 2011/12): 41–78.

3. The figure for China's average annual growth is from C. Fred Bergsten, Charles Freeman, Nicholas R. Lardy, and Derek J. Mitchell, *China's Rise: Challenges and Opportunities* (Washington, D.C.: Peterson Institute for International Economics and the Center for Strategic and International Studies, 2008), 105.

4. U.S. annual GDP growth during the information technology boom peaked at 4.8 percent in 1999. From U.S. Department of Commerce, Bureau of Economic Analysis, *Gross Domestic Product: Percent Change from Preceding Period*, January 30, 2014, http://www.bea.gov/national/xls/gdpchg.xls. Comparisons of aggregate GDP are based on purchasing power parity figures from World Bank, World Development Indicators Online. The latest available are for 2012.

5. PricewaterhouseCoopers, *The World in 2050*, London, January 2011, 8.

6. Calculations based on figures from World Bank, World Development Indicators Online. The latest trade data available is for 2012.

7. The year 1990 is the base year because China's military expenditures during the 1980s were inflated by lingering tensions with the Soviet Union.

8. Calculation based on information from the Stockholm International Peace Research Institute (SIPRI), *Military Expenditure Database*, 2013, http://sipri.org/research/armaments/milex/milex_database.

9. National Science Foundation, Division of Science Resources Statistics, *Asia's Rising Science and Technology Strength: Comparative Indicators for Asia, the European Union, and the United States* (Arlington, Va.: National Science Foundation, May 2007), 15, table 7, "Gross Expenditures on Research and Development, by Selected Region and Country/Economy: 1990–2004"; James Wilsdon and James Keeley, *China: The Next Science Superpower?* (London: Demos, 2007), 6–8.

10. Calculation based on data from Battelle, *2014 Global R&D Funding Forecast*, December 2013, http://www.battelle.org/docs/tpp/2014_global_rd_funding_forecast.pdf, 7.

11. Andrew J. Nathan and Robert S. Ross, *The Great Wall and the Empty Fortress: China's Search for Security* (New York: Norton, 1997), 146.

12. The 1992 Defense Planning Guidance, a Pentagon document leaked to the *New York Times*, is sometimes cited as heralding a change in American perceptions of Chinese military power. Yet far from anticipating a rapid shift in the U.S.-China military balance, the document appears to have simply identified China as one of several potential competitors to be deterred "from even aspiring to a larger regional or global role." Patrick E. Tyler, "U.S. Strategy Plan Calls for Insuring No Rivals Develop," *New York Times*, March 8, 1992.

13. Joseph S. Nye, Jr., "East Asian Security: The Case for Deep Engagement," *Foreign Affairs* 74, 4 (July/August 1995): 91–92.

14. James Mann, *About Face: A History of America's Curious Relationship with China from Nixon to Clinton* (New York: Knopf, 1999): 332.

15. U.S. National Intelligence Council, *Global Trends 2010*, Washington, D.C., November 1997.

16. U.S. Department of Defense, *Quadrennial Defense Review Report*, Washington, D.C., May 19, 1997.

17. Condoleezza Rice, "Campaign 2000: Promoting the National Interest," *Foreign Affairs* 79, 1 (January/February 2000): 56.

18. U.S. Department of Defense, *Quadrennial Defense Review Report*, Washington, D.C., September 30, 2001, 4.

19. U.S. Department of Defense, *Quadrennial Defense Review Report*, Washington, D.C., February 6, 2006, 29.

20. U.S. Department of Defense, *Secretary Gates Remarks at Air Force Association's Annual Conference, National Harbor, Md.*, September 16, 2009; Andrew F. Krepinevich, *Why AirSea Battle?* (Washington, D.C.: Center for Strategic and Budgetary Assessments, February 2010), 13–25.

21. Interview with Charlene Barshefsky, former U.S. trade representative, October 14, 2009.

22. Ibid.

23. Phone interview with Winston Lord, former assistant secretary of state, October 13, 2009.

24. National Science Foundation, Division of Science Resources Statistics, *Asia's Rising Science and Technology Strength*, vii.

25. National Academy of Sciences, National Academy of Engineering, and Institute of Medicine, *Rising Above the Gathering Storm: Energizing and Employing America for a Brighter Economic Future* (Washington, D.C.: National Academies Press, 2007), 72–73, 209, 216.

26. Roger Altman, "The Great Crash, 2008: A Geopolitical Setback for the West," *Foreign Affairs* 88, 1 (January/February 2009): 11.

27. U.S. National Intelligence Council, *Global Trends 2025: A Transformed World*, Washington, D.C., November 2008, vi.

28. National Public Radio, "Transcript: Obama's State of the Union Address," January 25, 2011.

29. Alexander Burns, "GOP Sees Red over China," *Politico*, May 24, 2011.

30. Data from Center for Systemic Peace, Polity IV Annual Time-Series, 1800–2012. The most recent available data are from 2012.

31. James C. F. Wang, *Contemporary Chinese Politics: An Introduction* (Upper Saddle River, N.J.: Prentice Hall, 2002), 95.

32. Murray Scot Tanner, "The National People's Congress," in Merle Goldman and Roderick MacFarquhar, eds., *The Paradox of China's Post-Mao Reforms* (Cambridge, Mass.: Harvard University Press, 1999), 120. In a more recent work on the Chinese Communist Party, David Shambaugh describes the National People's Congress as a "puppet legislature." See David Shambaugh, *China's Communist Party: Atrophy and Adaptation* (Washington, D.C.: Woodrow Wilson Center Press, 2008), 179.

33. Quotations from *Constitution of the People's Republic of China*, http://english. people.com.cn/constitution/constitution.html.

34. Human Rights Watch, *China: Events of 2008*, http://www.hrw.org/en/node/ 79301; Committee to Protect Journalists, *Falling Short: Olympic Promises Go Unfulfilled as China Falters on Press Freedom*, June 2008, 25, 27, 38–43, http://cpj.org/Briefings/2007/Falling_Short/China/china_updated.pdf; Freedom House, *Freedom of the Press 2008: A Global Survey of Media Independence* (Lanham, Md.: Rowman and Littlefield, 2009), 89–92.

35. Interview with Charlene Barshefsky, October 14, 2009. Similar perspectives on China's membership in the WTO can be found in Bill Clinton, *My Life* (New York: Knopf, 2004), 794; Madeline Albright, *Madame Secretary* (New York: Miramax, 2003), 432–33.

36. Mann, *About Face*, 356; Robert L. Suettinger, *Beyond Tiananmen: The Politics of U.S.-China Relations 1989–2000* (Washington, D.C.: Brookings Institution Press, 2001), 359–65; Bonnie S. Glaser, "Challenged by New Crises," *Comparative Connections* 1, 1 (July 1999): 13–14.

37. Mann, *About Face*, 356; Suettinger, 322.

38. "Classified Report to Congress on the Non-Proliferation Policies and Practices of the People's Republic of China," 1997, 20, in William Burr, ed., *China, Pakistan, and the Bomb: The Declassified File on U.S. Policy, 1977–1997*, National Security Archive Electronic Briefing Book 114, March 5, 2004; Wendy Frieman, *China, Arms Control, and Non-Proliferation* (New York: RoutledgeCurzon, 2004), 32.

39. Frieman, 97; David M. Lampton, *Same Bed, Different Dreams: Managing U.S.-China Relations, 1989–2000* (Berkeley: University of California Press, 2001), 74.

40. Suettinger, 346; Nuclear Threat Initiative, *Military Maritime Consultative Agreement (MMCA)*," http://www.nti.org/db/china/mmcaorg.htm.

41. Suettinger, 356, 385, 401.

42. Shirley A. Kan, *Taiwan: Major U.S. Arms Sales Since 1990* (Washington, D.C.: Congressional Research Service, September 24, 2009), 2–3.

43. Japan Ministry of Foreign Affairs, *The Guidelines for Japan-U.S. Defense Cooperation*, September 1997; Michael D. Swaine, Rachel M. Swanger, and Takashi Kawakami, *Japan and Ballistic Missile Defense* (Santa Monica, Calif.: Rand, 2001), 34–35.

44. Bonnie S. Glaser, "First Contact: Qian Qichen Engages in Wide-Ranging, Constructive Talks with President Bush and Senior U.S. Officials," *Comparative Connections* 3, 1 (April 2001): 28; Bonnie S. Glaser, "Mid-Air Collision Cripples Sino-U.S. Relations," *Comparative Connections* 3, 2 (July 2001): 32–33; Bonnie S. Glaser, "Face to Face in Shanghai: New Amity and Perennial Differences," *Comparative Connections* 3, 4 (January 2002): 29–30.

45. To give one concrete example, after a Chinese jet collided with a U.S. spy plane in April 2001, resulting in a diplomatic showdown, the American side attempted to discuss procedures for interception of reconnaissance flights. However, this was a nonstarter. In every meeting, the Chinese side contended that such flights were illegal. Dennis C. Blair and David V. Bonfili, "The April 2001 EP-3 Incident: The U.S. Point of View," in Michael D. Swaine, Zhang Tuosheng, and Danielle F. S. Cohen, eds., *Managing Sino-American Crises: Case Studies and Analysis* (Washington, D.C.: Carnegie Endowment for International Peace, 2006), 387.

46. In February 2003, Secretary of State Colin Powell visited Beijing. There, he recruited the Chinese government to sponsor three-party nuclear disarmament. Karen DeYoung, *Soldier: The Life of Colin Powell* (New York: Knopf, 2006), 474–76.

47. U.S. Department of the Treasury, *Fact Sheet: Second Meeting of the U.S.-China Strategic and Economic Dialogue*, Washington, D.C., May 23, 2007; U.S. Department of the Treasury, Office of Public Affairs, *U.S. Fact Sheet: The Third Cabinet-Level Meeting of the U.S.-China Strategic Economic Dialogue*, Beijing, December 13, 2007; idem, *Joint U.S.-China Fact Sheet: Fourth U.S.-China Strategic Economic Dialogue*, Washington, D.C., June 18, 2008.

48. Alan D. Romberg, *Rein In at the Brink of the Precipice: American Policy Toward Taiwan and U.S.-PRC Relations* (Washington, D.C.: Henry L. Stimson Center, 2003), 195; Kirsten McNeil, "Long-Delayed Arms Sales to Taiwan Announced," *Arms Control*

Today, November 4, 2008; Bonnie S. Glaser, "China Signals Irritation with U.S. Policy," *Comparative Connections* 9, 4 (January 2008): 27.

49. Japan Ministry of Foreign Affairs, *Joint Statement U.S.-Japan Security Consultative Committee*, Washington, D.C., February 19, 2005.

50. Jim Lobe, "Indonesia: U.S. Lifts Ban on Sale of Lethal Arms," *Inter Press Service News Agency*, March 30, 2006.

51. Richard Armitage, R. Nicholas Burns, and Richard Fontaine, *Natural Allies: A Blueprint for the Future of U.S.-India Relations* (Washington, D.C.: Center for a New American Security, October 2010), 3.

52. Ronald O'Rourke, *Sea-Based Ballistic Missile Defense—Background and Issues for Congress* (Washington, D.C.: Congressional Research Service, September 18, 2009), 1, 7–8.

53. Ronald O'Rourke, *China Naval Modernization: Implications for U.S. Navy Capabilities—Background and Issues for Congress* (Washington, D.C.: Congressional Research Service, September 23, 2009), 23–24; Shirley A. Kan and Larry A. Niksch, *Guam: U.S. Defense Deployments* (Washington, D.C.: Congressional Research Service, May 22, 2009), 1–2.

54. David Barboza, "Geithner Softens Tone in Approach to Beijing," *New York Times*, June 2, 2009.

55. "Geithner: U.S. Wants Bigger Role for China in IMF," *Associated Press*, September 24, 2009.

56. Christi Parsons, John M. Glionna, and Don Lee, "G-20 Summit Ends with Watered-Down Agreement," *Los Angeles Times*, November 12, 2010; Don Lee, "G-20 moves to allay fears of 'currency war,'" *Los Angeles Times*, February 16, 2013.

57. "China Overtakes U.S. in Greenhouse Gas Emissions," *New York Times*, June 20, 2007.

58. John M. Broder and James Kanter, "China and U.S. Hit Strident Impasse at Climate Talks," *New York Times*, December 14, 2009; Anthony Faiola, Juliet Eilperin, and John Pomfret, "Copenhagen Climate Deal Shows New World Order May Be Led by U.S., China," *Washington Post*, December 20, 2009; Lenny Bernstein, "Warsaw climate conference produces little agreement," *Washington Post*, November 22, 2013.

59. U.S.-China Business Council, *USCBC Special Report: China Delinks Innovation and Procurement Policies*, May 10, 2011.

60. Weapons sales announced by the Obama administration in early 2010 were actually part of a Taiwan arms package approved by the Bush administration. John Pomfret, "U.S. Sells Weapons to Taiwan, Angering China," *Washington Post*, January 30, 2010.

61. Blaine Harden, "South Korea Says Probe Points to North in Sinking of Ship," *Washington Post*, May 20, 2010; Mark McDonald, "'Crisis Status' in South Korea After North Shells Island," *New York Times*, November 23, 2010; Michael Armacost et al., *"New Beginnings" in the U.S.-ROK Alliance: Recommendations to the Obama Administration* (Stanford, Calif: Freeman Spogli Institute for International Studies, May 2010).

62. Daniel Kliman and Abe Denmark, "How to Get Southeast Asia Right," *Diplomat*, February 2, 2011.

63. For an early articulation of AirSea Battle, see Krepinevich, *Why AirSea Battle?*

64. Paul K. Davis and Peter A. Wilson, *Looming Discontinuities in U.S. Military Strategy and Defense Planning: Colliding RMAs Necessitate a New Strategy* (Santa Monica, Calif.: Rand, March 2011), xiii.

65. Ellen Nakashima, "Gates Establishes Cyber-Defense Command," *Washington Post*, June 24, 2009; Siobhan Gorman and Yochi J. Dreazen, "New Military Command to Focus on Cybersecurity," *Wall Street Journal*, April 22, 2009.

66. Hillary Clinton, "America's Pacific Century," *Foreign Policy*, October 11, 2011; Mark E. Manyin et al., *Pivot to the Pacific? The Obama Administration's "Rebalancing" Toward Asia* (Washington, D.C.: Congressional Research Service, March 28, 2012).

67. Interview with former U.S. Department of Defense official, September 17, 2009; interview with Robert Suettinger, September 22, 2009; interview with U.S. State Department official involved in China affairs, September 29, 2009; interview with Dan Blumenthal, former U.S. Department of Defense official, September 29, 2009; interview with former senior U.S. official, October 2, 2009.

68. Interview with U.S. State Department official involved in China affairs, September 29, 2009.

69. Interview with James Kelly, former assistant secretary of state, September 16, 2009.

70. Interview with Robert Suettinger, September 22, 2009.

71. Interview with former U.S. Department of Defense official, September 17, 2009; interview with Dan Blumenthal, September 29, 2009; interview with U.S. State Department official involved in China affairs, September 29, 2009; interview with former senior U.S. official, October 9, 2009; interview with Randall Schriver, former deputy assistant secretary of state, October 13, 2009. This point is directly made in a U.S. Department of Defense report on China. "The PLA's role as an organ of the CCP rather than the State is also a factor to consider, adding another element of uncertainty with respect to decisions to use force." U.S. Department of Defense, *Annual Report to Congress: Military Power of the People's Republic of China 2006*, Washington, D.C., May 23, 2006, 13.

72. Interview with former senior U.S. official, October 2, 2009.

73. Interview with Marc Grossman, former under secretary of state, October 7, 2009.

74. Interview with U.S. State Department official involved in China affairs, September 29, 2009.

75. Michael J. Green and Daniel M. Kliman, "China's Risky Bet Against History," *Diplomat*, December 23, 2010.

76. Chico Harlan, "China creates new air defense zone in East China Sea amid dispute with Japan," *Washington Post*, November 23, 2013.

77. Interview with former senior U.S. State Department official, September 22, 2009.

78. Interview with Walter Slocombe, September 23, 2009.

79. Excerpt from U.S. Department of Defense, *Annual Report to Congress: Military*

Power of the People's Republic of China 2006, 1. Editions published during other years of the Bush administration contain similar language, http://www.defenselink.mil/pubs/china.html.

80. Robert B. Zoellick, *Whither China: From Membership to Responsibility*, Remarks to National Committee on United States-China Relations (NCUSCR), New York, September 21, 2005.

81. Condoleezza Rice, "Rethinking the National Interest: American Realism for a New World," *Foreign Affairs* 87, 4 (July/August 2008): 4.

82. U.S. Department of Defense, *Annual Report to Congress: Military Power of the People's Republic of China 2009*, Washington, D.C., March 25, 2009, 1.

83. James B. Steinberg, *Administration's Vision of the U.S.-China Relationship*, keynote address at Center for a New American Security, Washington, D.C., September 24, 2009; Josh Rogin, "The End of the Concept of 'Strategic Reassurance'?" *Foreign Policy*, November 6, 2009.

84. John Pomfret, "Hu Faces an Obama Administration More Hard-Nosed About Chinese Government," *Washington Post*, January 18, 2011.

85. Interview with Robert Suettinger, September 22, 2009.

86. Interview with U.S. State Department official involved in China affairs, September 29, 2009.

87. Green and Kliman, "China's Risky Bet Against History."

88. Interview with Walter Slocombe, September 23, 2009.

89. Interview with former U.S. military officer, September 18, 2009.

90. According to a 2007 study, the state was the major shareholder in China's top 100 corporations. Roman Tomasic and Neil Andrews, "Minority Shareholder Protection in China's Top 100 Listed Companies," *Australian Journal of Asian Law* 9, 1 (2007): 88–119.

91. Interview with Douglas Paal, September 16, 2009; phone interview with former senior Bush administration official, November 25, 2009.

92. Interview with former U.S. Department of Defense official, September 17, 2009.

93. Green and Kliman, "China's Risky Bet Against History."

94. Sewell Chan, "China and U.S. Businesses See Gains in Deeper Ties," *New York Times*, January 21, 2011.

95. Calculations based on the U.S. International Trade Commission Interactive Tariff and Trade Database, http://dataweb.usitc.gov, and U.S. Department of Commerce, Bureau of Economic Analysis, *Current-Dollar and "Real" Gross Domestic Product*, http://www.bea.gov/national/xls/gdplev.xls. The most recent annual data are for 2013.

96. U.S. Department of Commerce, Bureau of Economic Analysis, *U.S. Direct Investment Abroad on a Historical-Cost Basis: Country Detail by Selected Industry, 1997*; U.S. Department of Commerce, Bureau of Economic Analysis, *U.S. Direct Investment Position Abroad on a Historical-Cost Basis: Country Detail by Industry, 2012*. The most recent annual data are for 2012.

97. U.S. Department of the Treasury, *Major Foreign Holders of Treasury Securities*, January 16, 2014.

98. Daniel H. Rosen and Thilo Hanemann, *An American Open Door? Maximizing the Benefits of Chinese Foreign Direct Investment* (New York: Asia Society, May 2011), 8, 25.

99. Interview with U.S. Senate staffer, September 11, 2009; interview with James Kelly, September 16, 2009; interview with former senior U.S. State Department official, September 22, 2009; interview with Randall Schriver, October 13, 2009; interview with Charlene Barshefsky, October 14, 2009.

100. A high-profile case of a U.S. firm pressing for relaxation of export controls occurred in 1998. That year, Loral Space and Communications successfully lobbied the Clinton administration to permit the launch of its satellite atop a Chinese rocket. Mann, *About Face*, 364; Warren I. Cohen, *America's Response to China: A History of Sino-American Relations* (New York: Columbia University Press, 2000), 236–37.

101. Phone interview with Robert Kapp, former president of the U.S.-China Business Council, November 13, 2009.

102. Guy Dinmore and Geoff Dyer, "Immelt Hits Out at China and Obama," *Financial Times*, July 1, 2010.

103. Noam Scheiber makes this point in "Peking over Our Shoulder," *New Republic*, September 15, 2009.

104. Joe McDonald, "Asia to Keep Buying US Debt Despite Downgrade," *Associated Press*, August 9, 2011.

105. William J. Clinton, "Remarks to the Asia Society and the United States-China Education Foundation Board," quoted in Scott Kennedy, ed., *China Cross Talk: The American Debate over China Policy Since Normalization* (Lanham, Md.: Rowman and Littlefield, 2003), 172.

Chapter 7. Neighboring Titan

1. That a common Anglo-American strategic outlook exists is the central point of Walter Russell Mead's *God and Gold: Britain, America, and the Making of the Modern World* (New York: Vintage, 2008). However, Mead's argument pertains to visions of global order rather than strategies for managing the rise of new powers.

2. The figure for China's average annual growth is from C. Fred Bergsten, Charles Freeman, Nicholas R. Lardy, and Derek J. Mitchell, *China's Rise: Challenges and Opportunities* (Washington, D.C.: Peterson Institute for International Economics and Center for Strategic and International Studies, 2008), 105.

3. On Japanese GDP growth in the early 2000s, see Japan Ministry of Internal Affairs and Communications, Statistics Bureau, "table 3.5: Kokunai Souseisan no Jisshitsu Seichouritsu" [Real GDP growth rate], in *Sekai no Toukei 2009* [World statistics 2009], March 2009, 82; Martin Sommer, *Why Has Japan Been Hit So Hard by the Global Recession?* IMF Staff Position Note (Washington, D.C.: International Monetary Fund, March 18, 2009), 2–4.

4. Comparisons of aggregate GDP are based on purchasing power parity figures from World Bank, World Development Indicators online. Latest available data are for 2012.

5. Calculations based on trade figures from World Bank, World Development Indicators online. Latest available data are for 2012.

6. Calculation based on information from the Stockholm International Peace Research Institute (SIPRI), *Military Expenditure Database*, 2013, http://sipri.org/research/armaments/milex/milex_database; Isabel Reynolds, "Japan Defense Budget to Increase for First Time in 11 Years," *Bloomberg*, January 30, 2013.

7. National Science Foundation, Division of Science Resources Statistics, *Asia's Rising Science and Technology Strength: Comparative Indicators for Asia, the European Union, and the United States* (Arlington, Va.: National Science Foundation, May 2007), 15, table 7, "Gross Expenditures on Research and Development, by Selected Region and Country/Economy: 1990–2004"; James Wilsdon and James Keeley, *China: The Next Science Superpower?* (London: Demos, 2007), 6–8.

8. Calculation based on data from Battelle, *2014 Global R&D Funding Forecast*, December 2013, 7.

9. China's Medium- to Long-Term Science and Technology Development Program aims to boost R&D expenditures to 2.5 percent of total GDP by 2020; Wilsdon and Keeley, 7.

10. Michael J. Green and Benjamin L. Self, "Japan's Changing China Policy: From Commercial Liberalism to Reluctant Realism," *Survival* 38, 2 (Summer 1996): 48.

11. "'Tou igo' he kouzou kaikaku isogu chugoku" [Post-Deng China rushes toward structural reforms], *Yomiuri Shimbun*, November 11, 1993.

12. Interview with Hitoshi Tanaka, former Japanese diplomat, March 31, 2009.

13. Liberal Democratic Party, Research Commission on Foreign Affairs, *Jiyuminshutou gaikou seisaku no shishin I: Nihon no ajia taiheiyou senryaku: Henka no chousen* [Foreign policy of the Liberal Democratic Party, Part I: Japan's Asia-Pacific strategy: The challenges of transformation], Tokyo, April 11, 1997, 110–11. The first excerpt from the report is a translation from Michael J. Green, *Japan's Reluctant Realism: Foreign Policy Challenges in an Era of Uncertain Power* (New York: Palgrave, 2001), 99. This author translated the second excerpt.

14. "Shasetsu: Katsuryoku aru 21 seiki he: 'touzai yugou' de yutaka na sekai jitsugen wo" [Editorial: Toward a vital twenty-first century: Realizing a rich world through "Unification of East and West"], *Yomiuri Shimbun*, January 7, 1997.

15. Interview with Japan Ministry of Economy, Trade, and Industry official, April 16, 2009.

16. Japan Cabinet Office, *Science and Technology Basic Plan* (Provisional translation), March 28, 2006, 11. Also surveyed were Japan Cabinet Office, *Science and Technology Basic Plan (2001–2005)* (tentative version), March 30, 2001; Japan Cabinet Office, *Science and Technology Basic Plan* (unofficial translation), July 2, 1996, all at http://www8.cao.go.jp/cstp/english/basic/index.html.

17. David Barboza, "China Passes Japan as Second-Largest Economy," *New York Times*, August 15, 2010.

18. Japan Defense Agency, *Heisei 5 nenban: Nihon no Bouei: Bouei Hakusho* [Heisei 5th edition: Defense of Japan: Defense white paper], Tokyo, 1993.

19. Interview with retired senior Japanese defense official, March 19, 2009.

20. Interview with three Japanese Ministry of Defense officials, April 16, 2009. On China's initial purchases of Kilo-class submarines and Sovremenny destroyers, see David L. Shambaugh, *Modernizing China's Military: Progress, Problems, and Prospects* (Berkeley: University of California Press, 2004), 267, 273.

21. Interview with Japan Maritime Self-Defense Forces officer, March 24, 2009.

22. These activities are described in Japan Ministry of Defense, *Defense of Japan 2010: Defense White Paper*, Tokyo, 2010, 61–62.

23. Fumio Ota, "The Carrier of Asia-Pacific Troubles," *Wall Street Journal,* August 11, 2011.

24. Japan Ministry of Economy, Trade, and Industry, *Chugoku no WTO kamei koushou no genjou* [The current state of China's WTO membership negotiations], February 21, 2001; James Przystup, "Slowed But Not Soured," *Comparative Connections* 1, 1 (July 1999): 54; James Przystup, "Progressing, But Still Facing History," *Comparative Connections* 1, 2 (October 1999): 58; James Przystup, "A Search for Understanding," *Comparative Connections* 1, 3 (January 2000): 63; Interview with former senior Japan Ministry of Foreign Affairs official, March 19, 2009; interview with Takeo Hiranuma, LDP member of parliament, March 26, 2009; interview with Hitoshi Tanaka, March 31, 2009; interview with Sakutaro Tanino, former Japanese diplomat, April 2, 2009; interview with former Japan External Trade Organization executive, April 3, 2009; interview with Japan Ministry of Economy, Trade, and Industry official, April 16, 2009.

25. Annex B of the Kyoto Protocol to the United Nations Framework Convention on Climate Change, which lists parties with binding emission limitation or reduction commitments, contains no developing countries.

26. John Vidal and David Adam, "China Overtakes US as World's Biggest CO2 Emitter," *Guardian,* June 19, 2007.

27. Interview with Sakutaro Tanino, April 2, 2009.

28. Japan Ministry of Foreign Affairs, *First Japan-China High-Level Economic Dialogue,* Press communiqué, December 2, 2007.

29. Japan delineates each country's maritime sphere as the median line between overlapping EEZs, while China asserts control to the edge of the underwater continental shelf—an area subsuming Japanese claims.

30. James Przystup, "Waiting for Zhu . . . ," *Comparative Connections* 2, 3 (October 2000): 94–96; Mike M. Mochizuki, "Japan's Shifting Strategy Toward the Rise of China," *Journal of Strategic Studies* 30, 4–5 (August–October 2007): 753. James Przystup, "The Past Is Always Present," *Comparative Connections* 3, 1 (April 2001): 99–100.

31. James Przystup, "Trying to Get Beyond Yasukuni," *Comparative Connections* 7, 1 (April 2005): 115–16; James Przystup, "Progress in Building a Strategic Relationship," *Comparative Connections* 10, 2 (July 2008): 124–25.

32. Japan Ministry of Foreign Affairs, *The Guidelines for Japan-U.S. Defense Cooperation*, September 1997.

33. Michael D. Swaine, Rachel M. Swanger, and Takashi Kawakami, *Japan and Ballistic Missile Defense* (Santa Monica, Calif.: Rand, 2001), 34–35.

34. Ibid., 5; Japan Cabinet Office, *Statement by the Chief Cabinet Secretary*, December 19, 2003.

35. On changes in Japanese security policy after 2001, see Daniel M. Kliman, *Japan's Security Strategy in the Post-9/11 World: Embracing a New Realpolitik* (Westport, Conn.: Praeger, 2006).

36. Japan Ministry of Foreign Affairs, *Joint Statement U.S.-Japan Security Consultative Committee*, Washington, D.C., February 19, 2005.

37. Junichiro Koizumi, *Japan and ASEAN in East Asia: A Sincere and Open Partnership*, Singapore, January 14, 2002; Japan Ministry of Foreign Affairs, *Entry into Force of the Japan-ASEAN Comprehensive Economic Partnership Agreement*, December 1, 2008.

38. Japan Ministry of Foreign Affairs, *Free Trade Agreement (FTA) and Economic Partnership Agreement (EPA)*; Mochizuki, 757.

39. For a timeline of both EPA negotiations, see Japan Ministry of Foreign Affairs, *Japan-Australia Economic Partnership Agreement*, last updated June 2012; Japan Ministry of Foreign Affairs, *Japan-India Economic Partnership Agreement*, last updated February 2012.

40. William Tow, "The Trilateral Strategic Dialogue: Facilitating Community-Building or Revisiting Containment," in William Tow et al., *Assessing the Trilateral Strategic Dialogue* (Seattle: National Bureau of Asian Research, December 2008), 1–10; Japan Ministry of Foreign Affairs, *Japan-Australia Joint Declaration on Security Cooperation*, Tokyo, March 13, 2007.

41. Japan Ministry of Foreign Affairs, *Joint Declaration on Security Cooperation Between Japan and India*, Tokyo, October 22, 2008.

42. "Asia's Biggest Economies Promise Greater Cooperation," *New York Times*, October 11, 2009.

43. Abraham M. Denmark and Daniel M. Kliman, *Cornerstone: A Future Agenda for the U.S.-Japan Alliance* (Washington, D.C.: Center for a New American Security, June 2010).

44. Patrick M. Cronin, Daniel M. Kliman, and Abraham M. Denmark, *Renewal: Revitalizing the U.S.-Japan Alliance* (Washington, D.C., Center for a New American Security, October 2010).

45. Martin Fackler, "Japan Announces Defense Policy to Counter China," *New York Times*, December 16, 2010.

46. "Japan, Australia Sign 'Historic' Military Deal," *Agence France-Presse*, May 19, 2010.

47. Harumi Ozawa, "Mass Display of Aircraft, Warships at Japan-U.S. Exercise," *Agence France-Presse*, December 1, 2010.

48. Raja Mohan, "India's New Non-Alignment: Trilateral Dialogue with Japan and U.S.," *Indian Express*, April 8, 2011.

49. See for example Japan Ministry of Foreign Affairs, *Overview of Japan-China Foreign Ministers' Meeting*, October 29, 2010.

50. "Tokyo in FTA Talks with Seoul, Beijing," *Jiji Press*, March 27, 2013.

51. Reiji Yoshida, "Abe Declares Japan Will Join TPP Free-Trade Process," *Japan Times*, March 16, 2013; Isabel Reynolds, "Japan Defense Budget to Increase for First Time in 11 Years," *Bloomberg*, January 30, 2013; Pranab Dhal Samanta, "In Signal to China, Manmohan Singh Embraces Japan's Idea," *Indian Express*, May 29, 2013.

52. Interview with Sakutaro Tanino, April 2, 2009; interview with Japan Ministry of Foreign Affairs official, April 20, 2009.

53. Simultaneous interview with two Japan Ministry of Defense officials, April 21, 2009.

54. Ibid.

55. Interview with Shigeru Ishiba, former defense minister, April 6, 2009.

56. Interview with Japan Maritime Self-Defense Forces officer, March 24, 2009; interview with Japan Ministry of Foreign Affairs official, April 20, 2009.

57. Interview with two Japan Ministry of Defense officials, April 21, 2009.

58. Martin Fackler and Ian Johnson, "Arrest in Disputed Seas Riles China and Japan," *New York Times*, September 19, 2010.

59. Interview with three Japan Ministry of Defense officials, April 16, 2009.

60. Based on a content analysis of Japan Ministry of Defense, *Defense of Japan: Defense White Paper*, published from 2001 to 2008 (in Japanese). The 2005 through 2008 versions are available in English at http://www.mod.go.jp/e/publ/w_paper/.

61. Japan Defense Agency, *Heisei 18 nenban: Nihon no Bouei: Bouei Hakusho* [Heisei 18 edition: Defense of Japan: Defense white paper], Tokyo, 2006 (author's translation).

62. Interview with three Japan Ministry of Defense officials, April 16, 2009. China claimed the incursion was caused by a technical mistake, but this was dismissed by the Japanese government as mere pretext. "China 'Sorry' over Mystery Sub," *BBC News*, November 16, 2004.

63. Interview with three Japan Ministry of Defense officials, April 16, 2009.

64. Interview with Vice Admiral (ret.) Fumio Ota, April 9, 2009; interview with Lieutenant General (ret.) Noboru Yamaguchi, April 9, 2009.

65. Interview with Shigenobu Tamura, LDP staffer, March 3, 2009; interview with Fumio Kyuma, April 2, 2009.

66. "Japan Alarmed by Chinese 'Threat,'" *BBC News*, December 22, 2005.

67. Interview with Nobutaka Machimura, April 16, 2009.

68. Interview with Sadakazu Tanigaki, April 3, 2009.

69. Martin Fackler, "Cables Show U.S. Concern on Japan's Disaster Readiness," *New York Times,* May 3, 2011.

70. National Institute for Defense Studies, *NIDS China Security Report*, Tokyo,

February 2012; Martin Fackler and Ian Johnson, "Arrest in Disputed Seas Riles China and Japan," *New York Times*, September 19, 2010; Keith Bradsher, "Amid Tension, China Blocks Vital Exports to Japan," *New York Times*, September 22, 2010; Sachiko Sakamaki, "Four Japanese Held in China as Fishing Boat Tensions Escalate," *Bloomberg*, September 23, 2010.

71. Interview with former senior Japan Ministry of Foreign Affairs official, March 19, 2009.

72. Interview with Japan Ministry of Foreign Affairs official, April 20, 2009; Masahiko Sasajima, "Japan's Domestic Politics and China Policymaking," in Benjamin L. Self and Jeffrey W. Thompson, eds., *An Alliance for Engagement: Building Cooperation in Security Relations with China* (Washington, D.C.: Henry L. Stimson Center, 2002), 84. Interview with Japan Ministry of Foreign Affairs official, April 20, 2009; interview with two Japan Ministry of Defense officials, April 21, 2009.

73. A case in point is the DPJ delegation that visited Beijing in December 2009 for photographs with China's leadership. Although portrayed in the media as a coup for Chinese diplomacy, it failed to solidify meaningful personal ties. Martin Fackler, "In Japan, U.S. Losing Diplomatic Ground to China," *New York Times*, January 23, 2010.

74. Interview with Ryozo Kato, April 13, 2009.

75. Interview with Japan Maritime Self-Defense Forces officer, March 24, 2009. One retired military officer reported close relationships with Chinese counterparts, but admitted that he received little information about the internal workings of the Chinese government from them.

76. Interview with Japan Ministry of Foreign Affairs official, April 20, 2009.

77. Martin Fackler, "Cables Show U.S. Concern on Japan's Disaster Readiness," *New York Times*, May 3, 2011.

78. Calculation based on economic statistics assembled by Japan Ministry of Finance and Japan Cabinet Office, data available at http://www.customs.go.jp/toukei/suii/html/data/d42ca001.csv; http://www.esri.cao.go.jp/jp/sna/data/data_list/sokuhou/files/2013/qe131_2/__icsFiles/afieldfile/2013/06/07/gaku-mcy1312.csv (in Japanese). Latest available GDP data are from 2012.

79. Japan External Trade Organization, "Japan's Total Outward FDI by Country/Region (International Investment position)," 2013, http://www.jetro.go.jp/en/reports/statistics/data/12fdistocken01.xls. Latest available data are from 2012.

80. Monami Yui and Shigeki Nozawa, "China's Net Purchases of Japan Long-Term Debt Reach Record," *Bloomberg*, June 7, 2011.

81. Interview with Tomohiko Taniguchi, former Japan Ministry of Foreign Affairs deputy press secretary, March 31, 2009; interview with Sakutaro Tanino, April 2, 2009; interview with former Japan External Trade Organization executive, April 3, 2009; interview with Yotaro Kobayashi, former CEO of Fuji Xerox, April 9, 2009.

82. James Przystup, "Dialogue of the Almost Deaf," *Comparative Connections* 6, 1 (April 2004): 105; James Przystup, "Spring Thaw," *Comparative Connections* 8, 2 (July 2006): 122.

83. "China-Japan Dispute Takes Rising Toll on Top Asian Economies," *Bloomberg*, January 9, 2013.

Chapter 8. Implications for the Twenty-First Century

1. This section draws from Michael J. Green and Daniel M. Kliman, "China's Risky Bet Against History," *Diplomat*, December 23, 2010. The fourth section draws from Daniel M. Kliman, "Advantage India: Why China Will Lose the Contest for Global Influence," *Global Asia* 7, 2 (Summer 2012). The fifth section draws from a coauthored report, Daniel M. Kliman and Richard Fontaine, *Global Swing States: Brazil, India, Indonesia, Turkey, and the Future of International Order* (Washington, D.C.: German Marshall Fund of the United States and Center for a New American Security, November 2012).

2. U.S. Department of Defense, *Annual Report to Congress: Military and Security Developments Involving the People's Republic of China 2010*, Washington, D.C., August 16, 2010, 19.

3. Minxin Pei, *Political Reform in China: Leadership Differences and Convergence*, Carnegie Endowment for International Peace, 2008, http://carnegieendowment.org/files/Pei_Revised.pdf.

4. Bates Gill, Michael Green, Kiyoto Tsuji, and William Watts, *Strategic Views on Asian Regionalism: Survey Results and Analysis* (Washington, D.C.: Center for Strategic and International Studies, February 2009), 7.

5. Robert Hartmann, "China Rising: Back to the Future," *Asia Times*, March 16, 2007.

6. For example, see Foreign Secretary Shivshankar Menon, *India-Pakistan: Understanding the Conflict Dynamics*, speech at Jamia Millia Islamia, April 11, 2007; India, Press Information Bureau, "PM Addresses the Chinese Academy of Social Sciences," January 15, 2008; General Deepak Kapoor, Chief of the Army Staff, *Changing Global Security Environment with Specific Reference to Our Region and Its Impact on the Indian Army*," lecture at Institute for Defence Studies and Analyses, July 3, 2008.

7. Ashok Malik and Rory Medcalf, *India's New World: Civil Society in the Making of Foreign Policy* (Sydney: Lowy Institute, 2011).

8. Gill, Green, Tsuji, and Watts, 7.

9. The seminal work on today's rules-based international order is G. John Ikenberry, *Liberal Leviathan: The Origins, Crisis, and Transformation of the American World Order* (Princeton, N.J.: Princeton University Press, 2011).

10. Angus Maddison, "The West and the Rest in the International Economic Order," *OECD Observer*, 2002.

11. Samuel P. Huntington, *The Third Wave: Democratization in the Late Twentieth Century* (Norman: University of Oklahoma Press, 1993); and Laza Kekic, "The Economist Intelligence Unit's Index of Democracy," 2007, 2.

Appendix 1: Omitted Cases

1. In the first four omitted cases, GDP calculations are based on figures from Angus Maddison, *Historical Statistics for the World Economy: 1–2003 AD*, table 2, last updated

August 2007, http://www.ggdc.net/maddison. Trade figures are calculated using data from Katherine Barbieri, Omar Keshk, and Brian Pollins, *COW Trade Data, Version 2.01*, 2008, http://correlatesofwar.org. Relative figures on military spending reflect data from the COW *National Material Capabilities dataset, Version 3.02*, http://correlatesofwar.org.

2. For example, British leaders viewed Japan as critical to the naval balance of power in the Far East. See Ian H. Nish, *The Anglo-Japanese Alliance: The Diplomacy of Two Island Empires, 1894–1907* (London: Athlone, 1966), 174–84.

3. Akira Iriye, *Across the Pacific: An Inner History of American-East Asian Relations* (New York: Harcourt, Brace, 1967), 179, 217; Norman A. Graebner, "Hoover, Roosevelt, and the Japanese," in Dorothy Borg and Shumpei Okamoto, eds., *Pearl Harbor as History: Japanese-American Relations 1931–1941* (New York: Columbia University Press, 1973), 26–28, 36–40, 43, 45–46, 50.

4. Keith Neilson, *Britain, Soviet Russia, and the Collapse of the Versailles Order, 1919–1939* (New York: Cambridge University Press, 2006), 52–53, 207–10; Curtis Keeble, *Britain and the Soviet Union, 1917–89* (London: Macmillan, 1990), 99–103, 129, 138.

5. GDP and trade comparisons are based on figures from World Bank, World Development Indicators online. Relative figures on military spending reflect data from the COW *National Material Capabilities dataset, Version 3.02*.

Appendix 2: Coding Checks and Balances

1. This coding procedure is taken directly from Philip Keefer, *Database of Political Institutions: Changes and Variable Definitions*, World Bank Research Group, December 2007, 19–20.

Appendix 3: Measuring Freedom of the Press

1. Keith Werhan, *Freedom of Speech: A Reference Guide to the United States Constitution* (Westport, Conn.: Praeger, 2004), 9.

2. Gary D. Stark, "Trials and Tribulations: Authors' Responses to Censorship in Imperial Germany, 1885–1914," *German Studies Review* 12, 3 (October 1989): 448.

3. Richard Labunski, *Libel and the First Amendment: Legal History and Practice in Print and Broadcasting* (New Brunswick, N.J.: Transaction Books, 1987), 56–57.

4. Stark, 448; Alex Hall, "The War of Words: Anti-Socialist Offensives and Counter-Propaganda in Wilhelmine Germany 1890–1914," *Journal of Contemporary History* 11, 2/3 (July 1976): 15–16, 36.

5. During the 1890s, independent newspapers dominated the twenty-five largest U.S. cities. Ted C. Smythe, *The Gilded Age Press, 1865–1900* (Westport, Conn.: Praeger, 2003), 17–18, 56, 206.

6. Paul Kennedy, *The Rise of the Anglo-German Antagonism, 1860–1914* (London: Allen and Unwin, 1980), 363–65, 377; Hall, 13–15, 19–20.

7. Hall, 20.

8. John Nerone, *Violence Against the Press: Policing the Public Sphere in U.S. History* (Oxford: Oxford University Press, 1994), 128–58; Hall, 16.

9. Smythe, 212–13.

10. Hall, 12.

11. Peter J. Fliess, *Freedom of the Press in the German Republic, 1918–1933* (Baton Rouge: Louisiana State University Press, 1955), 9–15.

12. William L. Shirer, *The Rise and Fall of the Third Reich: A History of Nazi Germany* (New York: Simon and Schuster, 1960), 194.

13. Reich Press Law quoted in ibid., 245.

14. Richard J. Evans, *The Third Reich in Power, 1933–1939* (New York: Penguin, 2005), 144.

15. Oron J. Hale, *The Captive Press in the Third Reich* (Princeton, N.J.: Princeton University Press, 1964), 86.

16. Shirer, 244–45; Evans, 146; Richard Grunberger, *The 12-Year Reich: A Social History of Nazi Germany, 1933–1945* (New York: Holt, Rinehart and Winston, 1971), 395.

17. Shirer, 190, 245; Grunberger, 393; Hale, 86, 144, 151.

18. Hale, 131–34; Evans, 141–43. On the general assault against the left, which included the trade union press, see Richard Bessel, "The Nazi Capture of Power," *Journal of Contemporary History* 39, 2 (April 2004): 181–82.

19. Hale, 131, 137–38, 151; Evans, 133, 144, 146; Shirer, 246.

20. Mark W. Hopkins, *Mass Media in the Soviet Union* (New York: Pegasus, 1970), 100; James W. Markham, *Voices of the Red Giants: Communications in Russia and China* (Ames: Iowa State University Press, 1967), 105.

21. Article 58 in the appendix to Richard Weisberg, "Review: Solzhenitsyn's View of Soviet Law in 'The First Circle,'" *University of Chicago Law Review* 41, 2 (Winter 1974): 435–38.

22. Hopkins, 129–30.

23. Stalin quoted in Markham, 100.

24. Hopkins, 29, 139, 140; Markham, 120–21.

25. Markham, 125–26; Hopkins, 95, 128.

26. Markham, 131.

27. Hopkins, 29.

28. Quotations from Constitution of the People's Republic of China, http://english.people.com.cn/constitution/constitution.html.

29. Gordon Adams, "The List: The 10 Worst Chinese Laws," *Foreign Policy*, August 2008.

30. Human Rights Watch, *World Report 2013: China* (New York: Seven Stories Press, 2013), http://www.hrw.org/world-report/2013/country-chapters/china; Committee to Protect Journalists, *Falling Short: Olympic Promises Go Unfulfilled as China Falters on Press Freedom*, updated ed., June 2008, 38–41.

31. Committee to Protect Journalists, *Falling Short*, 25–27.

32. Ibid., 8; Freedom House, *Freedom of the Press 2008: A Global Survey of Media Independence* (Lanham, Md.: Rowman and Littlefield, 2009), 93.

33. In mid-2013, China had 591 million web users. "China Smartphone Owners Swell Number of Internet Users," *BBC*, July 17, 2013.

34. David Bandurski, "China's Guerrilla War for the Web," *Far Eastern Economic Review*, July 2008.

35. Committee to Protect Journalists, *Falling Short*, 24.

36. Ibid., 27; Freedom House, *Freedom of the Press 2008*, 89–90.

37. Committee to Protect Journalists, *Falling Short*, 42–43.

38. Ibid., 31; *Freedom of the Press 2008*, 90; and Reporters Without Borders, "Blogger Confined to Psychiatric Hospital Against His Will," August 23, 2007, http://www.rsf.org/Blogger-confined-to-psychiatric.html.

39. Committee to Protect Journalists, *Falling Short*, 25; Freedom House, *Freedom of the Press 2008*, 92.

Bibliography

Direct Attribution Interviews

Charlene Barshefsky, former U.S. trade representative
Dan Blumenthal, former Department of Defense official
Douglas Paal, former director of the American Institute in Taiwan
Fumio Kyuma, former defense minister
Fumio Ota, vice admiral (ret.)
Hitoshi Tanaka, former Japanese diplomat
James Kelly, former assistant secretary of state
Marc Grossman, former under secretary of state
Noboru Yamaguchi, lieutenant general (ret.)
Nobutaka Machimura, former foreign minister
Randall Schriver, former deputy assistant secretary of state
Robert Kapp, former president of the U.S.-China Business Council
Robert Suettinger, former national intelligence officer for East Asia
Ryozo Kato, former Japanese diplomat
Sadakazu Tanigaki, former finance minister
Sakutaro Tanino, former Japanese diplomat
Shigenobu Tamura, Liberal Democratic Party staffer
Shigeru Ishiba, former defense minister
Takeo Hiranuma, LDP member of parliament
Tomohiko Taniguchi, former Ministry of Foreign Affairs deputy press secretary
Walter Slocombe, former under secretary of defense
Winston Lord, former assistant secretary of state
Yotaro Kobayashi, former CEO of Fuji Xerox

News Sources

Agence France-Presse
Arms Control Today
Asia Times
Associated Press

BBC News
Bloomberg
Business Week
Far Eastern Economic Review
Financial Times
Foreign Policy
Guardian
Indian Express
Inter Press Service News Agency
Japan Times
Jiji Press
Los Angeles Times
National Public Radio
New York Journal of Commerce
New York Times
New York World
Politico
Times (London)
Wall Street Journal
Washington Post
Yomiuri Shimbun

Data Sources

Barbieri, Katherine, Omar Keshk, and Brian Pollins. *Correlates of War Project Trade Data, Version 2.01*, 2008. http://correlatesofwar.org.

Batelle. *2014 Global R&D Funding Forecast*. December 2013. http://www.battelle.org/docs/tpp/2014_global_rd_funding_forecast.pdf.

Center for Systemic Peace. *Polity IV Annual Time-Series, 1800–2012*. http://www.systemicpeace.org/inscr/inscr.htm.

Correlates of War Project. *National Material Capabilities Dataset, Version 3.02*. http://correlatesofwar.org/.

Keefer, Philip. *Database of Political Institutions: Changes and Variable Definitions*. World Bank Research Group, December 2007.

Japan Cabinet Office, Economic and Social Research Institute.

Japan External Trade Organization. *Japan's Total Outward FDI by Country/Region (International Investment Position)*. 2013.

Japan Ministry of Finance. Trade Statistics of Japan.

Japan Ministry of Internal Affairs and Communications. *World Statistics 2009*.

League of Nations. *World Economic Survey 1932–1933*. Geneva: Economic Intelligence Service, 1933.

Maddison, Angus. *Historical Statistics for the World Economy: 1–2003 AD*. Last updated August 2007.

National Science Foundation, Division of Science Resources Statistics. *Asia's Rising Science and Technology Strength: Comparative Indicators for Asia, the European Union, and the United States.* Arlington, Va.: National Science Foundation, May 2007.

Russett, Bruce, and John R. Oneal. Trade Data. *Triangulating Peace: Democracy, Interdependence, and International Organizations.* New York: Norton, 2001. http://pantheon.yale/edu/~brusset/PeaceStata.zip.

Stockholm International Peace Research Institute (SIPRI). *Military Expenditure Database.* 2013. http://sipri.org/research/armaments/milex/milex_database.

U.S. Department of Commerce, Bureau of Economic Analysis. *Current-Dollar and "Real" Gross Domestic Product. 2014.*

———. *Gross Domestic Product: Percent Change from Preceding Period.* January 30, 2014.

———. *U.S. Direct Investment Abroad on a Historical-Cost Basis: Country Detail by Selected Industry. 1997.*

———. *U.S. Direct Investment Position Abroad on a Historical-Cost Basis: Country Detail by Industry. 2012.*

U.S. Department of Treasury. *Major Foreign Holders of Treasury Securities.* Washington, D.C., January 16, 2014.

U.S. International Trade Commission. *Interactive Tariff and Trade Database.* http://dataweb.usitc.gov.

World Bank. *World Development Indicators Online.*

Books, Documents, and Articles

Acheson, Dean. *Present at the Creation: My Years in the State Department.* New York: Norton, 1969.

Albright, Madeline. *Madame Secretary.* New York: Miramax, 2003.

Altman, Roger. "The Great Crash, 2008: A Geopolitical Setback for the West." *Foreign Affairs* 88, 1 (January/February 2009): 2–14.

Angell, Norman. *The Great Illusion: A Study of the Relation of Military Power in Nations to Their Economic and Social Advantage.* London: Putnam's, 1911.

Armacost, Michael et al. *"New Beginnings" in the U.S.-ROK Alliance: Recommendations to the Obama Administration.* Stanford, Calif.: Freeman Spogli Institute for International Studies, May 2010.

Armitage, Richard, R. Nicholas Burns, and Richard Fontaine. *Natural Allies: A Blueprint for the Future of U.S.-India Relations.* Washington, D.C.: Center for a New American Security, October 2010.

Art, Robert. "The United States and the Rise of China: Implications for the Long Haul." *Political Science Quarterly* 125, 3 (Fall 2010): 359–91.

Barbieri, Katherine. "Economic Interdependence: A Path to Peace or Source of Interstate Conflict?" *Journal of Peace Research* 33, 1 (February 1996): 29–49.

Barnett, Correlli. *Engage the Enemy More Closely: The Royal Navy in the Second World War.* London: Hodder and Stoughton, 1991.

Bates, Darrell. *The Fashoda Incident of 1898: Encounter on the Nile*. New York: Oxford University Press, 1984.

Beck, Thorsten, George Clarke, Alberto Groff, Philip Keefer, and Patrick Walsh. "New Tools in Comparative Political Economy: The Database of Political Institutions." *World Bank Economic Review* 15, 1 (September 2001): 165–76.

Beckley, Michael. "China's Century: Why America's Edge Will Endure." *International Security* 36, 3 (Winter 2011/12): 41–78.

Bergsten, C. Fred, Charles Freeman, Nicholas R. Lardy, and Derek J. Mitchell. *China's Rise: Challenges and Opportunities*. Washington, D.C.: Peterson Institute for International Economics and Center for Strategic and International Studies, 2008.

Bertram, Marshall. *The Birth of Anglo-American Friendship: The Prime Facet of the Venezuelan Boundary Dispute: A Study of the Interreaction of Diplomacy and Public Opinion*. Lanham, Md.: University Press of America, 1992.

Bessel, Richard. "The Nazi Capture of Power." *Journal of Contemporary History* 39, 2 (April 2004): 169–88.

Bialer, Uri. *The Shadow of the Bomber: The Fear of Air Attack and British Politics, 1932–1939*. London: Royal Historical Society, 1980.

Blair, Dennis C., and David V. Bonfili. "The April 2001 EP-3 Incident: The U.S. Point of View." In *Managing Sino-American Crises: Case Studies and Analysis*, ed. Michael D. Swaine, Zhang Tuosheng, and Danielle F. S. Cohen, 377–90. Washington, D.C.: Carnegie Endowment for International Peace, 2006.

Bourne, Kenneth. *Britain and the Balance of Power in North America, 1815–1908*. Berkeley: University of California Press, 1967.

Bremmer, Ian. *The End of the Free Market: Who Wins the War Between States and Corporations?* New York: Portfolio, 2010.

Buckle, George Earle, ed. *The Letters of Queen Victoria, Third Series: A Selection from Her Majesty's Correspondence and Journal Between the Years 1886 and 1901*. Vol. 3. New York: Longmans, Green, 1932.

Bueno de Mesquita, Bruce, and David Lalman. *War and Reason: Domestic and International Imperatives*. New Haven, Conn.: Yale University Press, 1992.

Bueno de Mesquita, Bruce, James D. Morrow, Randolph M. Siverson, and Alastair Smith. *The Logic of Political Survival*. Cambridge, Mass.: MIT Press, 2003.

———. "An Institutional Explanation of the Democratic Peace." *American Political Science Review* 93, 4 (December 1999): 791–807.

Bullock, Alan. *Hitler and Stalin: Parallel Lives*. London: HarperCollins, 1991.

———. *Hitler: A Study in Tyranny*. New York: Harper Perennial, 1991.

Burr, William, ed. *China, Pakistan, and the Bomb: The Declassified File on U.S. Policy, 1977–1997*. National Security Archive Electronic Briefing Book 114. March 5, 2004.

Campbell, Charles S. *Anglo-American Understanding, 1898–1903*. Baltimore: Johns Hopkins University Press, 1957.

Carley, Michael J. *1939: The Alliance That Never Was and the Coming of World War II.* Chicago: Ivan Dee, 1999.

Carlton, David. *Anthony Eden: A Biography.* London: Allen Lane, 1981.

Carr, William. *Arms, Autarky and Aggression: A Study in German Foreign Policy, 1933–1939.* London: Edward Arnold, 1972.

Cherny, Andrei. *The Candy Bombers: The Untold Story of the Berlin Airlift and America's Finest Hour.* New York: Putnam's 2008.

Churchill, Winston S. *The Second World War.* Vol. 1, *The Gathering Storm.* Boston: Houghton Mifflin, 1948.

———. *Great Contemporaries.* London: Thornton Butterworth, 1937.

Clinton, Bill. *My Life.* New York: Knopf, 2004.

Clinton, Hillary. "America's Pacific Century." *Foreign Policy,* October 11, 2011.

Cohen, Warren I. *America's Response to China: A History of Sino-American Relations.* New York: Columbia University Press, 2000.

Colvin, Ian. *Vansittart in Office: An Historical Survey on the Origins of the Second World War Based on the Papers of Sir Robert Vansittart.* London: Gollancz, 1965.

Committee to Protect Journalists. *Falling Short: Olympic Promises Go Unfulfilled as China Falters on Press Freedom,* updated ed. June 2008. http://cpj.org/Briefings/2007/Falling_Short/China/china_updated.pdf.

Copeland, Dale. "Economic Interdependence and War: A Theory of Trade Expectations." *International Security* 20, 4 (Spring 1996): 5–41.

———. *The Origins of Major Wars.* Ithaca, N.Y.: Cornell University Press, 2000.

Coppock, D. J. "The Causes of the Great Depression, 1873–1896." *Manchester School of Economic and Social Studies* 29, 3 (1961): 205–32.

Cronin, Patrick M., Daniel M. Kliman, and Abraham M. Denmark. *Renewal: Revitalizing the U.S.-Japan Alliance.* Washington, D.C.: Center for a New American Security, October 2010.

Crowson, N. J. *Facing Fascism: The Conservative Party and the European Dictators, 1935–1940.* London: Routledge, 1997.

Crozier, Andrew J. *Appeasement and Germany's Last Bid for Colonies.* Basingstoke: Macmillan, 1988.

Davis, Lynn Etheridge. *The Cold War Begins: Soviet-American Conflict over Eastern Europe.* Princeton, N.J.: Princeton University Press, 1974.

Davis, Paul K., and Peter A. Wilson. *Looming Discontinuities in U.S. Military Strategy and Defense Planning: Colliding RMAs Necessitate a New Strategy.* Santa Monica, Calif.: Rand Corporation, March 2011.

Deane, John R. *The Strange Alliance: The Story of Our Efforts at Wartime Co-Operation with Russia.* New York: Viking, 1946.

Denmark, Abraham M., and Daniel M. Kliman. *Cornerstone: A Future Agenda for the U.S.-Japan Alliance.* Washington, D.C.: Center for a New American Security, June 2010.

Denmark, Abraham M., and James Mulvenon, eds. *Contested Commons: The Future of American Power in a Multipolar World*. Washington, D.C.: Center for a New American Security, January 2010.

de Soysa, Indra, John R. Oneal, and Yong-Hee Park. "Testing Power-Transition Theory Using Alternative Measures of National Capabilities." *Journal of Conflict Resolution* 41, 4 (August 1997): 509–28.

DeYoung, Karen. *Soldier: The Life of Colin Powell*. New York: Knopf, 2006.

Dixon, William J. "Democracy and Peaceful Settlement of International Conflict." *American Political Science Review* 88, 1 (March 1994): 14–32.

Dockrill, M. L. "British Policy During the Agadir Crisis of 1911." In *British Foreign Policy Under Sir Edward Grey*, ed. F. H. Hinsley, 271–86. Cambridge: Cambridge University Press, 1977.

Donovan, Robert J. *Conflict and Crisis: The Presidency of Harry S. Truman, 1945–1948*. New York: Norton, 1977.

Douglas-Home, Alec. *The Way the Wind Blows: An Autobiography*. New York: Quadrangle/New York Times, 1976.

Dower, John W. *Embracing Defeat: Japan in the Wake of World War II*. New York: Norton, 1999.

Doyle, Michael W. "Kant, Liberal Legacies, and Foreign Affairs." In *Debating the Democratic Peace*, ed. Michael E. Brown, Sean M. Lynn-Jones, and Steven E. Miller, 3–57. Cambridge, Mass.: MIT Press, 1997.

———. "Three Pillars of the Liberal Peace." *American Political Science Review* 99, 3 (August 2005): 463–66.

Dutton, David. *Simon: A Political Biography of Sir John Simon*. London: Aurum Press, 1993.

Eckstein, Harry. "Case Study and Theory in Political Science." In *Handbook of Political Science*, vol. 1, *Political Science: Scope and Theory*, ed. Fred I. Greenstein and Nelson W. Polsby, 79–133. Reading, Mass.: Addison-Wesley, 1975.

Edelstein, David M. "Managing Uncertainty: Beliefs About Intentions and the Rise of Great Powers." *Security Studies* 12, 1 (Autumn 2002): 1–40.

Ekstein, Michael G., and Zara Steiner. "The Sarajevo Crisis." In *British Foreign Policy Under Sir Edward Grey*, ed. F. H. Hinsley, 397–410. Cambridge: Cambridge University Press, 1977.

Etzold, Thomas H., and John Lewis Gaddis, eds. *Containment: Documents on American Policy and Strategy, 1945–1950*. New York: Columbia University Press, 1978.

Evans, Richard J. *The Third Reich in Power, 1933–1939*. New York: Penguin, 2005.

Fliess, Peter J. *Freedom of the Press in the German Republic, 1918–1933*. Baton Rouge: Louisiana State University Press, 1955.

Forbes, Neil. "London Banks, the German Standstill Agreements, and 'Economic Appeasement' in the 1930s." *Economic History Review* n.s. 40, 4 (November 1987): 571–87.

Freedom House. *Freedom of the Press 2008: A Global Survey of Media Independence.* Lanham, Md.: Rowman and Littlefield, 2009.

Freedom House. *Freedom of the Press 2013: Middle East Volatility Amidst Global Decline.* Washington, D.C.: Freedom House, 2013.

Friedberg, Aaron L. *The Weary Titan: Britain and the Experience of Relative Decline, 1895–1905.* Princeton, N.J.: Princeton University Press, 1988.

Frieman, Wendy. *China, Arms Control, and Non-Proliferation.* New York: Routledge-Curzon, 2004.

Funabashi, Yoichi. "Japan and the New World Order." *Foreign Affairs* 70, 5 (Winter 1991/1992): 58–74.

Gaddis, John Lewis. *George F. Kennan.* New York: Penguin, 2011.

———. "The Long Peace: Elements of Stability in the Postwar International System." *International Security* 10, 4 (Spring, 1986): 99–142.

———. *Strategies of Containment: A Critical Appraisal of Postwar American National Security Policy.* New York: Oxford University Press, 1982.

———. *The United States and the Origins of the Cold War, 1941–1947.* New York: Columbia University Press, 1972.

Gartzke, Erik. "Kant We All Just Get Along? Opportunity, Willingness, and the Origins of the Democratic Peace." *American Journal of Political Science* 42, 1 (January 1998): 1–27.

Gartzke, Erik, Quan Li, and Charles Boehmer. "Investing in the Peace: The Impact of Economics on International Conflict." *International Organization* 55, 2 (Spring 2001): 391–438.

Gaubatz, Kurt Taylor. "Democratic States and Commitment in International Relations." *International Organization* 50, 1 (Winter 1996): 109–39.

Gilbert, Bentley B. "Pacifist to Interventionist: David Lloyd George in 1911 and 1914. Was Belgium an Issue?" *Historical Journal* 28, 4 (December 1985): 863–85.

Gilbert, Martin. *Churchill: A Life.* London: Heinemann, 1991.

Gilbert, Martin, and Richard Gott. *The Appeasers.* Boston: Houghton Mifflin, 1963.

Gill, Bates, Michael Green, Kiyoto Tsuji, and William Watts. *Strategic Views on Asian Regionalism: Survey Results and Analysis.* Washington, D.C.: Center for Strategic and International Studies, February 2009.

Gilpin, Robert. *War and Change in World Politics.* New York: Cambridge University Press, 1981.

Glaser, Bonnie S. "Challenged by New Crises." *Comparative Connections* 1, 1 (July 1999): 13–21.

———. "China Signals Irritation with U.S. Policy." *Comparative Connections* 9, 4 (January 2008): 25–35.

———. "Face to Face in Shanghai: New Amity and Perennial Differences." *Comparative Connections* 3, 4 (January 2002).

———. "First Contact: Qian Qichen Engages in Wide-Ranging, Constructive Talks with President Bush and Senior U.S. Officials." *Comparative Connections* 3, 1 (April 2001): 22–33.

———. "Mid-Air Collision Cripples Sino-U.S. Relations." *Comparative Connections* 3, 2 (July 2001): 23–37.

Glaser, Charles. *Rational Theory of International Politics: The Logic of Competition and Cooperation*. Princeton, N.J.: Princeton University Press, 2010.

———. "Will China's Rise Lead to War? Why Realism Does Not Mean Pessimism." *Foreign Affairs* 90, 2 (March/April 2011).

Gooch, G. P., and Harold Temperley, eds. *British Documents on the Origins of War, 1898–1914*. Vol. 3, *The Testing of the Entente, 1904–1906*. London: HMSO, 1928.

Gorlizki, Yoram, and Oleg Khlevniuk. *Cold Peace: Stalin and the Soviet Ruling Circle, 1945–1953*. Oxford: Oxford University Press, 2004.

Gowa, Joanne. *Allies, Adversaries, and International Trade*. Princeton, N.J.: Princeton University Press, 1995.

———. *Ballots and Bullets: The Elusive Democratic Peace*. Princeton, N.J.: Princeton University Press, 1999.

Gowa, Joanne, and Edward D. Mansfield. "Power Politics and International Trade." *American Political Science Review* 87, 2 (June 1993): 408–20.

Graebner, Norman A. "Hoover, Roosevelt, and the Japanese." In *Pearl Harbor as History: Japanese-American Relations 1931–1941*, ed. Dorothy Borg and Shumpei Okamoto. New York: Columbia University Press, 1973.

Green, Michael J. *Japan's Reluctant Realism: Foreign Policy Challenges in an Era of Uncertain Power*. New York: Palgrave, 2001.

Green, Michael J., and Daniel M. Kliman. "China's Hard Power and the Potential for Conflict in Asia." *SERI Quarterly* 4, 2 (April 2011): 33–41.

———. "China's Risky Bet Against History." *Diplomat*, December 23, 2010.

Green, Michael J., and Benjamin L. Self. "Japan's Changing China Policy: From Commercial Liberalism to Reluctant Realism." *Survival* 38, 2 (Summer 1996): 35–57.

Grenville, J. A. S. *Lord Salisbury and Foreign Policy: The Close of the Nineteenth Century*. London: Athlone, 1970.

Grunberger, Richard. *The 12-Year Reich: A Social History of Nazi Germany, 1933–1945*. New York: Holt, Rinehart, 1971.

Gwynn, Stephen, ed. *The Letters and Friendships of Sir Cecil Spring-Rice, a Record*. Vol. 1. Boston: Houghton Mifflin, 1929.

Hale, Oron J. *The Captive Press in the Third Reich*. Princeton, N.J.: Princeton University Press, 1964.

Hall, Alex. "The War of Words: Anti-Socialist Offensives and Counter-Propaganda in Wilhelmine Germany 1890–1914." *Journal of Contemporary History* 11, 2/3 (July 1976): 11–42.

Harriman, W. Averell, and Elie Abel. *Special Envoy to Churchill and Stalin, 1941–1946*. New York: Random House, 1975.

Hegre, Havard, John R. Oneal, and Bruce Russett. "Trade Does Promote Peace: New Simultaneous Estimates of the Reciprocal Effects of Trade and Conflict." *Journal of Peace Research* 47, 6 (November 2010): 763–74.

Herring, George C., Jr. *Aid to Russia, 1941–1946: Strategy, Diplomacy, the Origins of the Cold War*. New York: Columbia University Press, 1973.

Hilderbrand, Robert C. *Dumbarton Oaks: The Origins of the United Nations and the Search for Postwar Security*. Chapel Hill: University of North Carolina Press, 1990.

Hill, John S. "American Efforts to Aid French Reconstruction Between Lend-Lease and the Marshall Plan." *Journal of Modern History* 64, 3 (September 1992): 500–524.

Hirschman, Albert O. *Exit, Voice, and Loyalty: Responses to Decline in Firms, Organizations, and States*. Cambridge, Mass.: Harvard University Press, 1970.

———. *National Power and the Structure of Foreign Trade*. Berkeley: University of California Press, 1945.

Hoffman, Ross J. S. *Great Britain and the German Trade Rivalry, 1875–1914*. Philadelphia: University of Pennsylvania Press, 1933.

Holloway, David. *Stalin and the Bomb: The Soviet Union and Atomic Energy, 1939–1956*. New Haven, Conn.: Yale University Press, 1994.

Hopkins, Mark W. *Mass Media in the Soviet Union*. New York: Pegasus, 1970.

Human Rights Watch. *World Report 2013: China*. New York: Seven Stories Press, 2013.

Huntington, Samuel P. *The Third Wave: Democratization in the Late Twentieth Century*. Norman: University of Oklahoma Press, 1993.

Hyde, H. Montgomery. *British Air Policy Between the Wars, 1918–1939*. London: Heinemann, 1976.

Ikenberry, G. John. *After Victory: Institutions, Strategic Restraint, and the Rebuilding of Order After Major Wars*. Princeton, N.J.: Princeton University Press, 2001.

———. *Liberal Leviathan: The Origins, Crisis, and Transformation of the American World Order*. Princeton, N.J.: Princeton University Press, 2011.

———. "The Rise of China and the West: Can the Liberal System Survive?" *Foreign Affairs* 81, 1 (January/February 2008): 23–37.

India Press Information Bureau. *PM Addresses the Chinese Academy of Social Sciences*. January 15, 2008.

Iriye, Akira. *Across the Pacific: An Inner History of American-East Asian Relations*. New York: Harcourt, Brace, 1967.

Japan Cabinet Office. *Science and Technology Basic Plan* (Provisional translation). March 28, 2006.

———. *Science and Technology Basic Plan* (Unofficial translation). July 2, 1996.

———. *Science and Technology Basic Plan (2001–2005)* (Tentative version). March 30, 2001.

———. "Statement by the Chief Cabinet Secretary." December 19, 2003.

Japan Defense Agency. *Heisei 5 nenban: Nihon no Bouei: Bouei Hakusho* [Heisei 5 edition: Defense of Japan: Defense white paper]. Tokyo, 1993.

———. *Heisei 18 nenban: Nihon no Bouei: Bouei Hakusho* [Heisei 18 edition: Defense of Japan: Defense white paper]. Tokyo, 2006.

Japan External Trade Organization. *China Overtakes the US as Japan's Largest Trading Partner.* February 28, 2008.

Japan Ministry of Defense. *Defense of Japan 2010: Defense White Paper.* Tokyo, 2010.

Japan Ministry of Economy, Trade, and Industry. *Chugoku no WTO kamei koushou no genjou* [The current state of China's WTO membership negotiations]. February 21, 2001.

Japan Ministry of Foreign Affairs. *Entry into Force of the Japan-ASEAN Comprehensive Economic Partnership Agreement.* December 1, 2008.

———. *First Japan-China High-Level Economic Dialogue.* Press communiqué, December 2, 2007.

———. *Free Trade Agreement (FTA) and Economic Partnership Agreement (EPA).* http://www.mofa.go.jp/policy/economy/fta/index.htm.

———. *The Guidelines for Japan-U.S. Defense Cooperation.* September 1997.

———. *Japan-Australia Joint Declaration on Security Cooperation.* Tokyo, March 13, 2007.

———. *Japan-India Economic Partnership Agreement.* Last updated February 2012.

———. *Japan-Australia Economic Partnership Agreement.* Last updated June 2012.

———. *Joint Declaration on Security Cooperation Between Japan and India.* Tokyo, October 22, 2008.

———. *Joint Statement U.S.-Japan Security Consultative Committee.* Washington, D.C., February 19, 2005.

———. *Overview of Japan-China Foreign Ministers' Meeting.* October 29, 2010.

Jervis, Robert. "Cooperation Under the Security Dilemma." *World Politics* 30, 2 (January 1978): 167–214.

———. *Perceptions and Misperceptions in International Politics.* Princeton, N.J.: Princeton University Press, 1976.

Kan, Shirley A. *Taiwan: Major U.S. Arms Sales Since 1990.* Washington, D.C.: Congressional Research Service, September 24, 2009.

Kan, Shirley A., and Larry A. Niksch. *Guam: U.S. Defense Deployments.* Washington, D.C.: Congressional Research Service, May 22, 2009.

Kaplan, Lawrence S. *NATO 1948: The Birth of the Transatlantic Alliance.* Lanham, Md.: Rowman and Littlefield, 2007.

Kapoor, Deepak. *Changing Global Security Environment with Specific Reference to Our Region and Its Impact on the Indian Army.* Lecture at the Institute for Defence Studies and Analyses, July 3, 2008.

Katzenstein, Peter J. *Cultural Norms and National Security: Police and Military in Postwar Japan.* Ithaca, N.Y.: Cornell University Press, 1996.

Kee, Robert. *Munich: The Eleventh Hour.* London: Hamilton, 1988.

Keeble, Curtis. *Britain and the Soviet Union, 1917–89.* London: Macmillan, 1990.

Keefer, Philip, and David Stasavage. "The Limits of Delegation: Veto Players, Central

Bank Independence, and the Credibility of Monetary Policy." *American Political Science Review* 77, 3 (August 2003): 407–23.

Kennan, George F. *Memoirs: 1925–1950*. Boston: Little, Brown, 1967.

Kennedy, Paul M. *The Rise and Fall of the Great Powers: Economic Change and Military Conflict from 1500 to 2000*. New York: Random House, 1987.

———. *The Rise of the Anglo-German Antagonism, 1860–1914*. London: Allen & Unwin, 1980.

———. *The Samoan Tangle: A Study in Anglo-German-American Relations, 1878–1900*. New York: Barnes and Noble, 1974.

———. "The Tradition of Appeasement in British Foreign Policy, 1865–1939." In *Strategy and Diplomacy, 1870–1945*, 13–39. London: Allen and Unwin, 1983.

Kennedy, Scott, ed. *China Cross Talk: The American Debate over China Policy Since Normalization*. Lanham, Md.: Rowman and Littlefield, 2003.

Keohane, Robert O. *After Hegemony: Cooperation and Discord in the World Economy*. Princeton, N.J.: Princeton University Press, 1984.

Keshk, Omar M. G., Brian M. Pollins, and Rafael Reuveny. "Trade Still Follows the Flag: The Primacy of Politics in a Simultaneous Model of Interdependence and Armed Conflict." *Journal of Politics* 66, 4 (November 2004): 1155–79.

Kim, Hyung Min, and David L. Rousseau. "The Classical Liberals Were Half Right (or Half Wrong): New Tests of the 'Liberal Peace,' 1960–88." *Journal of Peace Research* 42, 5 (September 2005): 523–43.

Kim, Soo Yeon. "Ties That Bind: The Role of Trade in International Conflict Processes, 1950–1992." Ph.D. Dissertation, Yale University, 1998.

Kim, Woosang, and James D. Morrow. "When Do Power Shifts Lead to War?" *American Journal of Political Science* 36, 4 (November 1992): 896–922.

King, Gary, Robert O. Keohane, and Sidney Verba. *Designing Social Inquiry: Scientific Inference in Qualitative Research*. Princeton, N.J.: Princeton University Press, 1994.

Kinsella, David. "No Rest for the Democratic Peace." *American Political Science Review* 99, 3 (August 2005): 453–57.

Kliman, Daniel M. "Advantage India: Why China Will Lose the Contest for Global Influence." *Global Asia* 7, 2 (Summer 2012).

———. *Japan's Security Strategy in the Post-9/11 World: Embracing a New Realpolitik*. Westport, Conn.: Praeger, 2006.

Kliman, Daniel M., and Abe Denmark. "How to Get Southeast Asia Right." *Diplomat*, February 2, 2011.

Kliman, Daniel M., and Richard Fontaine. *Global Swing States: Brazil, India, Indonesia, Turkey and the Future of International Order*. Washington, D.C.: German Marshall Fund of the United States and Center for a New American Security, November 2012.

Koizumi, Junichiro. *Japan and ASEAN in East Asia: A Sincere and Open Partnership*. Singapore, January 14, 2002.

Krepinevich, Andrew F. *Why AirSea Battle?* Washington, D.C.: Center for Strategic and Budgetary Assessments, February 2010.

Krock, Arthur. *Memoirs: Sixty Years on the Firing Line.* New York: Funk and Wagnalls, 1968.

Kuniholm, Bruce. *The Origins of the Cold War in the Near East: Great Power Conflict and Diplomacy in Iran, Turkey, and Greece.* Princeton, N.J.: Princeton University Press, 1980.

Kupchan, Charles A. *How Enemies Become Friends: The Sources of Stable Peace.* Princeton, N.J.: Princeton University Press, 2010.

Kynge, James. *China Shakes the World: A Titan's Troubled Rise—and the Challenge for America.* Boston: Houghton Mifflin, 2007.

Labunski, Richard. *Libel and the First Amendment: Legal History and Practice in Print and Broadcasting.* New Brunswick, N.J.: Transaction Books, 1987.

Lampton, David M. *Same Bed, Different Dreams: Managing U.S.-China Relations, 1989–2000.* Berkeley: University of California Press, 2001.

Langhorne, Richard T. B. "Great Britain and Germany, 1911–1914." In *British Foreign Policy Under Sir Edward Grey,* ed. F. H. Hinsley, 288–314. Cambridge: Cambridge University Press, 1977.

———. "The Naval Question in Anglo-German Relations, 1912–1914." *Historical Journal* 14, 2 (June 1971): 359–70.

Layne, Christopher. "Kant or Cant: The Myth of the Democratic Peace." *International Security* 19, 2 (Fall 1994): 5–49.

Leffler, Melvyn P. "National Security and U.S. Foreign Policy." In *Origins of the Cold War: An International History,* ed. Melvyn P. Leffler and David S. Painter, 15–52. London: Routledge, 1994.

———. *A Preponderance of Power: National Security, the Truman Administration, and the Cold War.* Stanford, Calif.: Stanford University Press, 1992.

Lemke, Douglas, and Jacek Kugler. "The Evolution of the Power Transitions Perspective." In *Parity and War: Evaluations and Extensions of the War Ledger,* ed. Douglas Lemke and Jacek Kugler, 3–34. Ann Arbor: University of Michigan Press, 1996.

Lemke, Douglas, and Suzanne Werner. "Power Parity, Commitment to Change, and War." *International Studies Quarterly* 40, 2 (June 1996): 235–60.

Levy, James P. *Appeasement and Rearmament: Britain, 1936–1939.* Lanham, Md.: Rowman and Littlefield, 2006.

Liberal Democratic Party. Research Commission on Foreign Affairs. *Jiyuminshutou gaikou seisaku no shishin I: Nihon no ajia taiheiyou senryaku: Henka no chousen* [Foreign policy of the Liberal Democratic Party, Part I: Japan's Asia-Pacific strategy: The challenges of transformation]. Tokyo, April 11, 1997.

Lipson, Charles. *Reliable Partners: How Democracies Have Made a Separate Peace.* Princeton, N.J.: Princeton University Press, 2003.

Lloyd George, David. *War Memoirs of David Lloyd George, 1914–1915*. Boston: Little, Brown, 1933.

Loewenheim, Francis L., Harold D. Langley, and Manfred Jonas, eds. *Roosevelt and Churchill: Their Secret Wartime Correspondence*. New York: Dutton, 1975.

MacDonald, C. A. "Economic Appeasement and the German 'Moderates' 1937–1939. An Introductory Essay." *Past and Present* 56, 1 (August 1972): 105–35.

MacDonald, Paul K., and Joseph M. Parent. "Graceful Decline? The Surprising Success of Great Power Retrenchment." *International Security* 35, 4 (Spring 2011): 7–44.

Macmillan, Margaret. *Paris 1919: Six Months That Changed the World*. New York: Random House, 2003.

Maddison, Angus. "The West and the Rest in the International Economic Order." *OECD Observer*, 2002.

———. *The World Economy: A Millennial Perspective*. Paris: OECD, 2001.

Maiolo, Joseph A. *The Royal Navy and Nazi Germany, 1933–1939: A Study in Appeasement and the Origins of the Second World War*. New York: St. Martin's, 1998.

Malik, Ashok, and Rory Medcalf. *India's New World: Civil Society in the Making of Foreign Policy*. Sydney: Lowy Institute, 2011.

Mann, James. *About Face: A History of America's Curious Relationship with China from Nixon to Clinton*. New York: Knopf, 1999.

Mansfield, Edward. *Power, Trade, and War*. Princeton, N.J.: Princeton University Press, 1994.

Mansfield, Edward D., and Rachel Bronson. "Alliances, Preferential Trading Arrangements, and International Trade Patterns." *American Political Science Review* 91, 1 (March 1997): 94–107.

Mansfield, Edward D., and Jack Snyder. "Democratic Transitions, Institutional Strength, and War." *International Security* 56, 2 (Spring 2002): 297–337.

———. "Democratization and the Danger of War." *International Security* 20, 1 (Summer 1995): 5–38.

———. *Electing to Fight: Why Emerging Democracies Go to War*. Cambridge, Mass.: MIT Press, 2007.

Manyin, Mark E. et al. *Pivot to the Pacific? The Obama Administration's "Rebalancing" Toward Asia*. Washington, D.C.: Congressional Research Service, March 28, 2012.

Maoz, Zeev, and Bruce Russett. "Normative and Structural Causes of the Democratic Peace, 1946–1986." *American Political Science Review* 87, 3 (September 1993): 624–38.

Marder, Arthur J. *The Anatomy of British Sea Power: A History of British Naval Policy in the Pre-Dreadnought Era, 1880–1905*. New York: Knopf, 1940.

Markham, James W. *Voices of the Red Giants: Communications in Russia and China*. Ames: Iowa State University Press, 1967.

Marsden, Arthur. "The Blockade." In *British Foreign Policy Under Sir Edward Grey*, ed. F. H. Hinsley, 488–515. Cambridge: Cambridge University Press, 1977.

Marshall, Monty G., Keith Jaggers, and Ted Robert Gurr. *Polity IV Project: Dataset Users' Manual*. November 2010.

Mastanduno, Michael. *Economic Containment: CoCom and the Politics of East-West Trade*. Ithaca, N.Y.: Cornell University Press, 1992.

———. "The United States Political System and International Leadership: A 'Decidedly Inferior' Form of Government?" In *American Foreign Policy: Theoretical Essays*. 2nd ed., ed. G. John Ikenberry, 328–48. New York: HarperCollins, 1996.

Matloff, Maurice. *Strategic Planning for Coalition Warfare, 1943–1944*. Washington, D.C.: Office of the Chief of Military History, Department of the Army, 1959. Reprint, Government Reprints Press, 2002.

May, Ernest R. *Imperial Democracy: The Emergence of America as a Great Power*. New York: Harcourt, Brace, 1961.

McDonough, Frank. *Neville Chamberlain, Appeasement, and the British Road to War*. New York: Manchester University Press, 1998.

McFaul, Michael. "Are New Democracies War-Prone?" *Journal of Democracy* 18, 2 (2007): 160–67.

Mead, Walter Russell. *God and Gold: Britain, America, and the Making of the Modern World*. New York: Vintage, 2008.

Mearsheimer, John J. *The Tragedy of Great Power Politics*. New York: Norton, 2001.

Medeiros, Evan S. "Strategic Hedging and the Future of Asia-Pacific Stability." *Washington Quarterly* 29, 1 (Winter 2005–2006): 145–67.

Menon, Shivshankar. *India-Pakistan: Understanding the Conflict Dynamics*. Speech at Jamia Millia Islamia, April 11, 2007.

Millis, Walter, ed. *The Forrestal Diaries*. New York: Viking, 1951.

Miscamble, Wilson D. *From Roosevelt to Truman: Potsdam, Hiroshima, and the Cold War*. New York: Cambridge University Press, 2007.

Mochizuki, Mike M. "Japan's Shifting Strategy Toward the Rise of China." *Journal of Strategic Studies* 30, 4–5 (August–October 2007): 739–76.

Modelski, George. "The Long Cycle of Global Politics and the Nation-State." *Comparative Studies in Society and History* 20, 2 (April 1978): 214–35.

———. *Long Cycles in World Politics*. Seattle: University of Washington Press, 1987.

Monger, George. *The End of Isolation: British Foreign Policy, 1900–1907*. London: Thomas Nelson, 1963.

Morgan, Kenneth O. "Lloyd George and Germany." *Historical Journal* 39, 3 (September 1996): 755–66.

Morrow, James D. "Arms Versus Allies: Trade-Offs in the Search for Security." *International Organization* 47, 2 (Spring 1993): 207–33.

———. "How Could Trade Affect Conflict?" *Journal of Peace Research* 36, 4 (July 1999): 481–89.

Morrow, James D., Randolph M. Siverson, and Tressa E. Tabares. "The Political Determinants of International Trade: The Major Powers, 1907–90." *American Political Science Review* 92, 3 (September 1998): 649–61.

Morton, Walter A. *British Finance, 1930–1940*. Madison: University of Wisconsin Press, 1943.

Narang, Vipin, and Rebecca M. Nelson. "Who Are These Belligerent Democratizers? Reassessing the Impact of Democratization on War." *International Organization* 63, 2 (Spring 2009): 357–79.

Narizny, Kevin. "The Political Economy of Alignment: Great Britain's Commitments to Europe, 1905–39." *International Security* 27, 4 (Spring 2003): 184–219.

———. *The Political Economy of Grand Strategy*. Ithaca, N.Y.: Cornell University Press, 2007.

Nathan, Andrew J., and Robert S. Ross. *The Great Wall and the Empty Fortress: China's Search for Security*. New York: Norton, 1997.

National Academy of Sciences, National Academy of Engineering, and Institute of Medicine. *Rising Above the Gathering Storm: Energizing and Employing America for a Brighter Economic Future*. Washington, D.C.: National Academies Press, 2007.

National Institute for Defense Studies. *NIDS China Security Report*. Tokyo, February 2012.

Neilson, Keith. *Britain, Soviet Russia, and the Collapse of the Versailles Order, 1919–1939*. New York: Cambridge University Press, 2006.

Nerone, John. *Violence Against the Press: Policing the Public Sphere in U.S. History*. Oxford: Oxford University Press, 1994.

Neville, Peter. *Hitler and Appeasement: The British Attempt to Prevent the Second World War*. London: Hambledon, 2006.

Newton, Scott. *Profits of Peace: The Political Economy of Anglo-German Appeasement*. New York: Oxford University Press, 1996.

Newton, Thomas Wodehouse. *Lord Lansdowne: A Biography*. London: Macmillan, 1929.

Nish, Ian H. *The Anglo-Japanese Alliance: The Diplomacy of Two Island Empires, 1894–1907*. London: Athlone, 1966.

Norris, Robert S., and William M. Arkin. "NRDC Nuclear Notebook: Global Nuclear Stockpiles, 1945–1997." *Bulletin of the Atomic Scientists* 53, 6 (November/December 1997).

Nye, Joseph S., Jr. "The Changing Nature of World Power." *Political Science Quarterly* 102, 2 (Summer 1990): 177–92.

———. "East Asian Security: The Case for Deep Engagement." *Foreign Affairs* 74, 4 (July/August 1995): 90–102.

Oneal, John R., Frances H. Oneal, Zeev Maoz, and Bruce Russett. "The Liberal Peace: Interdependence, Democracy, and International Conflict, 1950–1985." *Journal of Peace Research* 33, 1 (February 1996): 11–28.

Oneal, John R., and James Lee Ray. "New Tests of the Democratic Peace Controlling for Economic Interdependence, 1950–1985." *Political Research Quarterly* 5, 4 (December 1997): 751–75.

Oneal, John R., and Bruce Russett. "Assessing the Liberal Peace with Alternative Specifications: Trade Still Reduces Conflict." *Journal of Peace Research* 36, 4 (1999): 423–42.

————. "The Kantian Peace: The Pacific Benefits of Democracy, Interdependence, and International Organizations." *World Politics* 52, 1 (October 1999): 1–37.

Oneal, John R., Bruce Russett, and Michael L. Berbaum. "Causes of Peace: Democracy, Interdependence, and International Organizations." *International Studies Quarterly* 47, 3 (September 2003): 371–93.

Oren, Ido. "The Subjectivity of the 'Democratic' Peace: Changing U.S. Perceptions of Imperial Germany." *International Security* 20, 2 (Fall 1995): 147–84.

Organski, A. F. K. *World Politics.* New York: Knopf, 1958.

Organski, A. F. K., and Jacek Kugler. *The War Ledger.* Chicago: University of Chicago Press, 1980.

O'Rourke, Ronald. *China Naval Modernization: Implications for U.S. Navy Capabilities— Background and Issues for Congress.* Washington, D.C.: Congressional Research Service, September 23, 2009.

————. *Sea-Based Ballistic Missile Defense—Background and Issues for Congress.* Washington, D.C.: Congressional Research Service, September 18, 2009.

Owen, John M. "How Liberalism Produces Democratic Peace." *International Security* 19, 2 (Fall 1994): 87–125.

————. *Liberal Peace, Liberal War: American Politics and International Security.* Ithaca, N.Y.: Cornell University Press, 1997.

Papayoanou, Paul A. "Interdependence, Institutions, and the Balance of Power: Britain, Germany, and World War I." *International Security* 20, 4 (Spring 1996): 42–76.

————. *Power Ties: Economic Interdependence, Balancing, and War.* Ann Arbor: University of Michigan Press, 1999.

Parker, R. A. C. *Chamberlain and Appeasement: British Policy and the Coming of the Second World War.* Basingstoke: Macmillan, 1993.

————. *Churchill and Appeasement.* London: Macmillan, 2000.

Paterson, Thomas G. *Soviet-American Confrontation: Postwar Reconstruction and the Origins of the Cold War.* Baltimore: Johns Hopkins University Press, 1973.

Peden, G. C. *British Rearmament and the Treasury: 1932–1939.* Edinburgh: Scottish Academic Press, 1979.

Pei, Minxin. *China's Trapped Transition: The Limits of Developmental Autocracy.* Cambridge, Mass.: Harvard University Press, 2008.

————. *Political Reform in China: Leadership Differences and Convergence.* Carnegie Endowment for International Peace, 2008.

Perkins, Bradford. *The Great Rapprochement: England and the United States, 1895–1914.* New York: Atheneum, 1968.

Peters, Anthony R. *Anthony Eden at the Foreign Office, 1931–1938.* New York: St. Martin's, 1986.

Post, Gaines, Jr. *Dilemmas of Appeasement: British Deterrence and Defense, 1934–1937.* Ithaca, N.Y.: Cornell University Press, 1993.

Powell, Robert. *In the Shadow of Power: States and Strategies in International Politics.* Princeton, N.J.: Princeton University Press, 1999.

PricewaterhouseCoopers. *The World in 2050.* London, January 2011.

Przystup, James. "Dialogue of the Almost Deaf." *Comparative Connections* 6, 1 (April 2004): 103–15.

———. "The Past Is Always Present." *Comparative Connections* 3, 1 (April 2001): 93–109.

———. "Progress in Building a Strategic Relationship." *Comparative Connections* 10, 2 (July 2008): 119–32.

———. "Progressing, But Still Facing History." *Comparative Connections* 1, 2 (October 1999): 57–62.

———. "A Search for Understanding." *Comparative Connections* 1, 3 (January 2000): 60–65.

———. "Spring Thaw." *Comparative Connections* 8, 2 (July 2006): 117–26.

———. "Trying to Get Beyond Yasukuni." *Comparative Connections* 7, 1 (April 2005): 109–21.

———. "Waiting for Zhu . . ." *Comparative Connections* 2, 3 (October 2000): 92–101.

Reuveny, Rafael, and Heejoon Kang. "International Trade, Political Conflict/Cooperation, and Granger Causality." *American Journal of Political Science* 40, 3 (August 1996): 943–70.

Rice, Condoleezza. "Campaign 2000: Promoting the National Interest." *Foreign Affairs* 79, 1 (January/February 2000): 45–62.

———. "Rethinking the National Interest: American Realism for a New World." *Foreign Affairs* 87, 4 (July/August 2008): 2–26.

Roberts, Andrew. *"The Holy Fox": A Biography of Lord Halifax.* London: Weidenfeld and Nicolson, 1991.

———. *Salisbury: Victorian Titan.* London: Weidenfeld and Nicolson, 1999.

Rock, Stephen R. *Appeasement in International Politics.* Lexington: University Press of Kentucky, 2000.

———. *When Peace Breaks Out: Great Power Rapprochement in Historical Perspective.* Chapel Hill: University of North Carolina Press, 1989.

Romberg, Alan D. *Rein In at the Brink of the Precipice: American Policy Toward Taiwan and U.S.-PRC Relations.* Washington, D.C.: Henry L. Stimson Center, 2003.

Rosato, Sebastian. "The Flawed Logic of Democratic Peace Theory." *American Political Science Review* 97, 4 (November 2003): 585–602.

Rose, Norman. *Churchill: An Unruly Life.* London: Simon and Schuster, 1994.

Rosecrance, Richard. *The Rise of the Trading State: Commerce and Conquest in the Modern World.* New York: Basic Books, 1986.

Rosen, Daniel H., and Thilo Hanemann. *An American Open Door? Maximizing the Benefits of Chinese Foreign Direct Investment.* New York: Asia Society, May 2011.

Rugierro, John. *Neville Chamberlain and British Rearmament: Pride, Prejudice, and Politics.* Westport, Conn.: Greenwood Press, 1999.

Russett, Bruce. *Grasping the Democratic Peace: Principles for a Post-Cold War World.* Princeton, N.J.: Princeton University Press, 1993.

Russett, Bruce, and John R. Oneal, *Triangulating Peace: Democracy, Interdependence, and International Organizations.* New York: Norton, 2001.

Russett, Bruce, John R. Oneal, and David R. Davis. "The Third Leg of the Kantian Tripod for Peace: International Organizations and Militarized Disputes." *International Organization* 52, 3 (Summer 1998): 442–43.

Sasajima, Masahiko. "Japan's Domestic Politics and China Policymaking." In *An Alliance for Engagement: Building Cooperation in Security Relations with China,* ed. Benjamin L. Self and Jeffrey W. Thompson, 79–110. Washington, D.C.: Henry L. Stimson Center, 2002.

Schaller, Michael. *The American Occupation of Japan: The Origins of the Cold War in Asia.* New York: Oxford University Press, 1985.

Scheiber, Noam. "Peking Over Our Shoulder." *New Republic,* September 15, 2009.

Schoppa, Leonard J. "Two-Level Games and Bargaining Outcomes: Why Gaiatsu Succeeds in Japan in Some Cases But Not Others." *International Organization* 37, 43 (Summer 1993): 353–86.

Schroeder, Paul W. "Alliances, 1815–1945: Weapons of Power and Tools of Management." In *Historical Dimensions of National Security Problems,* ed. Klaus Knorr, 227–62. Lawrence: University Press of Kansas, 1975.

Schweller, Randall L. "Domestic Structure and Preventive War: Are Democracies More Pacific?" *World Politics* 44, 2 (January 1992): 235–69.

———. "Managing the Rise of Great Powers: History and Theory." In *Engaging China: The Management of an Emerging Power,* ed. Alastair Iain Johnston and Robert S. Ross, 1–31. New York: Routledge, 1999.

Self, Robert. *Neville Chamberlain: A Biography.* Aldershot: Ashgate, 2006.

———. ed. *The Neville Chamberlain Diary Letters.* Vol. 4, *The Downing Street Years, 1934–1940.* Aldershot: Ashgate, 2005.

Shambaugh, David. *China's Communist Party: Atrophy and Adaptation.* Washington, D.C.: Woodrow Wilson Center Press, 2008.

———. *Modernizing China's Military: Progress, Problems, and Prospects.* Berkeley: University of California Press, 2004.

Shay, Robert, Jr. *British Rearmament in the Thirties: Politics and Profits.* Princeton, N.J.: Princeton University Press, 1977.

Shirer, William L. *The Rise and Fall of the Third Reich: A History of Nazi Germany.* New York: Simon and Schuster, 1960.

Shrader, Charles R. *The Withered Vine: Logistics and the Communist Insurgency in Greece, 1945–1949.* Westport, Conn.: Praeger, 1999.

Slantchev, Branislav L., Anna Alexandrova, and Erik Gartzke. "Probabilistic Causality, Selection Bias, and the Logic of the Democratic Peace." *American Political Science Review* 99, 3 (August 2005): 459–62.

Smythe, Ted C. *The Gilded Age Press, 1865–1900*. Westport, Conn.: Praeger, 2003.

Sommer, Martin. *Why Has Japan Been Hit So Hard by the Global Recession?* IMF Staff Position Note. Washington, D.C.: International Monetary Fund, March 18, 2009.

Spiro, David E. "The Insignificance of the Liberal Peace." *International Security* 19, 2 (Fall 1994): 50–86.

Stark, Gary D. "Trials and Tribulations: Authors' Responses to Censorship in Imperial Germany, 1885–1914." *German Studies Review* 12, 3 (October 1989): 447–67.

Steele, David. *Lord Salisbury: A Political Biography*. London: UCL Press, 1999.

Steinberg, James B. *Administration's Vision of the U.S.-China Relationship*. Keynote address at the Center for a New American Security. Washington, D.C., September 24, 2009.

Steiner, Zara S. *Britain and the Origins of the First World War*. London: Macmillan, 1977.

Stewart, Graham. *Burying Caesar: Churchill, Chamberlain and the Battle for the Tory Party*. London: Weidenfeld and Nicolson, 1999.

Suettinger, Robert L. *Beyond Tiananmen: The Politics of U.S.-China Relations 1989–2000*. Washington, D.C.: Brookings Institution Press, 2001.

Swaine, Michael D., Rachel M. Swanger, and Takashi Kawakami. *Japan and Ballistic Missile Defense*. Santa Monica, Calif.: Rand Corporation, 2001.

Sweet, D. W. "Great Britain and Germany, 1905–1911." In *British Foreign Policy Under Sir Edward Grey*, ed. F. H. Hinsley, 216–35. Cambridge: Cambridge University Press, 1977.

Tanner, Murray Scot. "The National People's Congress." In *The Paradox of China's Post-Mao Reforms*, ed. Merle Goldman and Roderick MacFarquhar, 100–128. Cambridge, Mass.: Harvard University Press, 1999.

Temin, Peter. *Lessons from the Great Depression*. Cambridge, Mass.: MIT Press, 1989.

Tomasic, Roman, and Neil Andrews. "Minority Shareholder Protection in China's Top 100 Listed Companies." *Australian Journal of Asian Law* 9, 1 (2007): 88–119.

Tooze, Adam. *The Wages of Destruction: The Making and Breaking of the Nazi Economy*. London: Allen Lane, 2006.

Tow, William. "The Trilateral Strategic Dialogue: Facilitating Community-Building or Revisiting Containment." In William Tow et al., *Assessing the Trilateral Strategic Dialogue*, 1–10. Seattle: National Bureau of Asian Research, 2008.

Truman, Harry S. *Memoirs*. Vol. 1, *Year of Decisions*. vol. 2, *Years of Trial and Hope*. Garden City, N.Y.: Doubleday, 1955, 1956.

Ulam, Adam B. *The Rivals: America and Russia Since World War II*. New York: Viking, 1971.

"United States: Mutual Defense Assistance Act of 1949." *American Journal of International Law* 44, 1, Supplement: Official Documents (January 1950): 29–38.

U.S.-China Business Council. *USCBC Special Report: China Delinks Innovation and Procurement Policies*. May 10, 2011.

U.S. Department of Defense. *Annual Report to Congress: Military and Security*

Developments Involving the People's Republic of China 2010. Washington, D.C., August 16, 2010.

———. *Annual Report to Congress: Military Power of the People's Republic of China 2006.* Washington, D.C., May 23, 2006.

———. *Annual Report to Congress: Military Power of the People's Republic of China 2009.* Washington, D.C., March 25, 2009.

———. *Quadrennial Defense Review Report.* Washington, D.C., May 19, 1997.

———. *Quadrennial Defense Review Report.* Washington, D.C., September 30, 2001.

———. *Quadrennial Defense Review Report.* Washington, D.C., February 6, 2006.

———. *Secretary Gates Remarks at Air Force Association's Annual Conference, National Harbor, Md.* September 16, 2009.

U.S. Department of State. *Foreign Relations of the United States: Diplomatic Papers, 1945.* Vol. 5, *Europe.* Washington, D.C.: Government Printing Office, 1945.

U.S. Department of the Treasury. *Fact Sheet: Second Meeting of the U.S.-China Strategic Economic Dialogue.* Washington, D.C., May 23, 2007.

———. *Joint U.S.-China Fact Sheet: Fourth U.S.-China Strategic Economic Dialogue.* Washington, D.C., June 18, 2008.

———. *U.S. Fact Sheet: The Third Cabinet-Level Meeting of the U.S.-China Strategic Economic Dialogue.* Beijing, December 13, 2007.

U.S. National Intelligence Council. *Global Trends 2010.* Washington, D.C., November 1997.

———. *Global Trends 2025: A Transformed World.* Washington, D.C., November 2008.

Van Dormael, Armand. *Bretton Woods: Birth of a Monetary System.* New York: Holmes and Meier, 1978.

Van Evera, Stephen. "Primed for Peace: Europe After the Cold War." *International Security* 15, 3 (Winter 1990–1991): 7–57.

Vansittart, Robert. *The Mist Procession: The Autobiography of Lord Vansittart.* London: Hutchinson, 1958.

Walt, Stephen. *The Origins of Alliances.* Ithaca, N.Y.: Cornell University Press, 1987.

Wang, James C. F. *Contemporary Chinese Politics: An Introduction.* Upper Saddle River, N.J.: Prentice Hall, 2002.

Wark, Wesley K. *The Ultimate Enemy: British Intelligence and Nazi Germany, 1933–1939.* Ithaca, N.Y.: Cornell University Press, 1985.

Watt, Donald Cameron. "British Intelligence and the Coming of the Second World War in Europe." In *Knowing One's Enemies: Intelligence Assessment Before the Two World Wars,* ed. Ernest R. May, 237–70. Princeton, N.J.: Princeton University Press, 1984.

Weart, Spencer R. *Never at War: Why Democracies Will Not Fight One Another.* New Haven, Conn.: Yale University Press, 1998.

Weil, Martin. *A Pretty Good Club: The Founding Fathers of the U.S. Foreign Service.* New York: Norton, 1978.

Weisberg, Richard. "Review: Solzhenitsyn's View of Soviet Law in 'The First Circle.'" *University of Chicago Law Review* 41, 2 (Winter 1974): 417–38.

Wendt, Alexander. *Social Theory of International Politics*. New York: Cambridge University Press, 1999.

Werhan, Keith. *Freedom of Speech: A Reference Guide to the United States Constitution*. Westport, Conn.: Praeger, 2004.

Williamson, Philip, and Edward Baldwin, eds. *Baldwin Papers: A Conservative Statesman, 1908–1947*. Cambridge: Cambridge University Press, 2004.

Wilsdon, James, and James Keeley. *China: The Next Science Superpower?* London: Demos, 2007.

Wilson, Trevor. "Britain's Moral Commitment to France in August, 1914." *History* 64, 212 (October 1979): 380–90.

Wohlforth, William C. "Unipolarity, Status Competition, and Great Power War." *World Politics* 61, 1 (2009): 28–57.

Yergin, Daniel. *Shattered Peace: The Origins of the Cold War and the National Security State*. Boston: Houghton Mifflin, 1977.

Zakaria, Fareed. *From Wealth to Power: The Unusual Origins of America's World Role*. Princeton, N.J.: Princeton University Press, 1998.

Zoellick, Robert B. *Whither China: From Membership to Responsibility?* Remarks to National Committee on U.S.-China Relations. New York, September 21, 2005.

Index

Acknowledgments

Audrey Emanuel Kliman and Wayne Kliman, my parents, have given me love and support every step of the way. I dedicate this book to them, to my late grandparents, Karoline and Max Emanuel, whose lives inspire, and to Carolyn Trager Kliman, who brightened my life as soon as she entered it.